The Pioneer Preacher

THE PIONEER PREACHER

Incidents of Interest, and Experiences in the Author's Life

Rev. Sherlock Bristol

With an Introduction and Notes by
Dewey D. Wallace, Jr.

Illustrated by
Isabelle Blood

University of Illinois Press
Urbana and Chicago

Introduction and Notes © 1989 by the Board of Trustees
of the University of Illinois

1 2 3 4 5 C P 6 5 4 3 2

This book is printed on acid-free paper.

Library of Congress Cataloging-in-Publication Data

Bristol, Sherlock, 1815–1906.
    The Pioneer preacher : incidents of interest and experiences in
the author's life / Sherlock Bristol ; with an introduction and
notes by Dewey D. Wallace, Jr. ; illustrated by Isabelle Blood.
        p.   cm.
    Originally published : Chicago : F. H. Revell, 1887.
    ISBN 0-252-01666-1 (cloth : alk. paper). — ISBN 0-252-06091-1
    (paper : alk. paper)
    ISBN 978-0-252-01666-0 (cloth : alk. paper). — ISBN 978-0-252-06091-5
    (paper : alk. paper)
    1. Bristol, Sherlock, 1815–1906. 2. Congregational churches—
United States—Biography. I. Wallace Dewey D. II. Title.
    BX7260.B67A3   1989
    285.8'092'4—dc19
    [B]   89-4757
                                                CIP

Printed and bound in Great Britain by
Marston Book Services Limited, Oxford

For my sisters Joan and Dorothy,
who live in Bristol's West

Contents

EDITOR'S PREFACE

My first encounter with Sherlock Bristol was the serendipitous discovery of *The Pioneer Preacher* in a second-hand bookstore. When I found time to read it, I realized that I had come upon a lively, interesting, and revealing text, and further inquiry disclosed both its neglect by students of the history of the American West and of American religion, and its rarity (especially the first edition) in American libraries. I was convinced that it deserved a better fate, more for its representative and illustrative character than its inherent merit (though I do not consider it to be without such merit), and after presenting a paper on Bristol to a session of the American Society of Church History at its meeting in Fort Worth, Texas, in April, 1986, I was also encouraged by others to seek its reprinting.

After comparing the first edition of 1887 with the later edition of 1898, I decided that the first edition best fit my purposes for reprinting. The later edition added an encomium by the president of Oberlin College, where Bristol had been educated; Bristol also took an additional and somewhat extraneous anecdote and turned it into a new chapter, and rewrote the final chapter by inserting further musings about what he had been doing between editions. The first edition seemed to me to be fresher and more striking as a historical artifact of revivalistic religion on the western frontier, so I added textual annotations that take note of the changes made for the 1898 edition, and summarized that material. Only a few minor changes have been made in the text of the first edition except for the emendation, on page 157, of the date 1884 to 1864. The same error reappeared in the later edition, but the narrative makes clear that the earlier of the two dates was meant.

There were no footnotes in Bristol's text, so all the annotations are mine. My intention in the notes is to elucidate textual references to significant matters of historical and religious background.

It is a pleasure to acknowledge the assistance of many persons who contributed to the final product. Dina Schoonmaker, head of

Special Collections at the library of Oberlin College, gave me access to several items concerning Bristol. Correspondence with Myron Fogde and Frederick Kuhns supplied useful suggestions. The encouragement of Jan Shipps was important in pointing this project toward publication. Many persons at the University of Illinois Press provided help: Elizabeth Dulany guided me through many stages of the publication process, Mary Lou Menches patiently answered the questions of a novice about how to get my work onto computer disks, and Becky Standard expertly edited the text. At George Washington University Kevin Stephenson aided me with various miscellaneous tasks in preparation for publication.

Finally, many members of my family helped this project along at different stages. Paul helped me formulate some of my attitudes toward Bristol in conversations about his adventures; Mark helped me improve the language and style of the introduction; and Marion helped me polish and proofread the final text.

INTRODUCTION

Sherlock Bristol's *The Pioneer Preacher*, first published in 1887, is a fascinating and revealing text that documents many aspects of religion in the American West from frontier Ohio to far-off California. Bristol himself was not an important leader of the frontier mission, and standard histories do not mention his name, but the relatively artless autobiography of this Congregationalist preacher on the frontier vividly portrays the everyday events and attitudes that illustrated and shaped culture and religion in western America.

Sherlock Bristol was born on June 5, 1815, near Cheshire, Connecticut, where his parents, Gideon and Julia Bristol, were farmers of modest means, descended from generations of farmers. The family cared little about religion, but Bristol first grew serious about religion as a boy and then was converted, by means of an earnest young man from a prominent family, who was his Sunday-school teacher. With little prospect of rising above life on the farm, Bristol nonetheless decided to be a minister. He gained financial support from the Congregational Church of his village and other patrons, enabling him to attend Phillips Academy in Andover, Massachusetts, where he prepared for college from 1833 to 1835. His conversion to abolitionist views jeopardized his stay there and cost him the support of his church. But he persisted in his intention to enter the ministry and found another patron who paid for some of his later expenses at Oberlin College. He arrived at Oberlin in 1835, at most only months after the famous evangelist Charles G. Finney had come there as Professor of Theology. Because of its commitment to revivalism and antislavery, Oberlin exerted considerable attraction upon young men such as Bristol. Its manual labor plan helped Bristol and others who had little money to attend. He graduated from Oberlin in 1839 and began his theological studies at the seminary at Yale, where he enthusiastically promoted the Oberlin outlook, especially with respect to the doctrine of holiness Finney and Asa Mahan first broached there in 1836. After one year at New Haven he returned to Oberlin and completed his theological studies in 1842. He was licensed to preach by the Central Ohio Congregational Association.

Sherlock Bristol's early career as a minister was marked by frequent changes. From 1841 to 1843 he was pastor of the Congregational Church at Franklin, Ohio, a fairly remote settlement. From 1843 to 1846 he traveled as a fundraiser for Oberlin College, the institution that had so largely shaped his social and theological ideas. His efforts in that position were described by his employers as "industrious, persistent, and self-sacrificing."[1] In 1846 he became pastor of the strongly abolitionist Trinitarian Congregational Church in Fitchburg, Massachusetts. He left that church two years later for the Sullivan Street Church in New York City, where he also remained only two years. From 1850 to 1851 he served as pastor of another abolitionist stronghold, the Free Church in Andover, Massachusetts, the scene of his early education and first abolitionist exploits.

In order to restore his failing health, Bristol left Massachusetts for an eighteen-month trip to the California mining camps and back, by way of the Isthmus of Panama, a route to California taken by only a minority of those who responded to the promise of riches so widely advertised to be found there. On the journey and in the camps he combined mining, hunting, and preaching. He returned with enough wealth to establish himself and his family on a farm in frontier Wisconsin, where from 1852 to 1862 he was pastor of several churches— at Dartford, Green Lake Prairie, and Metomon—with a detour to Elmwood, Illinois, during 1859-61.

In 1862 Bristol set out for Oregon as captain of a wagon train. From Oregon he moved to the Boise valley of Idaho, where he preached, ranched, mined again for gold, and fought Indians. Gold had been discovered in Idaho in 1860, and many who had been in the California goldfields flocked there. In 1864 he returned to his family in Wisconsin and was Congregational pastor at Springvale and Brandon, Wisconsin, until 1867. In 1868 he established his family in Ventura County, California, where he ranched and engaged in freelance preaching and writing until his death from pneumonia in 1906. He married twice, to Emily Ingraham in 1842, and after her death to Amelia Locke in 1865. He had eight children, three daughters and five sons, all of whom survived him.[2]

Of course the genre of *The Pioneer Preacher* is autobiography. It is a commonplace about autobiography that it speaks with a double voice: it attempts a recreation of its "I" at earlier stages of life, but also provides "a point of view on the writer's own past life," an exercise in memory and interpretation at some point later than the principal events. An obvious inference is that there is in autobiography an imaginative and even fictive element shaping the events that are described. Thus autobiography consists of what James Olney has called "metaphors of self."[3] Such metaphors often better recapture the culture that provides the context both for the time in which the events are set and the time in which they are remembered than would an exact and annalistic transcript of events as they occurred. Moreover, tales of the American West were well known for exaggeration. Sherlock Bristol knew this: at the beginning he warns the reader not to expect "literal correctness" in the details of conversations and stories of long ago. And at the end of his story he ponders the problem of memory and retrospection, like his greater predecessor St. Augustine.[4]

However, unlike Augustine's *Confessions, The Pioneer Preacher* is not primarily spiritual autobiography focusing on the inner life; instead it invites comparison with the *Autobiography* of Peter Cartwright, the Methodist circuit rider on the Ohio valley frontier, who recounted his adventures in western preaching. But in comparison with Cartwright, and also with *The Pioneer Preacher*'s closest counterpart, William Chauncey Pond's *Gospel Pioneering: Reminiscences of Early Congregationalism in California, 1833-1920,* Bristol's narrative does not chiefly describe his preaching and ecclesiastical adventures, though it has its share of revival incidents and "surprising conversions." Bristol is fairly indifferent to the spread of his denomination westward and works alone, whereas Cartwright and Pond were sectarian propagandists and denominational chauvinists who worked in close contact with or under the supervision of others. Instead Bristol delights in recounting his own adventures, ecclesiastical or otherwise, and seems less interested in larger purposes than in telling his story.

Proportion indicates Bristol's interests: almost one-third of the narrative of *The Pioneer Preacher* details the childhood, education, and Oberlin years of the author; the eighteen-month trip to California and back constitutes one-fifth of the text, and another sizable portion describes his two years on the Oregon Trail and in Idaho. The ending also reflects Bristol's own interests: arriving in California, "choicest spot for human residence on earth," he meditates on its similarity both to Canaan and the Garden of Eden, noting that it differs from the latter by the presence of sin. It is an easy step from a sin-infested paradise to meditation on the celestial paradise where there will be no sin, and accordingly Bristol ends with his own apocalypse, beginning with a sentence reminiscent both of St. John and John Bunyan: "I once had a dream of heaven." The images of heaven that follow take him back to scenes of his earlier life, to the green of New Haven, and to a place where no walls divide the mansions, just like "Euclid Street in Cleveland." And "every heart in that delightful land was intensely conscious of these throbbings of divine love, and was also joyfully responsive to them."[5]

The protagonist of an autobiography requires some dominating force to impel the narrative, which James Olney in his study of autobiography likens to the socratic daimon.[6] For example, Pond in *Gospel Pioneering* wakes as a young man to the romance of home missions and follows the gleam of his vision.[7] But the number of Bristol's brief pastorates (quite common in fact with western Congregationalists), along with his descriptions of the nervous disorders to which he fell prey whenever he stayed too long in one place, suggest the daimon of restlessness. Whether as a youth, student, or pastor, he is continually confronted with the need to pull up stakes and move on. He declares that from his boyhood he had the "dare-devil's spirit of adventure."[8] He turned down support from the American Home Missionary Society while preaching in Wisconsin, because it would have prevented him from homesteading at the same time—he needed to clear the forest and plow the land to retain his health while he preached. Home only a few weeks from California, he announced that he wanted a place on the frontier, and moved to Wisconsin. Soon he was invited to leave Wisconsin for a journey to Oregon—"Then came the happy thought of a trip across the plains, with covered wagon drawn by oxen or horses, and plodding along for six months, with little opportunity for reading books or mental exercise, and an abundance of calls for muscular employment."[9] Thus adventuring was justified for reasons of health; Bristol always returned from his adventures recuperated, living to the age of ninety-one. This theme runs throughout the literature of the period, and appeared in the lore about Daniel Boone as "the ability of the wilderness to redeem man by liberating him from melancholy."[10]

The restlessness that drove Bristol onward, and the adventuresomeness that he reveled in as he proceeded, make his narrative travel literature as well as an account of religious occurrences. But while Bristol's restless and adventuresome behavior may have qualified as that "muscular Christianity" popular at the time of his writing, his manner lacked the dignity and decorum that were thought proper for a member of the clergy. And as will be discussed later, his unsympathetic attitude to the Native Americans probably also had something to do with the eventual neglect of his account.

Bristol's style of writing fits his character. It is plain with short, direct sentences and vivid images. He makes no claim for literary merit.[11] He writes with none of the labored pretentiousness or bloated rhetoric of nineteenth-century clerical prose that mars even the pages of so rough-hewn an author as Peter Cartwright. He has an eye for a good story. There is much commonsensical humanity in his pages as well as humor — "a good, hearty laugh hurts no man," he declared at one point.[12] Such a direct style no doubt reflected his preaching on the frontier: in *Roughing It* Mark Twain caricatured a minister who could not communicate with western miners; but Bristol knew how to make himself understood.

Books such as *The Pioneer Preacher* were published because they were considered edifying and exemplary of Christian ideals. However, literary exemplifications of the Christian life inevitably drew upon an extensive heritage of motifs of sanctity, extending from patristic times through Puritan biographies to the ministerial and missionary narratives about American evangelicals. Elements of this heritage that are relevant to Bristol's autobiography include the depiction of personal sanctity, heroic pastoral labors, providential occurrences, and miraculous events of clairvoyance and answered prayer. Based on a study of lives of Methodist itinerants, Donald E. Byrne, Jr., has shown how such motifs became folkloristic in America. Bristol knew something of this literature, having spent time at Oberlin reading "religious biographies."[13]

Bristol's sanctity is evident from the depicted holiness of his life: though surrounded by profanity in his early years, after his conversion he never again engaged in it — no mean feat on the profanity-ridden frontier.[14] As an Oberlin student he often fasted.[15] So unselfish is he that he and a partner in the California goldfields each press an extra two hundred dollars in earnings upon the other, a story reminiscent of one from the lore of the Desert Fathers in which two saintly old men try to quarrel over who owns a certain tile, only to find themselves unable to do so.[16]

However, Sabbath-keeping was the principal external sign of Sherlock Bristol's holiness of life. He failed to keep the Sabbath as a day of prayer and meditation only once, under the duress of Indian attack. Bristol's exactitude about the Sabbath was the Protestant equivalent of the prayer vigils of medieval saints. Based on the Puritan example, American evangelical Protestants had raised the proper observance of the Sabbath to a place of eminence among the particulars of a sound Christian life, and it was especially important to them as evidence of the spread of "scriptural holiness" across America, a symbol that even though the nation recognized no particular denomination, it was nonetheless a Christian land. Thus the American Sabbath Union had a significant place among the various voluntary and benevolent societies by which evangelical Protestants hoped to influence the nation. Particularly in frontier communities, observance of the Sabbath was an important indication of a Christian presence. There were many other early California ministers besides Bristol who emphasized its importance.[17]

Inwardly, Bristol's sanctity is evidenced by his search for a higher and more sin-free Christian life, a matter that becomes the chief theological strand running through the narrative. Neither the spread of a denomination, such as motivated Cartwright and Pond, nor even the desire to preach the gospel seemed as important to Bristol, at the time when he wrote his narrative, as did this cultivation and spread of holiness. His autobiography, he says, was written for those men and women who "sigh and cry after holiness of heart," and it records not only his weaknesses and temptations but also "the power of Christ to deliver." Thus at Oberlin he quickly adopted the new doctrine of Christian perfection and attempted to teach it to others.[18] He devoted the only lengthy theological treatise he ever wrote to this subject, *Paracletos, or The Baptism of the Holy Ghost*, published in 1892 by Fleming H. Revell, also the publisher of his autobiography. In his additions to the final chapter of the 1898 edition of *The Pioneer Preacher* Bristol claimed that he had received so much response to his discussion of holiness in his autobiography that he decided to prepare an entire treatise on the subject. In *Paracletos* he appealed to Christians to seek total victory over sins through dependence on God's spirit, and to expect daily help from the Holy Spirit, something that he called "appropriating faith." The book shows him clearly conversant with the holiness tradition as it had developed to that time through both John Wesley and the Oberlin perfectionists, the evangelist Charles G. Finney and his colleague Asa Mahan. He is also aware of the work of Phoebe Palmer, a holiness teacher who did much to popularize the doctrine in the middle of the century. All of these had taught, to the horror of strict Calvinists, that it was possible to attain a piety of sinless perfection in this life, though they admitted there was no guarantee of remaining in that state. In his years of retirement in California Bristol corresponded extensively on the subject.[19]

Bristol's heroic pastoral labors were manifested in his vigorous and indefatigible preaching. Often, like other frontier preachers such as Peter Cartwright and many Methodist itinerants, he had to face down opponents. This paralleled ancient worthies such as St. Martin, who had to overcome demonic disturbers of their evangelistic efforts. At one place where he preached, "Campbellites," followers of Alexander Campbell's effort to restore Christianity through a simple adherence to the New Testament alone, opposed his preaching.[20] Sometimes opposition to Bristol's preaching arose because of his abolitionist views that had been reinforced by his years at Oberlin, a bastion of the cause. Other Finneyite frontier preachers had similar reputations as abolitionists. William Chauncey Pond was known in California as "the abolition preacher."[21]

Providential occurrences are rife in ancient hagiographies, Puritan lives, and in many biographies and autobiographies of heroic American evangelicals. Many variations of this motif in Methodist folklore have been recently catalogued.[22] Bristol continues this tradition by claiming he financed most his education through "special providences." Providence was also evident to him in some of the surprising conversions he narrated. In Bristol's account such providential occurrences shaded rather gradually into miraculous events of clairvoyance and answered prayer. Thus Bristol's boyhood pastor foresees that Bristol will become a minister, and Bristol observes that prayer precedes many of the providential events in the story.[23] Mark Twain ridiculed the frequent appearance of such things in contemporary narratives with his "Uncle Lem," who was appointed by special providence to break the fall of an Irish hod carrier who lost his balance, even though it broke Uncle Lem's back.[24]

But in Bristol's autobiography as a whole, the hoary motifs of Christian hagiography are overwhelmed by the more pervasive motifs of the West and the frontier. Rather than St. Martin, John Bunyan, or Peter Cartwright, the models most relevant to *The Pioneer Preacher* are Daniel Boone, Davy Crockett, Kit Carson, Bigfoot Wallace, and Buffalo Bill. And even though one western preacher, the Baptist John Mason Peck, wrote a biography of Boone portraying him as a protector of Christian values, the main motifs in the lives of these American heroes were not sanctity and providence, but those of the rough and violent westering pioneer, who boasted of exaggerated exploits and of acquaintance with forbidding terrain while yet seeking the Eden of the West; they are motifs of the explorer, the hunter, the Indian fighter, and the fiercely democratic foe of all aristocratic pretension.[25]

Sherlock Bristol was such a westering pioneer on the frontier. Already in the East he was a woodsman, familiar with the flora and fauna of the Connecticut wilds and skilled with the axe—"the sun had browned my face, my hands were hard with work."[26] For him the wilderness was a place of adventure, as it had been for James Fenimore Cooper.[27] When Bristol arrived at Oberlin in the mid-1830s, it was a scene ready for a *coureur des bois,* an academic Natty Bumppo, for it was a "little clearing" in the midst of a "dense, dark forest," with only a few log houses. There Bristol helped support himself by "chopping wood" and "clearing land," while sleeping in the attic of a "woodshed." He was descended from folk who thought that fame came from skill with an axe; the axe takes on a special symbolism when Bristol converts an Ohio backwoodsman by first praising his choice of an axe and then showing that he, though a preacher, can chop as well as anyone—"I knew the heart of a chopper."[28]

Like Daniel Boone, Bristol needed elbow room. He described his first Ohio pastorate as "a rude backwoods settlement." Eager to move to Wisconsin, he says that "The place I wanted was one on the frontier." But even in far-off Wisconsin he felt the urge to cross the plains.[29] On the trail he was selected as captain of the wagon train and scouted ahead to find camping sites and detect signs of hostile Indians. Back in Wisconsin, he soon sold out, and headed for California. Crossing a California desert, he and some companions almost died of thirst. In his travels he recapitulated the images of woodsman, homesteader, prairie trailblazer, and forty-niner. The frontier was not a single place, but a continuously moving borderland, waiting to be chased by the adventuresome. According to Dixon Wecter, "The winning of the west is the great fantasy of the Republic," and the frontier is for American heroes "the proving-ground" of their courage.[30]

"But they were rough in those times!" proclaimed Mark Twain of the western mining towns,[31] and Bristol boasted of rough exploits from Connecticut to California. Shortly after his conversion and while still a schoolboy, seven young toughs tried to ride him on a rail because of his temperance advocacy: "a back-handed stroke sent one assailant against a bench over which he fell heavily, striking on his head. Seizing the rail I thrust it back against the wall, almost crushing out the bowels of him who stood at that end and held it. This put two out of the fight." He was not ridden on a rail. A pastor in Ohio, he was discouraged from calling on a man by the man's son, who declared, "My pa says he will shoot you, if you come"—which just whetted Bristol's appetite for a convert. To an aristocratic assailant he said, "Why you little whiffet, I can throw you out of that window, and I will do it if you attempt to strike me. I could break every bone in your little body in five minutes."[32] This is the clerical version of the boasting Mississippi River ruffians in *Huckleberry Finn.*[33]

While a pastor in New York he thrashed a Tammany Hall enforcer. When a rough miner in California warned him that he assailed all preachers who passed by, Bristol threw him into a puddle, leaving him "looking as foolish and crestfallen as a picked goose." Staying alone at a California ranch, he found out that three desperadoes were coming to rob him, and gathered in readiness "a Colt's navy revolver, an Allen's six-shooter, a double-barrel shot gun, a double-barrel pistol, a rifle, a musket, and a Mexican sword." So armed, he captured them all, and boasted, "They were cowed down and held in mortal fear by one man!" Returning home with his gold from the mining camp (which he carried sewn into a special vest that also provided protection against dagger thrusts), he bested a rowdy sailor who was terrorizing the other passengers: "seizing the middle fingers of both hands and turning them nearly out of joint, I held him in that condition."[34] No wonder that a frontier Episcopalian announced that "The physical weakling has no place in the missionary work in the west."[35] Richard Dorson has singled out the strong hero as the characteristic figure of American folklore, with Davy Crockett most typical.[36] Bristol was the ministerial version of such a strong hero, and like Crockett was also a mighty hunter and brave fighter.

Incidents of hunting constitute a significant portion of *The Pioneer Preacher*, as Bristol sought, like Isaac McCaslin in Faulkner's *The Bear*, "to earn for himself from the wilderness the name and state of hunter." After some early hunting exploits, Davy Crockett declared, "It was here that I began to distinguish myself as a hunter"; Bristol also was fond of hunting as a boy, and was like Nimrod or Esau, famed biblical hunters. When a man, he was acknowledged by others as the "best shot" among them.[37]

Bristol supported himself by hunting on the Isthmus of Panama while he awaited passage for California, and had narrow escapes from both a puma and alligators. When he killed a monstrous alligator, he was acclaimed by the natives of the region for delivering them from its menace. The alligator seems to have been as big and dangerous as those Mrs. Trollope was entertained with by storytellers on her trip up the Mississippi. Battles with fearsome alligators filled foreign accounts of the threats to be encountered in America.[38]

Bristol found California "a paradise of wild animals" and proceeded to shoot as many as he could. Undeterred by the danger, he trailed a grizzly bear for many miles (Davy Crockett commented in his autobiography, "that spring I killed ten bears"; on the frontier a person's worth was measured by the number of bears killed). Bristol hunted wild boar with equal courage, and described the encounter in epic terms: "there confronted me the famous wild boar of which I have spoken . . . he did not rush upon me at once, but approached steadily . . . his tusks protruding three inches outside his upper lip, and his mouth white with foam." In his California retirement he continued to hunt to maintain his health.[39]

Many frontier preachers earned the title of "fighting" because of their survival of encounters with Indians. Both on the Oregon Trail and while ranching in Idaho, Bristol was engaged in shoot-outs. He refused the offer of cavalry protection for the wagon train to Oregon, outraging most of the other travelers. "Better ten men who can crawl half a mile in the brush to shoot them singly, than a round hundred fighting as civilized soldiers usually do," he told them. Thus he avoided another defeat like that of General Braddock. On the trail he and another scout tracked and shot an Indian whom they thought had killed one of their companions. Unlike Bigfoot Wallace, Bristol did not boast of a milestone when he killed his first Indian, nor did he consent to scalping, but he accepted the frontier argument that nonresistance was more credible in the East than the West, where one confronted real Indians. He thought that those who felt whites were to blame for tribal disturbances would soon be disabused of such a notion were they to live on the frontier. When two Indians were killed in a battle with Idaho ranchers and miners, he commented that "there were two less of a race whose principal business is to rob and to kill."[40]

American attitudes toward Native Americans veered from considering them noble savages to regarding them as a race worthy of extermination, with the latter the usual view in the West. The violence of the Indian fighter was central to western myth; Bristol is not a dissenting voice from prevailing western views. It is perhaps surprising that one who was such a staunch abolitionist and friend of blacks (a free black accompanied him to the California goldfields and shared in his labors there; Bristol was proud of his associate's skill as a boxer when he defeated the white champion of the mining district) should not also have extended his sympathies to the Native American. In fact by the time Bristol wrote, many eastern evangelicals had made, however paternalistically, the cause of their protection one of their crusading efforts. So widespread was sympathy for Native Americans and concern for Indian missions among evangelicals by the end of the century that Bristol's lack of such concern in all likelihood is one of the reasons his narrative dropped out of currency among the pious.[41]

Frederick Jackson Turner's classical and influential interpretation of American history claimed that the pioneering experience of the continually westward-moving frontier was the most important form-

ative influence on American life and culture, providing it with a new
and different constellation of values from that of the older European
society. As Ray Allen Billington has restated Turner's outlook, on the
frontier a set of characteristic values emerged that became the values
of American culture as a whole: mobility, activism, optimism, willing-
ness to innovate, and democratic disdain for aristocracy. In addition,
Richard Slotkin has emphasized the violent streak endemic to western
(and American) life.[42] These frontier values are well illustrated by
Bristol's autobiography. From the beginning to the end of *The Pioneer
Preacher* the transformation of inherited Christian attitudes by these
values is apparent. Apart from the violence, the Oberlin and Finneyite
theological heritage by which Bristol was formed had in many ways
already adapted to such values. Bristol summed up his pioneering
spirit when he declared himself "ready for any adventure which called
for strength, and that ready and practical wit" of which he had full
supply. Tradition and reflection did not deter him: "No casuistry had
yet been allowed to impose on my common sense," for "an ounce of
prompt and resolute decision is often worth a ton of vacillation and
palaver."[43] Bristol illustrates a western and American naive shrewdness
that could overcome intellectuals and European sophisticates, and that
one hears in the crude wisdom voiced by Davy Crockett or Bigfoot
Wallace when they confront "city slickers." Bristol would certainly
not have disagreed with those representatives of the Congregationalists who asserted that the West would be especially receptive to the
founding of Congregational churches, for "our spirit of freedom,
democracy and fellowship appeals to western people."[44] In fact, western and Finneyite Congregationalists such as Bristol took it as a point
of great pride that their denomination, begun in America with the
Pilgrims, had kept alive their pioneering spirit ever since, and was
consequently the denomination that best represented a joining of the
Christian and the American way. The later nineteenth century particularly saw a great increase in this kind of denominational chauvin-
ism: as late as 1921 the theologian John Wright Buckham called Pond
and other early California Congregationalists "true Pilgrim Fathers
of the Pacific, of the same heroic mold and dauntless spirit as the
founders of Plymouth."[45]

No one applied the insights of Turner about the American frontier to religious life with more influence on later historians than
William Warren Sweet. But while Sweet chronicled the successes in
the West of those popular denominations which were most adaptive
to frontier conditions, such as the Methodists, he also significantly
shifted the focus to the role religious institutions played in civilizing

the frontier, presumably by stamping its character with the values those denominations represented. Thus the story of religion in the West has also been told as a story of the extension of social control to regions sadly in need of it, from the point of view of more established groups concerned with the problem of disorder. And so Christianity on the frontier was promoted as a stabilizing force, as Christians perceived the western wilderness as an obstacle to religion and civilization. Alarmed by what lay beyond the mountains, Lyman Beecher uttered his famous "Plea for the West" and Horace Bushnell wrote *Barbarism the First Danger.* The westering Baptist John Mason Peck was distressed by the slipping of western religion into an indolent primitivism, which he sought to head off by denominational organization, Sunday schools, and voluntary associations. Flavel Bascom, one of those western missionaries who was part of the famed "Yale Band" that labored in frontier Illinois, referred to his task as that of "promoting a true Christian civilization." Thus in their thrust westward the descendents of the New England Puritans brought along their churches, schools, colleges, and orderly towns. Chauncey Pond in California mused on "the wonderful adaptability of the polity and the spirit of the Pilgrims to solve the problem of the frontier." Bristol often saw his own labors as such an extension of social control, as he strove to impose temperance and Sabbath-keeping in the West, despite opposition (in California he first enrages and then wins over to the temperance cause a man who declared that he had left Maine and crossed a continent to escape temperance reformers). Bristol even brought some order to the mining camps where he labored; likewise a recent investigator has maintained that religion was quite important in creating social order in the Colorado mining towns.[46]

These western traits and labors for the control of the West by Christianity bespeak the spirit of Oberlin and of Charles G. Finney. Oberlin was founded to extend religious revival into the West, and it quickly became a center of enthusiasm for all the causes of that network of voluntary associations for missions and reform that have been collectively dubbed the "benevolent empire." Oberlin stood for temperance and abolition as well as revivalism; the barely functioning college was saved in the fall of 1834 when its founder, John Jay Shipherd, persuaded the so-called Lane rebels who left Lyman Beecher's Lane seminary in Cincinnati to come to Oberlin, where antislavery sentiments were not so restricted. Oberlin also became a center for such advanced movements in evangelicalism as the holiness awakening. According to this movement, conversion was expected to lead to an activist Christian life of holiness and reform, carried out in a spirit of optimism. Finney and Oberlin were strongly committed to an optimistic postmillennialist eschatology whereby the second coming of Christ would be at the end of a period of world improvement achieved through revival and reform. Finney had also been important as an innovator in the practice of revivals. His practical "new measures," which he hoped would lead to a much more effective revivalism, included the protracted meeting, in which length itself became a means of breaking down the resistance of sinners, the "anxious bench," by means of which those ripe for conversion could be brought forward and made available for further and more personal exhortation, and the practice of calling upon those known to be in need of conversion by name. These new measures were roundly condemned by conservative opponents, but Finney, who thought one had to understand the laws of mind, the psychology of sinners, to be an effective revivalist, protested against the older method of telling inquirers that they must wait upon God and hope that at some future point they would begin to feel the workings of grace in their hearts. He was convinced that individuals had the moral ability to be converted if they chose to do so, and that it was the task of the revivalist to bring them to the point where they would so choose.[47]

Bristol was not only educated at Oberlin by Finney and Mahan, but also recurred constantly to their ideas. His commitment to Finneyite and Oberlin views is clear from *The Pioneer Preacher.* He was scornful of the notion that God does not want everyone to repent, echoing Finney's rejection of Calvinist predestination; he luxuriated in the "perpetual revival" of Oberlin; he brought about conversions through straightforward argument meant to break down the resistance of sinners; he sought the total consecration advocated by Oberlin perfectionism; and he was an optimistic postmillennialist.[48]

The other published writings of Sherlock Bristol also provide evidence of the persistence of the Oberlin and Finneyite strain in his thought. Two small tracts of 1903 and 1906 respectively, *The Sin of Not Doing* and *Human Sinfulness,* as well as his one major theological work that treated Christian perfection, echo that earlier theology. *The Sin of Not Doing* is a published sermon developing the theme that since one has the ability to believe, one has the duty to be converted. The refusal to do so dishonors God, and is the sin of not loving God as one ought.[49] *Human Sinfulness* asserts that under the terms of God's moral government of the world, persons are responsible for the particulars of their own moral record. The various sins Bristol had long deplored — Sabbath-breaking, profanity, and intemperance — are mentioned, and their denunciation is updated (he is disturbed by the working of threshing machines on Sundays), but the ultimate sin is impenitence. Impenitence is described as an especially heinous sin in a land such as America, where so many opportunities for repentance and reform are at hand.[50] The work on holiness not only provided a detailed exposition of that doctrine, but also expressed his post-millennial optimism: Bristol thought that an emphasis on Christian perfection through the power of the Holy Spirit would lead to a "world-wide Pentecostal revival" and that when this had arrived "the millennium will have come, and the earth will be but a vestibule of heaven!" Then the church would regain the courage it had when it fought slavery.[51]

The Finneyite and Oberlin theology still being expressed by Bristol at the turn of the new century had a rather old-fashioned ring by that time, outdated by newer theological currents, both liberal and conservative. However, there is considerable evidence for the persistence of this outlook among western Congregationalists, as well as members of other denominations in the West. Charles Oliver Brown, who had significant pastorates in Dubuque and San Francisco in the 1880s and 1890s, was equally Finneyite in his theology. So were Chauncey Pond and another venerable western Congregationalist, John C. Holbrook.[52] It would seem as though there was a kind of theological culture lag in many western pulpits, whereas eastern Congregationalists were absorbing the insights of Horace Bushnell and developing the "new theology" of liberalism.

But a question remains as to why this Finneyite theological formation did not lead these ministers to a more positive attitude concerning the emerging liberal theology, especially since there seem to have been so many connections between Oberlin Arminianism, post-millennialism, and moral reformism on the one hand, and the newer liberal theological currents on the other. Did not the Finneyite program of practical theological simplification point forward to the liberal dismantling of dogma?

Evidence drawn from Sherlock Bristol's later years suggests a more complex pattern. Already in *Paracletos, or The Baptism of the Holy Ghost,* he had evinced a Fundamentalist kind of alarm over German and American theological professors who had never experienced the baptism of the Holy Spirit that would have kept them faithful to belief in the divine authority of the scripture.[53] It was a common complaint of the early Fundamentalists that ungodly German biblical critics were having a bad influence on American seminaries. Over ten years later he fired an early Fundamentalist salvo with his *An Address to the Congregational Brotherhood,* a brief tract of sixteen pages in which he

attacked the Congregationalist seminaries and associations for allowing in their midst those who employed infidel methods of biblical
scholarship and who denied central doctrines of the faith. Bristol
blamed this trend on the young men who had studied in Germany,
and was especially shocked that such persons were even teaching at
Oberlin. Once again he noted that these professors would have been
inoculated against such false teachings if they had ever received the
baptism of the Holy Spirit. But the particular doctrinal concerns of
his "Fundamentalism" appear to be more the issues of earlier Finneyite arguments than those related to the issues of the new theology:
thus he stressed belief in the Bible rather than infidelity (Thomas
Paine is mentioned), Trinitarianism instead of Unitarianism, and belief
in hell as opposed to Universalism. Where these fundamentals were
eroded, he thought, there would be no authentic revivals and no
spiritual life in the Holy Ghost.[54]

Thus Bristol exemplifies a transition from Oberlin or "new school"
theology to Fundamentalism of the kind that George M. Marsden has
described for some Presbyterians. In fact, many of the later elements
of Fundamentalism were much closer to new school evangelicalism
than to strict Calvinism: for example, revivalism, moralism, reformist
nationalism, lack of interest in the sacraments, and a view of the
church as a voluntary society bringing together those who had been
soundly converted. A recent scholar has even pointed out how commonly the path from abolitionist to Fundamentalist was trod at the
end of the nineteenth century. Much Fundamentalism also seemed to
carry on the program of theological simplification that characterized
Oberlin theology. Such simplification, with its reduction of religion
to the practical and its implied anti-intellectualism, may have flour-
ished in the churches in the West, as Fundamentalism eventually did,
because it was compatible with the frontier and western attitudes. An
examination of religious opinion in the Colorado mining towns found
it quite conservative.[55]

The new perfectionist teachings, especially in the more moderate
form that emanated from the Keswick conferences in England and
were adopted by the evangelist Dwight Moody, the Bible annotator
Cyrus I. Scofield, and A. B. Simpson, founder of the Christian and
Missionary Alliance, were an influence in Fundamentalism, although
orthodox Calvinists such as Benjamin Warfield at Princeton Theological Seminary would have nothing to do with them. The more
extreme version of perfectionist teaching that Bristol adopted became
central for such emerging holiness and Fundamentalist denominations
as the Church of the Nazarene.[56] But Bristol showed no signs of

participating in the growing enthusiasm of incipient Fundamentalists
for the premillennial doctrine of the return of Christ; he was faithful
to his postmillennial Oberlin heritage.

The Pioneer Preacher illustrates much about the culture of the
frontier and the West. One can learn from it the way western religion
was influenced by frontier values and attitudes, and also about how
religion in the West functioned to provide the stability of traditional
values. Bristol's narrative also provides hints about connections between his Finneyite theological formation and the later movements
of holiness and Fundamentalism, both of which had significant impact
on western churches.

Notes to Introduction

1. Robert Samuel Fletcher, *A History of Oberlin College: From Its Foundation through the Civil War*, 2 vols. (Oberlin, Ohio: Oberlin College, 1943), I, 492.

2. Sherlock Bristol, *The Pioneer Preacher: Incidents of Interest, and Experiences in the Author's Life*, passim; *The Congregational Year-Book, 1907* (Boston: Fort Hill Press), p. 14; Ray Allen Billington, *The Far Western Frontier*, 1830-1860 (New York: Harper & Row, 1956), p. 249.

3. James Olney, *Metaphors of Self: The Meaning of Autobiography* (Princeton, N.J.: Princeton University Press, 1972), pp. 30ff., 42.

4. Bristol, *Pioneer Preacher*, pp. xxxiii, 179.

5. Ibid., pp. 175-76, 181-83. Other early ministers in California also saw it as an Eden full of possibilities, Sandra Sizer Frankiel, *California's Spiritual Frontiers: Religious Alternatives in Anglo-Protestantism, 1850-1910* (Berkeley: University of California Press, 1988), pp. 1-17; Gregory H. Singleton, *Religion in the City of the Angels: American Protestant Culture and Urbanization, Los Angeles, 1850-1930* (n.p., UMI Research Press, 1977), p. 1.

6. Olney, *Metaphors of Self*, p. 39.

7. William Chauncey Pond, *Gospel Pioneering: Reminiscences of Early Congregationalism in California, 1833-1920* (Oberlin, Ohio: News Printing Co., 1921), p. 15.

8. Bristol, *Pioneer Preacher*, p. 3; cf. also p. 6.

9. Ibid., pp. 113, 116, 128.

10. Richard Slotkin, *Regeneration through Violence: The Mythology of the American Frontier, 1600-1860* (Middletown, Conn.: Wesleyan University Press, 1973), p. 270.

11. Bristol, *Pioneer Preacher*, p. xxxiii.

12. Ibid., p. 61.

13. Ibid, p. 27.

14. Ibid., pp. 6-7; Ray Allen Billington, *Land of Savagery, Land of Promise: The European Image of the American Frontier* (New York: Norton, 1981), pp. 191-92.

15. Bristol, *Pioneer Preacher*, p. 27.

16. Ibid., p. 106; Helen Waddell, *The Desert Fathers: Translations from the Latin with an Introduction* (Ann Arbor: University of Michigan Press, 1957), p. 142.

17. Bristol, *Pioneer Preacher*, p. 148; for the Puritan background, see Winton U. Solberg, *Redeem the Time: The Puritan Sabbath in Early America* (Cambridge, Mass.: Harvard University Press, 1977); for Puritan sabbath observance as an aspect of sanctity, see Dewey D. Wallace, Jr., "The Image of Saintliness in Puritan Hagiography, 1650-1700," in John E. Booty, ed., *The Divine Drama in History and Liturgy: Essays Presented to Horton Davies on His Retirement from Princeton University* (Allison Park, Pa.: Pickwick Publications, 1984), p. 38; for later American developments, see Roy Z. Chamlee, "The Sabbath Crusade: 1810-1920," unpub. doct. diss., George Washington University, 1968; Alice Cowan Cochran, *Miners, Merchants and Missionaries: The Roles of Missionaries and Pioneer Churches in the Colorado Gold Rush and Its Aftermath, 1850-1870* (Metuchen, N.J.: Scarecrow Press, 1980), p. 70; Frankiel, *California's Spiritual Frontiers*, pp. 48ff.

18. Bristol, *Pioneer Preacher*, pp. xxxiv, 29-31, 32-33, 35-36, 47-49.

19. Sherlock Bristol, *Paracletos, or The Baptism of the Holy Ghost* (Chicago: Fleming H. Revell, 1892), pp. 5-6, 33, 101; for the holiness movement, see John L. Peters, *Christian Perfection and American Methodism* (New York: Abingdon Press, 1956); Melvin Easterday Dieter, *The Holiness Revival of the Nineteenth Century* (Metuchen, N.J.: Scarecrow Press, 1980); and James E. Johnson, "Charles G. Finney and Oberlin Perfectionism," *Journal of Presbyterian History*, 46 (March, 1968 and June, 1968), pp. 42-57, 128-38; Bristol, *Pioneer Preacher* (1898 ed.), p. 327.

20. Bristol, *Pioneer Preacher*, pp. 37ff., 50-53ff., 55ff., 58ff., 60-61; Donald E. Byrne, Jr., *No Foot of Land: Folklore of American Methodist Itinerants* (Metuchen, N.J.: Scarecrow Press, 1975), pp. 91-97; *Autobiography of Peter Cartwright*, ed. Charles L. Wallis (New York: Abingdon Press, 1956), pp. 45-46, 70-72; Sulpicius Severus et al., *The Western Fathers: Being the Lives of Martin of Tours, Ambrose, Augustine of Hippo, Honoratus of Arles and Germanus of Auxerre*, ed. trans. F. R. Hoare (New York: Harper and Row, 1965), pp. 26, 29; for the early "Campbellites," see David Edwin Harrell, Jr., *Quest for a Christian America: The Disciples of Christ and American Society to 1866*, vol. I of *A Social History of the Disciples of Christ* (Nashville, Tenn.: Disciples of Christ Historical Society, 1966).

21. Fletcher, *A History of Oberlin College*, I, 395; Pond, *Gospel Pioneering*, p. 82.

22. Byrne, *No Foot of Land*, pp. 126-70.

23. Bristol, *Pioneer Preacher*, pp. 14, 43ff.

24. Mark Twain, *Roughing It* (New York: New American Library, 1962), pp. 80-81.

25. Slotkin, *Regeneration through Violence*, pp. 394-465, discusses the lore growing up around Daniel Boone; Henry Nash Smith, *Virgin Land: The American West as Symbol and Myth* (Cambridge, Mass.: Harvard University Press, 1950), pp. 88-98, 113-25, discusses Kit Carson and Buffalo Bill; *The Autobiography of David Crockett, with an Introduction by Hamlin Garland* (New York: Charles Scribner's Sons, 1923); John C. Duval, *The Adventures of Big-*

foot Wallace, the Texas Ranger and Hunter (Philadelphia: Claxton, Remsen, and Haffelfinger, 1891).

26. Bristol, *Pioneer Preacher*, p. 9.

27. Roderic Nash, *Wilderness and the American Mind* (New Haven, Conn.: Yale University Press, rev. ed. 1973), p. 76.

28. Bristol, *Pioneer Preacher*, pp. 1-2, 25, 26, 52.

29. Ibid., pp. 50, 113, 128.

30. Dixon Wecter, *The Hero in America: A Chronicle of Hero-Worship* (1941; rpt. Ann Arbor: University of Michigan Press, 1963), pp. 182, 344.

31. Mark Twain, *Roughing It*, p. 310.

32. Bristol, *Pioneer Preacher*, pp. 16-17, 50, 61.

33. The scene of the river ruffians was originally intended for *Huckleberry Finn* but was removed at an editor's suggestion. It later appeared in the third chapter of *Life on the Mississippi*. Some editors restore it to its original place. See Mark Twain, *Adventures of Huckleberry Finn*, ed. Henry Nash Smith (Boston: Houghton-Mifflin, 1958), pp. 247-51.

34. Bristol, *Pioneer Preacher*, pp. 68-69, 91-92, 102-4, 105-6, 109.

35. Cyrus Townsend Brady, *Recollections of a Missionary in the Great West* (New York: Charles Scribner's, 1901), p. 73.

36. Richard Dorson, *American Folklore* (Chicago: University of Chicago Press, 1959), p. 200.

37. William Faulkner, *Go Down, Moses* (New York: Modern Library, 1942), p. 192; *Autobiography of David Crockett*, p. 50; Bristol, *Pioneer Preacher*, pp. 5, 82.

38. Bristol, *Pioneer Preacher*, pp. 73-79; Frances Trollope, *Domestic Manners of the Americans*, ed. Donald Smalley (New York: Alfred Knopf, 1949), pp. 4, 21-22; Billington, *Land of Savagery, Land of Promise*, p. 103.

39. *Autobiography of David Crockett*, p. 101; Slotkin, *Regeneration through Violence*, p. 415; Bristol, *Pioneer Preacher*, pp. 168-70.

40. Ross Phares, *Bible in Pocket, Gun in Hand: The Story of Frontier Religion* (Lincoln: University of Nebraska Press, 1964), p. 157; Duval, *The Adventures of Big-foot Wallace*, pp. 33-34; Bristol, *Pioneer Preacher*, pp. 140-43, 145, 147, 154.

41. Richard Slotkin, *The Fatal Environment: The Myth of the Frontier in the Age of Industrialization, 1800-1890* (New York: Atheneum, 1985), p. 32; Robert M. Utley, *The Indian Frontier of the American West, 1846-1890* (Albuquerque: University of New Mexico Press, 1984), pp. 34, 102, 203ff.

42. Ray Allen Billington, *America's Frontier Heritage* (New York: Holt, Rinehart and Winston, 1966), pp. 1-2, 117ff., 122, 205; Billington, *Land of Savagery, Land of Promise*, pp. 246ff., 215-17; Slotkin, *Regeneration through Violence*, pp. 5, 18, 32.

43. Bristol, *Pioneer Preacher*, pp. 3, 19, 138.

44. Quoted in Myron Fogde, *The Church Goes West* (n.p., Consortium Books, 1977), p. 177.

45. Quoted from his introduction to Pond, *Gospel Pioneering*, p. iii.

46. For an analysis of Sweet's views, see James L. Ash, Jr., *Protestantism and the American University: An Intellectual Biography of William Warren Sweet* (Dallas, Tex.: Southern Methodist University Press, 1982); Nash, *Wilderness and the American Mind*, pp. 41-42; *Memoir of John Mason Peck, D.D., Edited from His Journals and Correspondence by Rufus Babcock*, intro. Paul M. Harrison (Carbondale: Southern Illinois University Press, 1965), pp. liii-lix, 94ff., 111, 129ff.; quoted in William Warren Sweet, *Religion on the American Frontier, 1783-1850*, vol. III, *The Congregationalists, a Collection of Source Materials* (Chicago: University of Chicago Press, 1939), p. 234; Pond, *Gospel Pioneering*, p. 170; Bristol, *Pioneer Preacher*, p. 98; Alice Cowan Cochran, *Miners, Merchants and Missionaries: The Roles of Missionaries and Pioneer Churches in the Colorado Gold Rush and Its Aftermath, 1859-1870* (Metuchen, N.J.: Scarecrow Press, 1980), pp. ix, 23-25, 102, 120-21; for a study that follows the social control approach generally, see T. Scott Miyakawa, *Protestants and Pioneers: Individualism and Conformity on the American Frontier* (Chicago: University of Chicago Press, 1964), pp. 3-5.

47. For Finney's biography, see Keith J. Hardman, *Charles Grandison Finney, 1792-1875: Revivalist and Reformer* (Syracuse, N.Y.: Syracuse University Press, 1987); for his career as a revivalist, see William G. McLoughlin, Jr., *Modern Revivalism: Charles Grandison Finney to Billy Graham* (New York: Ronald Press, 1959), pp. 3-122; for Finney's Rochester revival and its social significance, see Paul E. Johnson, *A Shopkeeper's Millennium: Society and Revivals in Rochester, New York, 1815-1837* (New York: Hill and Wang, 1978); for his theology, consult the older work by Frank Hugh Foster, *A Genetic History of the New England Theology* (1907; rpt. New York: Russell and Russell, 1963), pp. 453-70; for the religious character of Oberlin College, see John Barnard, *From Evangelicalism to Progressivism at Oberlin College, 1866-1917* (Columbus: Ohio State University Press, 1969), pp. 3-33, and James H. Fairchild, *Oberlin: The Colony and the College, 1833-1883* (1883; rpt. New York: Garland Publishers, 1984).

48. Bristol, *Pioneer Preacher*, pp. 10, 30-31, 32, 35-36, 49, 118-23.

49. Bistol, *The Sin of Not Doing* (n.p., 1903), passim.

50. Bristol, *Human Sinfulness* (n.p., 1906), passim.

51. Bristol, *Paracletos*, pp. 5-6, 10, 13, 33, 36-37, 50, 68, 101, 117-18, 120, 139, 146, 148, 150.

52. Dewey D. Wallace, Jr., "Charles Oliver Brown at Dubuque: A Study in the Ideals of Midwestern Congregationalists in the Late Nineteenth Century," *Church History*, 53 (March 1984), pp. 46-60; Pond, *Gospel Pioneering*, pp. 46, 51.

53. Bristol, *Paracletos*, pp. 62, 73-74.

54. Bristol, *An Address to the Congregational Brotherhood* (n.p., 1903), passim; for changing trends at Oberlin, see John Barnard, *From Evangelicalism to Progressivism at Oberlin College, 1866-1917* (Columbus: Ohio State University Press, 1969).

55. George M. Marsden, *The Evangelical Mind and the New School Pres-*

byterian Experience (New Haven, Conn.: Yale University Press, 1970); Cochran, *Miners, Merchants and Missionaries*, pp. 206-7, 219; Richard S. Taylor, "Beyond Immediate Emancipation: Jonathan Blanchard, Abolitionism, and the Emergence of American Fundamentalism," *Civil War History* XXVII, no. 3, 1981, pp. 260-74.

    56. George M. Marsden, *Fundamentalism and American Culture: The Shaping of Twentieth Century Evangelicalism, 1870-1925* (New York: Oxford University Press, 1980), pp. 77-85, 94-101, provides a good discussion of the Keswick teachings and Warfield's response.

PREFACE[1]

This book is not written and sent forth to the public because of anything remarkable in the abilities or success of the author. He puts forth no claim to have walked on a higher plane, or to have accomplished a more important work than is quite within the reach of the average man. And, because he occupies this position, he cherishes the hope that the successes and failures narrated in the following pages, will afford encouragement and warning to those who, like him, are moving forward in the common walks of life. No claim is put forth to any special literary merit in the book, but the writer hopes to have made himself clearly understood, and that his style and language express average English in writing and speech. Nor does the writer claim absolute and literal correctness in all the minute narrations he has given of conversations and speeches, many of which occurred long ago. The statements of all the principal facts may be relied upon. They are too deeply graven on the tablet of memory to be doubted or forgotten. Minute and unimportant variations from literal truth, in some cases it is freely admitted, are possible, and even probable. Let the reader make allowances for such.

Should references to self—which abound in this book—savor of egotism, in the view of the reader let him consider how difficult it is to write an autobiography, whose very nature it is to write about self and avoid amenability to this charge. If the question be asked, does this give the whole—the totality of my life, the answer is, Certainly not. Much is left out which lies solely between the author and God; much that is properly private—much in which the public have little or no interest. But the following classes of persons, it is hoped, will read these pages with interest, and some degree of profit.

1st. *The young people*—between the ages of twelve and twenty—who, at times, seriously ponder the propriety and duty of an early consecration of themselves to God. They will read, perhaps with interest, the story of the writer's conversion, just after he had finished his fifteenth year. The obstacles which blocked the entrance upon the narrow way, his struggles to overcome them, and success through the help of One mighty to save. He hopes it will stir some of them to like efforts and like success. Will they regret it when, like the writer, they stand by their seventy-third milestone, and look back over the years of the right hand of the Most High? Will they regret it when 10,000 years have passed?

2d. The author's struggles for an education under difficulties, and the timely helps, which strangely came to hand, all the way through the academy and college and theological seminary, may stimulate hope and courage and effort in those, who like him, sigh after a liberal education to fit them for the ministry, or other walks of eminent usefulness, but lack the means to obtain it. Who can limit the possibilities which lie before the devout young man or woman who is brimful of faith, energy and perseverance? Of the most eminent men in the church and State it may be said, "These are they who have come out of great tribulation."

3d. In all our churches there is a class of earnest, devout men and women who long for emancipation from sin, and sigh and cry after holiness of heart. Such will, perhaps, read with interest the writer's story of his experience of the weakness of human resolutions and favorable surroundings, in the contest with sinful habits and temptations, and the power of Christ to deliver and to keep the soul that casts itself on Him wholly for help.[2]

4th. To the theological student and young minister seeking a field of labor, these pages may suggest some special attraction in the home missionary[3] and pioneer fields. After a life spent upon the border, were the writer to choose his field again he would go among the poorer churches and spend his life, or at least begin it, upon the frontier.

And, finally, he hopes these pages will contain words fitly spoken to those who, like himself, have passed their threescore years and ten, and are soon to fold their tents and pass over the Jordan. To such he would speak only words of encouragement and cheer. He fully believes in the possibility of a serene, cheerful and even happy old age. Infirmities indeed there are, but the helps promised correspond, "For as thy day is, so shall thy strength be." Nearly all expect to be old some time, should life be prolonged; it will come full soon, and too soon we cannot begin to prepare for it. And if we do, it will, save in special cases, be the most joyful period of life. Farewell, kind reader, let us each act our part bravely in life — lay up abundant stores for old age, and when the end comes may those who stand round our graves be reminded of the sweet words of inspiration, "Mark the perfect man, and behold the upright, for the end of that man is peace."

San Buena Ventura, Cal., Oct. 1, 1887.

The Pioneer Preacher

CHAPTER
1

THE FIRST FIFTEEN YEARS
OF MY LIFE

I was born in Cheshire, New Haven County, Conn., on the 5th of June, 1815. My father had just been drafted into the army which served against Great Britain in the second war with that power. My grandfather had served six years in the War of the Revolution, and was one of the tall and well-built veterans selected to receive the arms of the British soldiers who surrendered at Yorktown. He was a powerfully-built man, brave and generous. He was an ardent patriot, and when he had enlisted with Washington's army he staid by it to the end of the war—six long and weary years—and was in at the death of English domination in America.

I was born on the farm where my father was born, where his father was born, where his father was born, and which his father cleared and cultivated and where, also, he died, five generations of us, successively living practically under the same roof, and deriving our sustenance from the same acres. Our original ancestor referred to was an emigrant from England. He was one of some forty heads of families who colonized a section of the Connecticut forest, claimed by the New Haven Colony, some fifteen miles north of New Haven Harbor. This section was some twelve miles square, and was at the time an almost unbroken forest, abounding in great oaks, some of which were from 500 to 1,000 years old. Other trees there were, such as beech, elm, walnut, chestnut, butternut, maple, ash, bass, alder, pepperidge, boxwood, ironwood, etc. There were no prairies in all the State. The dark and dense woods covered every square rod, from hilltop to valley. Every acre was pre-empted by them. The only exceptions were the water courses and an occasional pond created by beaver-dams, or flood wood piled up by freshets in the narrow gorge. It requires not a little of bone and muscle, and of courage, too, for a man with a family to settle down for life in a forest so wild and forbidding. But "a man was famous in those days, according as he

lifted up axes against the mighty oaks." Indian wigwams were here
and there in the valleys and along the streams, and not infrequent
were their calls upon the pale faces, asking tribute of them for the
privilege of dwelling in their vicinity. This part of Connecticut was a
very paradise for the Indian. Its winters were comparatively mild and
free from snow. For the warm ocean air melted it away soon after it
fell. Its rivers and brooks were full of fish, such as trout, suckers, pike
and small bass. Its ponds, small and great, abounded in eels, bull-
heads, frogs and turtles. Deer, wildcat and catamount wre numerous.
There, too, were raccoon, woodchuck and squirrels without number,
the latter, naturally daring and impudent, coming down the trees
almost within reach of the Indian's arm, and defying him to try his
arrow upon them. Partridges drummed in the thickets, pigeons crowed
and cooed in the oaks, while quail and thrush and blackbird and robin
made all the welkin ring with their morning orison and their noon-
day song. Night, too, had its minstrels, the lively whip-poor-will, the
solemn owl and the katy-did. Berries, too, and nuts in varieties far
exceeding those of any other land I have ever visited, were found on
every square mile, and in quantities almost incredible. The adjacent
shores and shoals of Long Island Sound were covered with oysters,
quohogs, clams, mussels, scallops and almost every species of the great
conch family. And when you add to all this long list upon the Indian's
bill of fare, the vast shoals of menhaden, haddock, codfish and black-
fish, which often, in those early days, nearly choked the entrances
into its small bays, inlets and rivers, then surely you have demonstrated
that this, indeed, was a very paradise for the Indians of New England.
Very naturally, it also became the fighting ground, where fierce tribes
strove for the possession of the coveted prize, a contest always ending,
not as Darwin says, in "the survival of the fittest" — that is, the most
peace loving, humane and gentle — but rather in the *survival of the
worst*, that is of the most warlike and war-loving, the most bloodthirsty,
cruel and treacherous. It was here on the north border of the New
Haven Colony, and among these warlike tribes our ancestor selected
his location and received from the colonial officials a liberal grant of
land. It was on the east line of the present township of Cheshire, and
on the west of that of Wallingford. Here our ancestor lived many
years, brought up a family, wrestled with the oaks and fought out the
battle of life. Little has come down to us respecting him. But the
ancestral acres are invested with a historic lore, more interesting to
us of the fifth generation than tongue can tell. Here a bear was chased
down, treed and killed. There a ghost was seen — a veritable ghost —
and somebody died soon after. In yonder secluded valley lived a witch

who was wont nightly to sally forth, and, transforming some innocent man or woman into a horse, she rode her victim unmercifully over corduroy roads and high hills, till just at daydawn she returned home and changed back the animal she rode from horse to man or woman again. All the next day she would smile on her visitors and chatter with them of all good things, as if she was, indeed, but a little lower than the angels. No so her hard ridden neighbor, who grunted all day with galled back, swollen legs, roweled sides and rheumatic joints. Yonder stood a house where once a man was shot! At the funeral one of his ten thumbs and fingers pointed straight toward a man in the crowd which gathered at his funeral! No doubt that was his murderer, else why did that finger point at him?

Not to tarry longer among the scenes of this prehistoric period, I pass to say that the first fifteen years of my life were, in the main, uneventful. They were passed in alternate attendance upon school (district) and working on the farm. The school term for us farmer boys was usually about four months, in winter, while the work on the farm occupied us the other eight months of the year. Happy and specially privileged was the youth who could average five months of schooling per year till he was sixteen. I do not think I was noted during this period of my life for anything save for uniform good nature, fearlessness and athletic feats. I had the name of being what they called a "dare-devil boy," ready for any adventure which called for strength, and that ready and practical wit which in some persons is only brought out by emergencies. My father, my uncles and even my grandfather, seeing this trait in me, used often to test it, even when I was but a small boy, by various endeavors to frighten me, and great was the zest with which they often told to each other the stories of their failures. I remember many of them, and will narrate one as a sample: It was a dark and stormy night, the windows in the old house rattled and shook fearfully, and all things seemed weird and ghostly, when my father proposed that I should go out into the back room, without a candle, feel my way to the cellar door and go down the rickety stairs. Reaching the floor of the cellar I was to lift up my voice and cry out in the darkness:

> "Old Grandpa Grey Beard,
>   Without a tooth or tongue,
>   Give me your little finger,
>   And I'll give you my thumb."

Then I was to march to the end of the cellar, and as I went was to stop at each vinegar cask, or whisky barrel, or cider hogshead, and, thumping three times on the head of each, I was to repeat the incantation; on my way back I was to do the same. Dared I to do it? Was I not too big a coward for that? What would he give me to do it? He drew out eighteen cents and said, "I will give you that." Well, put it in mother's hands. He did so, and I started; I fumbled and felt my way to the bottom of the stairs. There I made the cellar caverns resound with that dolorous incantation. I did not know what it meant, and I don't now, but it seemed to me I stood at the mouth of Pluto's pit, and was daring the very devil himself to come out and take me if he could. But I was bound to put it through now I had begun. I felt my way along and thumped vigorously on the cider hogshead and whisky barrel. What sepulchral sounds they gave back! I had reached the end and was on my way back when I was startled by lugubrious shrieks and moans proceeding from the center of the stairway! I was standing by a potato bin, and, taking out a big one, I threw it! It hit my father full in the face, and he cried out, "Take care! You hurt!" He retreated up stairs and I followed, and got my eighteen cents. Mother laughed at him as I never knew her to do before or since.

My grandfather, too, exhausted on me his stories of witches and ghosts and scenes of blood and robbery and murder, "to try the boy's mettle," he used to tell grandmother, when she remonstrated. He would keep us around his great fireplace, eating apples and drinking cider, the long winter evenings, entertaining us with his wonderfully interesting stories. But the blackest and bloodiest and most horrifying of all were reserved for the last of the evening. And great was the old man's glee when he could by this means induce any of his grandchildren to stay with him over night. But I have no recollection of ever gratifying the dear old grandsire by waiting till morning before I dared to go down into the foggy valley which lay between our house and grandfather's. The valley was pleasant enough by day, when we boys went there to fish or to skate, but in the dark and foggy night how dismal it was! A very valley of Gehenna to us! There were the ruins of the old distillery, the cellar of the old haunted house, and where, according to grandfather, "oft the sheeted dead did squeak and gibber as in the Roman streets," and where now, in these degenerate days, their successors, the bats, flitted and coursed their crooked ways up and down the creek; where the great owls flapped their dusky wings and muttered forebodings of bad luck to all wicked boys who, like me, dared to intrude upon their solemn meditations during the dark hours of night! Where, moreover 10,000 toads and frogs, from the great-mouthed bullfrog of aldermanic proportions and dignity, whose deep bass voice sounded like a bass drum in the distance, up through all the grades of lesser frogs, to the tiny tree toad, who sat above the rest on a willow branch, piping prophecies of rainfall and freshet, making, in the aggregate, a pandemonium of noises which burdened all the dank and sickly air! All this, and more, made the aforesaid valley little less than a gauntlet through which we children hastened home with bated breath and quickened steps.

Let not the reader think I have overdrawn this picture of the dismal valley. Ought not I to know, who bobbed for eels a hundred nights up and down the brook, ofttimes alone, and sometimes staying out till 12 o'clock, waiting for one more bite? Yes, I speak with authority! I know all about the dark valley, and how often I tripped lightly through it, my feet scarce touching the ground, and by no means as the ignorant poet says, "whistling to keep my courage up," but careful not to step upon a leaf, lest the evil one should awake and learn who was passing. I was courageous enough when I reached the top of the hill, and I could see the lights in my father's house near by. But how was it when down in the valley? But enough of this, so brook of my childhood, farewell!

THE WOODCHUCK STORY

While yet a boy and not old enough to handle a gun I became passionately fond of hunting and fishing. I doubt whether Nimrod or Esau[4] were naturally more so. I knew all about the haunts and habits of the game in our vicinity, and set snares and nets and traps, and figure fours and deadfalls to capture them. But, in one of my feats, I received a setback which ever after greatly modified my treatment of wild animals. I had set a steel trap for a woodchuck; when caught it proved to be *a mother*, from whose appearance I judged she had a litter of small sucking woodchucks in the hold. I did not like to kill her and leave her young ones to die the lingering death of starvation. I tried to get her leg out of the trap, but it was broken badly; I got a stick and pressed with all my weight upon the spring. It broke in two and I fell upon her. The teeth snapped vigorously about my clothes. In the melee I gave her a blow which killed her. The next day, toward evening, I visited the hole and found four young kitten woodchucks gathered at the mouth of the hole, waiting for the return of their mother. Seeing me they scampered back into the hole. Why should they not? Was not I the murderer of their mother? What harm had they ever done to me? And for that matter what wrong had I received from their mother? Who else had she wronged? Could we not spare her a few heads of clover? Well, I felt bad, went home and told my brother. He felt as I did. We would carry them some choice fresh clover heads! We did so. The next day, at evening, we went again. They were all there, looking off toward the clover patch, if possible, to catch a glimpse of their mother again. They ran back as we came nigh! Alas, the clover heads were untasted, they were too young, they wanted milk! What should we do? We would dig them out and feed them on cow's milk, or, at least, put them out of their misery. But the job was too much for us, the great oak roots were too large and strong for us, and the burrow too intricate and deep, and we had to give it up. In a few days they dug out, poor, gaunt and hollow-eyed creatures, one after another went into the hold and never came out again. The last one, after about eight days' starvation, was so weak that we caught it. We offered it milk, but it was too far gone, and it died in our hands. Since then there has been a tender spot in my heart when I have had to do with harmless brute creatures when rearing their young.

PROFANITY

Recurring to the "dare-devil fearlessness" attributed to me in my boyhood, there was one phase of it not usual with boys of that ilk. I never tried to show it by taking my Maker's name in vain. Swearing was in those days quite common; nearly all our relatives and neighbors, on the male side, were more or less addicted to it, so were not a few of the boys of my age. But to me, it was about the most unreasonable, low-down and contemptible of all the forms of sin. As I read the Decalogue, no one of the commandments seemed to me so reasonable, and indeed so pathetic as that which says: "Thou shalt not take the name of the Lord thy God in vain!" Could the dear Father, whose fingers fashioned us and brought us forth, and to whom we owe everything, could he ask less of us, as we went forth from His arms of love, than that we should *treat His name with respect?* And what language is competent to denounce in suitable terms of loathing and scorn the reckless wretch who tramples under foot ever that command, and goes out of his way, even on the most trivial occasions, to kick about, as an old hat, *the sacred name of God?* From a child I hated the words and scorned the man who used them. Years before I had reached my fifteenth, it had become a principle with me to avoid association with boys or men who were profane. Not a few altercations over the matter occurred between me and my playmates, when the profanity became unendurable. Sometimes the swearers twitted me with being pious, and while I said, "You know well I am not," yet, I added, I am not mean enough to insult the God that gave me being, and if you are and intend to keep it up, then let us separate right here." Usually others interposed, the swearing was suspended, and the play went on. I noted that these swearers seldom afterward troubled us with their profane speech. This abhorrence of profanity has amounted almost to a passion with me, down to the present time. The sentiment is very emphatic within, "*I cannot endure profanity and I will not.*" And I have two things in relation to it, for which I am profoundly grateful: First, I have never indulged in one word of profane swearing. Second, I have enjoyed during my life a wonderful exemption from annoyance from its use. In the course of a long life, spent largely on the frontier, in the mines, on the plains and elsewhere, where rough language is largely in vogue, I have been brought in frequent contact with it. Slight words I have seldom noticed at first, but when they waxed thicker and blacker, and the great words came out, then I have attacked the swearer in a very decided manner, and not one time in twenty, if my recollection serves me, have I failed of an essential suppression of the vice. Just what brought this about, whether the form and manner of the reproof, or something else, I know not, but it has surprised me a hundred times.

CHAPTER

2

THE SABBATH SCHOOL

W hen about twelve years old, in the year 1827, there came to
our place the pastor of a neighboring church, and addressed
the Congregational Church, which I attended, on the subject of Sabbath schools.[5] I had never heard of them before. The subject was
new to all the people. After a very interesting address all were invited
to retire to the basement of the church who were in favor of organizing
a school. A goodly number of boys and girls, and their elders too,
gathered there. A superintendent was chosen, and teachers were called
for. And while they were being called out or volunteering, the superintendent, observing a young lawyer in a back seat, and looking
on with great interest, called out: "Squire Foot! Wont you take a
class?" The young lawyer, who had scarce reached his twenty-first
year, and had just entered upon the practice of law, arose, and with
many blushes, begged to be excused. He alleged his incompetency,
being, he said, "better acquainted with Blackstone[6] than the Bible."
He sat down. But better thoughts came into his mind. After some
moments of reflection he rose and said, "Mr. Superintendent! I have
concluded I will take a class and do my best for it, provided you will
let me select my scholars." "Certainly! certainly!" said the superintendent, and a murmur of approbation and gladness passed over the
audience, for all loved "Squire Foot." He had grown up in Cheshire,
a natural gentleman, polite to everybody, and his life without a blem-
ish. Was he not the son of Hon. Samuel Augustus Foot, for many
years Governor of the State of Connecticut, and even then its honored
Senator in the National Congress, and accounted one of the great
men of the nation? Well, the young lawyer went forward and looked
fairly in the faces of the youths gathered before him, and then proceeded to select from among them his pupils. He laid his trembling
hand on one head and another. To my utter astonishment, as he came
near where I was sitting, he laid his hand on my head and asked so
tenderly, "Will you be a member of my class?" I assented. But surely,
there must be some mistake about it! Surely he does not know me,

and never heard of me! I was a plainly dressed farmer's boy, the sun had browned my face, my hands were hard with work, and though at church, possibly I even then was barefoot. Well, he led us apart to the seat we were to occupy, and gave us our lesson, the portion of Scripture we were to learn by heart, and repeat the next Sabbath. I was for the time dazed with astonishment, but I felt the honor and the stimulus of the notice taken of me by the young lawyer, more than now I would to be made Governor of the State. A new prospect opened before me, new hopes began to dawn, perhaps I could get to be something in the world — I would try. Squire Foot should have no occasion to regret his choice. There were eight of us. The next Sabbath we were all in our places; we all repeated our verses without failure, our teacher commended us, and that amply paid us for our effort. By degrees we grew familiar and dared to ask questions as well as to answer them. The young lawyer's interest in the Sabbath school increased, and he was enthusiastic in praise of his boys. For more than three years he was our teacher, and great and lasting was the impression he made upon us. He was a model teacher, and in some respects peculiar, especially for the personal interest he showed in each of his class. I was frequently sent to the village on errands; it was two miles distant, and in summer I sometimes went barefoot, but it made no difference with my teacher — if I met him on the street, he always greeted me cordially, took my hand and asked of my welfare, and that of our family. Sometimes he would even cross over the wide street to meet me on the opposite sidewalk. It mattered not who was with him, he always stopped to speak with us. On one occasion he was walking with (I believe) a Member of Congress, on a visit to his father. He stopped, shook hands with me and introduced me to the stranger as one of his Sabbath school class, and spoke to him of my diligence in my studies, and instanced some reply I had made the Sunday before to a question, which he regarded as specially sensible and perhaps, bright. When he met my father or mother he would make inquiries after me, and utter warm words in my praise. These things took strong hold of me; they stiffened my backbone, and sooner would I have lost my right arm than the confidence of my teacher. I do not suppose his treatment of me was peculiar; very likely he treated the whole class in like manner.

CONVERSION

T hree years passed and the boys of twelve had become the youths
of fifteen. We had become greatly attached to each other, and
had all of us come under Gospel influences which were daily modifying
our characters. Combined with other causes they culminated in my
conversion when a few weeks past fifteen, and in this way it was
brought about. The Congregationalists of that day were accustomed
to hold, occasionally, three days' meetings; such a meeting was held
in Cheshire; the preaching was principally by Rev. N. W. Taylor, of
the New Haven Theological Seminary.[7] I attended the second day
and heard the wonderful preacher portray the love of God toward
men, even sinful men, and his desire, sincere, heartfelt, and unequi-
vocal, that every man, woman and child on earth should repent, *and
do it now.* The dogma, that somehow God did not want all to repent,
he trod down with utmost scorn and indignation; then the terms of
salvation, repentance — what it is toward man, what it is toward God;
then faith — a leaning upon Christ's arm, mighty to save unto the
uttermost, all who submit and lean upon him. I was greatly interested,
and long before he had finished his sermon I had anticipated his
conclusions. I saw clearly just what I must do to be accepted and
forgiven. I must start off as I was then, as Peter did, in fisherman's
dress, and follow Christ, making the law of his lips the rule of my
life. That there was no need to wait for further convictions, or even
for deeper feeling, but that I could go to him as I was and in his
tutelage find, in due time, all the feeling and hate of sin I needed to
have. Manifestly the first step was a formal and sincere pledge to
count myself the Lord's servant from this moment onward. This I
did at once; leaning my head forward upon the back of the seat in
front of me, covering my face with my hands, three times I deliberately
repeated the consecration to Him who possessed my reins and my
heart, and asked Him to accept and ratify it. And now a great struggle
ensued. Obstacles, many and almost insurmountable, rose up before
me. I believe the evil spirits who had me in charge were furious at

my attempted escape, and they assailed me with objections and difficulties I had never thought of before. But I called upon the Lord,
and he helped me. He said to the winds and waves, Be still, and there
was great calm. When my assailants returned again, a resort to the
same great Helper brought a second deliverance. Indeed, I soon found
the throne of grace a refuge from temptation and the storm. My
tempters finding their violent assaults only drove me to the Lord,
they desisted in large measure, and resorted to other tactics better
calculated to further their designs.

CHRISTIAN WORK, IMMEDIATELY SUBSEQUENT
TO CONVERSION

At the time of my conversion I was at work by the month, for a man
who carried on extensive farming, ran a distillery, and employed quite
a number of men. None of them were religious, and at once they set
upon me, to ridicule me out of my allegiance to God—my religion.
I was the youngest of them all, and it seemed to me the devil helped
them when they were together, to make sport of my faith, and make
a mock at sin. When two or more of them were together they were
too much for me, but I soon found my way effectually to spike their
guns. *I took them one by one*, and, when alone with them, I talked with
them of my newborn faith, and love, and joy. Of the new life I was
trying to live, its present peace, and its hopes of the future, and
frequent foretaste of a bliss sweeter than earth could give. And I
entreated them not to hinder me, nor trifle in a matter of such infinite
importance to us all. Emboldened by going so far, I went farther; I
asked them to make a break for eternal life. Could they do it too
soon? Would not Christ help them? What if they should be lost forever,
etc.? When thus addressed, and alone, they could neither answer me,
nor scarce resist my appeals. Often they wept and sometimes asked
me to pray for them and with them. Thenceforward *that gun was
spiked*, that person troubled me no more; he knew I had his secret
and his conscience too. Thus I took them one by one, till the boss of
the gang was reached. He was harder than the rest, but God gave
me a mouth and wisdom in my appeals and arguments he could not
gainsay or resist, and so at the last they began to go to meeting with
me, and the ridicule was over. Sooner or later nearly all of them gave
evidence of conversion. Thus I found that the best method of self-
defence is to "carry the war into Africa."

The second prayer-meeting I attended after my conversion I
arose and tried to stand up for Jesus. I did not utter coherently and
distinctly the words I intended, which were—"He hath taken my feet

from the miry clay and placed them upon a rock," but I did succeed
in putting down that fear of man which brings a snare. From that
evening onward it was always expected that I would take a part in
every prayer-meeting I attended. Nor do I know that they were ever
disappointed. Usually I was the first one to speak or to pray. The
reason for that was this: I found *that the most difficult place* in the
prayer-meeting. As a general thing at that time—all are not there—
more or less are coming in—there is noise and disturbance. Then
too, the religious pulse has not been quickened, so as to make it easy
to take part. Yet I found this a most important place—*the starting off*
of the services. And I asked the Lord to help me *to do that work.* I
believe He did, and I was helped in it. Yet there were some—even
in the church—who misunderstood it. They attributed it to unwar-
rantable forwardness, especially in one so young. One of them, a man
of large wealth and influence, came to me and asked significantly,
"Aren't some of you young people getting beyond your years in
talking so much in meeting?" I remember well my reply. It was this:
"Mr. G—, if you will attend these prayer-meetings, and speak and
pray in them, and see that the time is well occupied, I will agree not
to open my mouth." "Humph!" said he, and dropped his head and
went away greatly disgusted, for he would not have prayed in a prayer-
meeting for a hundred dollars, much as he loved money. About this
time our beloved teacher, at the close of a session of the Sabbath
school, rose in his place and said: "I have a thank-offering to make
to the Lord, and before his people to-day. It has been known in the
school that for some months past a work of grace has been in progress
in my class. One after another has come out on the Lord's side. To-
day *the last one* in my class expresses the hope that he has been born
again!" He could say no more, but sat down and wept, and the whole
school bowed before the Lord and wept with him. Did ever sweeter
incense ascend to God from Jewish altars than rose from that congregation weeping its tears of joy? "And I say unto you there is joy
in the presence of the angels of God over one sinner that repenteth."
Two of these boys became preachers of the Gospel—one an honored
deacon—another a class leader and exhorter—two died early, and
went, we have no doubt, to the Father's house. Another became a
mechanic, honorable and true, whose latter history I have not been
able to follow. And the eighth was the only one who I believe never
made a profession of faith in Christ. "Who art thou that despiseth
the day of small things?" "Esquire Foot" practiced law in Cheshire
all these years, but his labors in that line have long since passed from

mind. But his labors in the Sabbath school and in his class, when will they be forgotten and when will their influence end?

THE FAMILY ALTAR ERECTED IN MY FATHER'S HOUSE

In the fall of the year after my conversion, in 1831, I returned home after my summer's work. Conversing one evening with my mother about the sad religious condition of our kindred, scarcely any of them even professing to be Christians, I asked her if there was a *family altar* in all our circle, or had there been one for a century back. She replied sadly—none that she could think of. My father coming in just then, I asked him the same question. It startled him. But he quickly replied—none that he knew of. I asked was he willing to have one set up here? To have a short prayer offered every day in the family, and a portion of Scripture read? He had no objection. Mother promptly got the big Bible, read a few verses, and then I dropped upon my knees and offered up the prayer! Thenceforward the fire was kept burning and a daily offering made theron, so long as I was an inmate of my father's house, and as often as I returned to it for a temporary visit. The news of this new altar to the Lord spread among our kindred and neighbors and perhaps had some influence in bringing about the great change—religiously—which has since come over them. Looking backward, from this present, over the lapse of fifty and seven years, it seems incredible that a boy of fifteen and a half should have ventured upon a thing so strange! so beyond his years! so fraught with responsibility! Stanger still it seems when I recall to mind that no one ever suggested that such was my duty. Not unfrequently a family gathering occurred at our house, and there gathered there uncles, aunts, cousins and others, and we sat down—a long table full of joyful kindred. In a moment all was hushed and a blessing asked. There was no sport made of it. It was too solemn for that! So when evening came the big Bible was brought out, all took seats, a chapter read and then the prayer went up as usual, nor was it ever omitted because much company was there.

A CALL TO PREPARE TO PREACH THE GOSPEL

Not long after my conversion I became impressed with the conviction that the Lord had called me to preach his Gospel. Gradually, it became the theme of earnest prayer. But immense difficulties were in the way. How could my father spare me from the work on the farm? He could not help me financially should I undertake a course of studies. Not one of my kindred were able to do it, or if they were able were disposed to do so. Nor did I know one person on earth to whom I could look for one dollar where ten would be needed. Yet the expense of going through the three schools necessary—The Academic, Collegiate and Theological—would be great. I could not do much toward it by my work, while keeping along with my classes. Had I not been working all the summer at six dollars a month, and the highest wages for farm hands were about ten dollars a month! The boss workman under whom I was working only got eleven dollars a month! While impressed with the call, and praying over it, our minister, Rev. Joseph Whiting, visited the family where I worked. He inquired for me. They would send and call me from the field. No, he would go out where I was—he wished to see me alone. After a little kindly talk about my trials, conflicts, etc., he laid his hand on my shoulder and said so solemnly as the tears filled his eyes: "My son, has not the Lord called you into his kingdom, to the end that you should preach his gospel? And has not the Spirit whispered this to you already?" I could not answer him for the moment. How had he got my secret? I had not breathed it to any mortal. At length I confessed it was so. That was on my mind much of the time, but the way seemed all hedged up. Where could I get the means? It was doubtful if my father would consent till I was of age,—six years hence! He replied that once he felt as I now did. But God had removed one obstacle after another and had led him through the long course of studies and into the ministry. His words were so tenderly dropped upon my ear, his experience so timely, his counsels so wise, that when he left the field he left a youth behind, hopeful and joyous, and with purpose settled, to reach the ministry if he could. Dear, blessed man of God! to this day I feel the influence of your words, the impulse of your love. Subsequently, he helped me by his counsels, by books lent, by hearing me recite, and teaching me the rudiments of Latin and Greek. An immense debt of gratitude yet remains unpaid and unspoken to this dear man, this father of my early spiritual life.

> "By and by we will go home and meet him
> Away over in the promised land."

The first step was to secure the consent of my parents, and the donation of my time, from sixteen and onward. My father was not very strong and my brother was by no means rugged at that time, while I was hardy, strong, and capable of great endurance. How could they spare me? Hard it was for them and hard for me to ask it. But at length consent was given and I entered the Episcopal Academy in Cheshire. At first I boarded at home, two miles distant, working Saturdays on the farm, and paying my tuition by ringing the bell, sweeping the rooms, building the fires, etc., etc. By and by some friends in the village, wishing to save me my long walk, offered to board me for my work mornings and evenings, and so I went forward toward the goal.

PERSECUTION FOR TEMPERANCE

In the latter part of the autumn of 1832 a lecturer on temperance visited our place and addressed a large congregation on the evils of intemperance, the feasibility of total abstinence, the utility of the pledge,[8] and the necessity of immediate action. There were abundant reasons for such a movement in our place. We had eight distilleries of cider brandy in full blast, from twenty to thirty cider mills, half a dozen taverns all selling brandy and whiskey at three cents a glass. All the stores kept it and there was scarce a well-to-do family in the township but boasted a sideboard sacred to strong drink and wherein were stored from five to ten kinds of liquor, catering to the tastes of the various visitors who called upon them. No sooner had a guest arrived and been fairly seated than they were set forth before him and he was urged and expected to partake of such as he chose. It was an insult not to ask him to drink. It was scarcely less to refuse to drink. Then too, cider, worked cider, "*hard* cider" it was properly called, was the common drink of the people. They drank it at the table, they drank it between meals, they carried it in bottles to the fields. Liquor ran free in those days. A very millennium of *no license!* I think if some of our good temperance people, who execrate the taxing of the selling business, where we cannot carry prohibition, or carrying it cannot execute the law, if they had lived in those good old days, when no license prevailed, they would hold as I do, if you cannot stop the sale entirely, you should restrict it and cripple it all you can. Was it strange then that drunkenness was in every other family nearly? Was it strange then that my mother and I counted over fifty drunkards within the circle of our acquaintance? I mean people who occasionally staggered and talked boosily through strong drink? Was it strange, that in one winter we buried ten men who had died with delirium tremens, out of a population of 2,000 people? Well, the address aforesaid was able and was heard by a large audience. At its close Squire Foot, my Sabbath school teacher, arose and made a speech, and at once drew up a pledge, signed it, and presented it to the audience. This was the first hard blow the liquor interest received, for everybody loved Squire Foot. He had won his way to the public heart by his irreproachable character, his agreeable manners, and his ready and often unpaid advocacy of the cause of the poor and of him who had no helper. While not a few signed the pledge, the opposition was open, outspoken, contemptuous, and even savage. In the academy which I attended, a meeting was held to denounce the Temperance movement. A resolution was passed, that if any student should sign the pledge, he should be ridden on a rail through the principal street of the town.

The academy at that time was little else than a Southern school in a Northern town. The students were largely sons of Southern planters, or from the West Indies. These young bloods dominated the meeting which passed the resolutions referred to. I well knew of this action before I had signed the pledge. But not having the fear of these young hoodlums before my eyes, I signed it on the first opportunity. The next Monday morning, hastening over my two-mile walk, I had reached the academy and was making the fire, when in rushed seven of the largest students *bearing a rail!* Shouting simultaneously, they ordered me to submit to my fate of being ridden on a rail! For some moments I stood them off, and asked what harm I had done to them? I said the school would open in half an hour, I must ring the bell, make the fire, and sweep the room. If they must do it, take some other time. But they swore great oaths that they *would do it now.* I saw clearly, I must either fight them with something more than words, or submit to be carried on a rail through the long street! The thought was terrible! to be thus shamefully abused by these young mobocrats! to be hooted at by the inmates of each tavern I passed! To be followed by a pack of boys and pelted perhaps with mud balls and stones! to be sneered at by servant girls, prompt to please their masters, leering out of the windows and shouting, "Good enough for you, young temperance fanatic!" All this was rapidly passing in my mind, as for a time I kept them at bay, deliberating what I should do. There were seven against me. But little I cared for that. I knew I could make it hot for them, and so did they, if I could really undertake it. But I had become a Christian, and they counted largely on a passive submission. I too, was troubled as to what was my duty and my right. Did not the Book say: "Resist not evil," etc., etc.? But the thought came over me, "*It is your duty* to put this house in order for the school! The powers that be require it! You have agreed to do it and you have no right to let these hoodlums prevent it if you can help it!" Instantly my duty was clear. It was to thrust them out of my way as I would a pack of dogs, or so many swine in the way of my duty. A back-handed stroke sent one assailant against a bench over which he fell heavily, striking on his head. Seizing the rail I thrust it back against the wall, almost crushing out the bowels of him who stood at that end and held it. This put two out of the fight. The rail was dropped, and now the fight commenced in earnest. How long it continued I don't know. In the course of it I was pushed against the brick wall with such force that a large bunch instantly rose on my head. Recovering I seized a large iron inkstand, before which my opponents shied and fled before me out of the house and ran in every direction! But though left alone I was too dizzy to do my work. Soon one of the teachers arrived, and seeing my swollen head, my bloody hands, the rail lying on the floor, the seats overturned, and other signs of a big melee, thought I had best go to the doctor's. But I went directly to Squire Foot, my Sabbath school teacher, and for once I saw him brimful of wrath. In less than an hour a writ of arrest for assault and battery was in the sheriff's hands and a posse were searching private residences and hiding places, and even the academy, for the miscreants. There was no school in the academy that day, and there was some excitement over the affray in our unusually quiet village. The temperance people of course took my side. They were glad the hoodlums were defeated. Seven of them tried in vain to ride one temperance boy on a rail! The law abiding thought the roughs had learned a lesson. On the whole, I do not think the cause of religion suffered at all from my vigorous use of the strong muscles and hard hands the Lord had given me. After that the students treated me respectfully, not deeming it quite prudent to presume very largely on my being a non-resistant. Subsequently reflection has led me to the conclusion, that the words of Jesus, which refer to this subject, really enjoin, as the general rule of life, *just what the civil laws of most civilized nations require*, to wit—that in all ordinary cases of collision with our fellow citizens, we are not to adjudge the case ourselves, or mete out judgment and justice with our own hands. We are too partial, too much personally interested. We are to suffer the wrong and leave it to be adjudicated by the impartial tribunals appointed for that purpose. That there are exceptions to this rule all admit, but neither the Bible nor the civil law specify just what they are. Before the trial came off my assailants settled with me, giving me quite a bonus to do so, and paying all the costs.

PHILLIPS' ACADEMY, ANDOVER

The following spring, under the advice of my pastor, I went to Phillips Academy,[9] Andover, Mass. When I arrived there I had but seven dollars in my pocket. Out of this I had to pay a five dollar entrance fee; this left me but two dollars with which to commence a two years' course of study in a place where I knew not a soul, and where I had no friend save the Lord. But I was kindly received and trusted, even to my board in the commons. Work fell into my hands imediately, such as sawing wood, gardening, well-digging, chopping wood, etc. These jobs I did between school hours, on Saturdays and in vacations. After a couple of terms friends began to appear to help me. The Education Society[10] gave me $60 a year. The church in my native town hearing a good report from my teachers, of my life and progress, voted me an annual aid of $50. I was progressing finely and had nearly completed my preparation for college when an event occurred which for a time blasted all my hopes and prospects of entering college the following autumn, at least. This was.

THE GREAT ANTI-SLAVERY REVIVAL

This occurred in the years 1834-'5. It swept over the United States and was especially powerful in the schools of learning, the colleges and seminaries, where were gathered the young men who were soon to go forth and mold public opinion and prepare the nation for the coming conflict, that battle of Armageddon in which slavery was to be overthrown, and cast into the bottomless pit. It was in that revival that I was converted to the doctrine of immediate emancipation, and this is how it was brought about: The literary society in the academy to which I belonged had selected as a question for discussion, this: "Is the American Colonization Society competent to deal with the matter of American Slavery?" I was appointed to speak on the affirmative, one Horace Eaton on the negative. Eaton had the name of being a rabid Abolitionist, a "fanatic" as such were then called. The Colonization Society,[11] presided over by Hon. Henry Clay, was immensely popular, North and South, and nowhere more so than in the churches and among the ministers. It was Janus faced, it looked in two opposite directions. In the Northern States it was looked upon as the great antidote for the evil of slavery. It was to establish a colony of freed men on the coast of Liberia, Africa, and there it was to transport black people, so fast as they could be freed, and educate and Christianize them. More and more were to be transported, year by year, till by and by every negro should be restored to Africa, and that country was to be civilized and evangelized. In the slave States it was regarded a happy scheme for getting rid of black men who were free, and carrying them out of sight of their brethren in bonds; no more to incite the slave to run away or to shield and shelter him after he had fled. My honored pastor was a strong advocate of colonization, that is of its Northern phase. He had little patience with the little Abolition clique, which just then was beginning to disturb the nation's slumber, over the crater of slavery. I regarded myself as a colonizationist, but I hated slavery. The stories my father had told of slave hunts with hounds and horses, and shot guns and pistols; the scenes of slave auctions and whippings and brandings; though they seemed necessary to him, and in the main right, they grated harshly on my ear. Indignantly I asked *"What for?"* and denounced the cruelty, and claimed the slave had as good a right to liberty as his master. No casuistry had yet been allowed to impose on my common sense, or override my spontaneous sense of justice. Well, such was the question we were to discuss. I was expected to make a good showing for the popular side, colonization. Documents were at hand and I thought I made a fair speech, but Eaton handled my arguments without gloves. He was not a genial speaker, but his logic was to my mind quite forcible. I replied to him and was applauded, the sympathies were all on my side, but I went home dissatisfied. The debate was adjourned over to the next week, and I was to open it on that evening. During the week I was greatly perplexed in my endeavor to answer Eaton, and sustain colonization. Brief after brief I constructed and then threw away. At last I began to feel that I was fighting against the truth. I knelt and asked the Lord to show me the truth, and promised I would receive it and advocate it whatever it might cost. Within a few hours all was clear, the fallacy of the colonization scheme, and the duty of immediate emancipation. Then there passed before me the cost of the step I had taken, the loss of friends, of reputation, of pecuniary helps, perhaps the necessity of giving up further study, possibly the ministry, too, to which I was looking forward. What else the step involved, who could tell! Was not Rev. Chas. Torry, a Congregational

minister, pining away in a Maryland prison because he was an Abolitionist, his right hand branded with the letters S.S.—sinner saved?
Were not $50,000 offered for the head of Garrison by the legislature
of South Carolina? Did not a pro-slavery mob control, not only every
Southern State, but Boston itself? What else there was in store for
Abolitionists, who could tell. Well! Be it so. I was no better than the
martyrs; why should I be exempt from suffering for the truth's sake?
I kept my counsels. The evening for reopening the discussion came
on. What a pressure was on me! I opened the debate and took up
Mr. Eaton's argument No. 1, examined it carefully, and at length, as
I laid it down, said: "Candor compels me to confess that, so far as I
can see, that argument is a good one, and I have no heart to dispute
it." Eaton left his seat and came and sat down before me, and looked
me fully in the face. I then took up argument No. 2, reviewed and
accepted that also. Eaton's eyes brightened and he moved a little
nearer. I then reviewed some of my own arguments of the evening
previous, and showed their fallacy, and how unsatisfactory they were.
I then laid down my brief and told to my astonished schoolmates the
story of my perplexity during the week, my prayer for light, my
promise to the Lord to follow the light, to confess it, to stand by it
at any cost, however great. How also, thereupon, the light came in,
and I saw the matter as I never saw it before. I then announced myself
an Abolitionist, with all the losses of good name and friends it might
imply. Eaton could stand it no longer; springing to his feet, he embraced me and cried out, "Thank God for an honest man!"

I had many friends in the institution, and they did not desert
me. Very candidly they conversed with me; one after another came
over to our views, till, within two or three months, a majority of our
200 students in the academy preparing for college, more than one-
half, were avowed Abolitionists! Meanwhile our beloved instructors
and the professors in the Theological Seminary were all hard at work
endeavoring to suppress the rising sentiments of hostility to American
slavery. But the Lord was in the movement, and how could they resist
its onward course? At this juncture, George Thompson, the famous
English anti-slavery orator, visited Andover. He was advertised to
lecture in the Methodist Church. I think no other church could be
secured for him. A mob had just driven him from Boston, and wherever he went the hand of violence was raised against him. It was hoped
he could be quietly heard in Andover. Was it not the school of the
Prophets and noted for its morality and for its religious spirit? So
Thompson came, but, as with Paul, bonds and affliction awaited him
there. A railroad was being built through the place. The contractor

was a rough pro-slavery character, and not a few roughs were in his employ. It was boldly given out that a mob would break up the meeting and probably tar and feather Mr. Thompson. The anti-slavery students got wind of it, and armed with heavy hickory clubs, which they used as staves, they were at the chapel as soon as the doors were opened and took possession of a couple of tier of front seats, which formed nearly a semicircle around the pulpit. As the house filled up the ushers besought us to vacate them and give place to ladies, but we knew our business, and not one of us could be ousted. There were about fifty of us, nearly all over twenty, the most of us farmers' sons, and with our long staves or clubs standing erect by our sides, I imagine the mobocratic portion of the audience studied us rather carefully. The speech was surpassingly eloquent. I remember some of its passages, one of them, his apostrophe to America, was very striking; it began with: "America! America! Thou art the anointed cherub, God's darling child! Apart from the nations God hath set thee! etc." It fairly raised the audience to his feet. The lecture was two hours long. When it closed, in an instant every light was blown out, and the mob rushed for the pubpit. But those fifty students closed around Thompson and Wilson the Methodist minister, in phalanx so compact, with clubs brandished so threateningly that the mob kept at respectful distance and finally dispersed. We saw Wilson and Thompson safe at home. After consultation it was agreed that six should stay down town (South Parish) and patrol the streets till morning. One should take his station half way up the hill toward the Seminary, another should take his stand at the corner leading to the dormitories of the classical school, the rest should retire to their rooms and sleep with their clothes on, ready for emergencies. I was one of the six who staid down town. I and my companion went into a vacant lot and concealed ourselves. After an hour or so a signal whistle was blown in a distant part of the town. It was answered by another, and then by a third close by us. We went for him with all speed, but he ran like a deer and we lost him. We sounded the alarm! It was taken up by the man half way up the hill, he sent it to the man at the corner, and he aroused the dormitories. Our squad of six guards rushed for Wilson's house and held at bay the gathering mob. Scarcely had we got there before we heard the tramp, tramp, tramp of a hundred students dashing down Andover hill at a two-forty pace. And it sounded out on the still hour of night like the coming of a regiment of cavalry. The mob, most of whom were Irish, listened a moment, then broke and fled in every direction. Thus was Andover saved from a crime against one of the noblest of men, which long years of penance could scarce have washed away.

ORGANIZING AN ANTI-SLAVERY SOCIETY

Up to this time we had not organized an Anti-Slavery Society. Fearing that we should do so, the faculty of the United Seminaries passed a regulation which read like this: "No student shall join any society in the town of Andover without leave of the principal of the institution with which he is connected." Alas! "The best laid schemes of mice and men aft gang aglee!" So it was in this case. A student whose room adjoined that in which the faculties met and discussed the matter, overheard enough to divine what was on the tapis. He at once informed us of what was up. In half an hour all the principal anti-slavery students were gathered in the Methodist chapel and then and there formed an Abolition society, chose officers, etc., and adjourned! The following Monday morning at prayers we beheld marshaled on the platform and around the desk, our four principal professors. Usually only one was present. There was something ominous in the air! Principal Johnson's voice was more tremulous than was usual. Professor McLane's face was unusually red and flushed. Professor Taylor's eyes were riveted to the floor, while Professor Sanborn sat uneasy and restless in his chair of state. Prayers over, Principal Johnson, in agitated tones, read the stern decree and then looked over the field to mark the effect of the shot! The other teachers also now looked up and took observations. But not a wing seemed broken, not a feather ruffled! We all took it serenely and it was noted that the anti-slavery leaders looked cross-wise at each other and smiled. What could it mean? After the students had gone to their rooms for recitations, or to the dormitories for study, Principal Johnson called up one Peter T. Woodbury, nephew of Hon. Levi Woodbury of New Hampshire fame,[12] and asked in a confidential tone: "Peter! what did it mean—those complacent smiles and glances between the Abolitionists when the new regulation was read?" "Why," said Peter brusquely, "they have stolen the march on you! They formed a society last Saturday night and all the Abolitionists joined it!" The color left Mr. Johnson's face. Recovering himself, he said plaintively: "You have not joined, have you Peter?" "*Yes Sir!*" said Peter. This was a stunner. The next effort was to induce the signers to withdraw their names, but without an instance of success. These young Abolitionists had been converted to stay. They believed in saints' perseverance and I have never yet heard of the apostacy of one of them, or even of their temporary falling from grace. Our professors, finding that neither coaxing nor flattery nor threatenings would do, proceeded to sterner measures. I was summoned before the Faculty to answer to the charge of combining with others, to destroy the good name of the academy and bring it into reproach before the public, etc., etc. Instead of standing on the defensive, I faced the music. I boldly charged upon them the sin of seeking to shield from exposure and condemnation, the great crime of slavery, of exerting themselves to make cowards and time-servers of the young men who were soon to go forth to help form and reform the opinions of mankind. I remember telling them if we were cowards here we would be cowards in college, cowards in the seminary and cowards in the ministry! In fact, during that interview I think they were in the prisoners' box quite as much as I was. At one time they actually all laughed aloud at the ridiculous turn the trial had taken. But they had resolved to make an example of me, and so they cast me out. No specific charges were voted as sustained. I was simply voted no longer a member of Phillips' academy, and to have no further right to a room or place in the recitation rooms. One other was dismissed with me. At once a meeting of the anti-slavery students was called, a remonstrance was gotten up and published. It was signed by some sixty students, all of whom left the institution without diplomas or other testimonials of character or scholarship. No sooner was I turned out of the academy than Mr. McLane wrote my pastor in Cheshire. He read the letter to the church and they voted not to help me any more. The letter from my pastor to me, though quite severe, was in parts very tender and parental. He regarded the anti-slavery revival as little better than a blast from the bottomless pit. I remember one sentence he used; "Oh, that God would hide you in his pavillion till this storm is overpast." Dear man! he was sadly mistaken! That strong wind and "the rushing mighty wind" of the day of Pentecost comes from the same quarter. Well, he sees it now and rejoices with us in the great deliverance from America's chiefest curse. My reply to him was said to be rather spirited. I kept no copy of it, but one who was present when it was received and heard it read told me that when the good pastor came to a place where I wrote, "Money given by a church on condition of keeping silence about slavery is not fit to buy a potter's field with," he laughed heartily and said: "He is plucky! is he not?" The Education Society also withdrew its aid and I was now cast upon my own resources again.

But I had two hands, the consciousness of being on the right side and an abiding faith that the Lord would in some way bring me out of all my troubles. I at once sold my books, paid my debts and then went out among the farmers seeking work. But the brand of "fanatic" was upon me and people were reluctant to employ me. But a rough outspoken man by the name of Holt said he did not think much of student farmers, but I looked stout and he would give me a trial. He took me to a meadow to mow grass with him. Before noon he quit, saying he was not going to mow while he had so good a hand. He took quite a fancy to me and much he talked in the stores and taverns about his expelled student, his strength and skill in farming. Friends began to gather around me. Two or three lawyers offered to lend me money if I would study law. But I told them if I plead any law it would be the law of God, that really I had no heart for anything else.

About this time I received an invitation from one Kimball of Maine, to come to his school. But just as I was about to start word was received that an anti-Abolition mob had broken up his school. Coming home from the field one evening, Mr. Holt said: "There has been a man to see you to-day, who is an Abolitionist like you and he wants to see you and if he takes a liking to you, you will not lack for money to go on with your studies, for he is rich and liberal. His name is John Smith—*money Smith* we call him. He is the chief owner of Fry village and the factory there. He will call this evening." Well! he did call and wished to hear the story of my expulsion. I narrated it to him. He asked me many questions and several times used his hand-kerchief freely, wiping his eyes. He wished me to call the next day at his office, he wished to introduce me to his partners. I went and was there put through a course of questions which showed they did not mean to be imposed upon. I was asked to call again some days after. They went after the seminary folks and found my statements were true. When I called again they only asked where I wished to take my College course. I preferred Oberlin, the new anti-slavery institution in Ohio, and where I could do something to pay my way. How much would I need to start with? One hundred dollars. They gave me one hundred and fifty, and I gave them my note. It was payable only after I had finished my course of studies, and not then in case I entered the ministry. What a burden here rolled off my back! Joyfully I retraced my steps to Mr. Holt's, packed my trunk and the next day was off for Oberlin.

CHAPTER

5

OBERLIN COLLEGE

From Andover I took stage for Troy, New York; from Troy to Buffalo, by canal; from Buffalo to Cleveland, Ohio, by steamboat; from Cleveland to Elyria, by stage, and thence to Oberlin, ten miles, on foot through a dense forest. How new, how wild, how weird and how chimerical the new enterprise looked, as I emerged from the dense, dark forest into the little clearing. The entire opening was scarce half a mile square, and that full of stumps, logs, fallen trees, fireweed and smoke. Yet there were *men there, and women too.* Some of the former were chopping down great trees, some with oxen hauling logs together to burn, some building log houses, some sowing grain and endeavoring to harrow it in, despite the roots and stumps. Ever and anon a tinkling bell called quite a flock of young men and women from their rooms to recitation, and sent as many back from recitation to study. For some hours I wandered round the clearing as a stranger taking in the situation. But I observed that every one was cheerful and hopeful, and unusually polite to strangers. Though not a soul knew me in the place, save one, no one passed me without a gentle bow and a kindly look, which seemed to say, "Call upon me if I can help you." A stranger to whom I introduced myself invited me to commons as the supper bell rang, and I went. It was a very plain meal; boiled potatoes, milk gravy, wheat bread and brown bread and butter, was about all there was of it. But there was no complaint, no dissatisfied looks and no criticisms. Nearly all seemed happy and even thankful and regarded themselves as privileged beyond the common walks even of the student's life. And indeed they were, for God, who from the first set the seal of his love upon Oberlin, was there, diffusing peace and joy and holy love in nearly every heart. the following day I introduced myself to President Mahan[13] and told him I came from Andover and wished to enter college. A Faculty meeting was called and I presented myself. My papers were called for. I had none. Why? I told the story of my expulsion on account of my anti-slavery views and action. Prof. Dascomb, whose relative was principal of the English school at Andover, expressed doubt of the truth of my statements. This nettled me somewhat, so I went farther and stated other things against his relative, more detrimental than the first. Dr. Dascomb was instructed to write to Andover and ask why my papers were withheld. Meanwhile I was allowed to enter the freshman class, conditionally. No answer was returned to Dr. Dascomb's letter. He wrote again and the reply came that they had no specific charges to make against the young man, and if Oberlin could make a useful man of him they should be glad of it. So I was received into college. The accommodations, so far as rooms were concerned, were, at the first, very plain and often quite uncomfortable. My room was, at the first, what might be called the attic or *garret of a woodshed*. It was a rough, one-story shed. Some joists were laid across overhead, and rough slabs were laid across them; the roof made the ceiling on two sides, and some thin factory cloth partitioned me off from another's claim. I could stand upright in the middle. There it was that I at the first set up my banners, and there I commenced my student life at Oberlin. But I was happy, for I was free, and literally I sang:

> "Oh, give me but a hollow tree,
> A crust of bread and liberty."

Largely I supported myself by chopping wood, clearing land and teaching school. One winter I acted as agent for the Cuyahoga County Bible Society. Meanwhile I kept up a correspondence with Messrs. Smith & Dove of Andover, and occasionally received from them fifty dollars.

A NEW PHASE OF CHRISTIAN LIFE

During the latter part of my Sophomore year, I passed through a phase of religious experience, whose influence has followed me down to the present time, a period of more than half a century. In my early Christian life, such were my besetments, my natural impulses, sinward, and the great obstacles in my way, that I felt that none could help me but the Lord; and on Him I leaned, and to Him I looked daily and hourly, for help. Nor did I look in vain. I was wonderfully upheld. I was divinely assisted. The life I lived was by faith in the Son of God. But as I grew in experience and knowledge, I began, gradually, to lose my sense of dependence on God, and unconsciously to lean on my power of will, my habits and my surroundings. This was particularly true when I went to Andover. Was it not famous as a school of the Prophets? Were not moral and religious principles predominant there? Two-thirds of my classmates were members of the church; one-half were preparing for the ministry, and several had the missionary field in view! "Surely," said I, "here I shall live a devoted and holy life; *the circumstances are so favorable!*"

Thus I began, insensibly, to lean upon my surroundings, and not upon Christ! The result was immediate stumbling and falling at almost every obstacle. Old sins, which I had fancied were slain, revived again. Like the tribes of Canaan, which Israel fancied they had suppressed forever—soon after they went over Jordan—they appeared again on the scene, and regained their lost territory. Again and again I rallied against them—resolved and re-resolved, wrote out my resolutions, like Edwards;[14] took solemn oaths in relation to them; tried the virtue of fastings; read religious biographies and other religious works, and did other things, but all to no purpose. More and more I fell under the power of sin; more and more I realized I was the slave of sin. For nearly two years I coursed up and down in the seventh chapter of Romans. Stopping ever and anon, and looking up to heaven I cried out, "Oh! wretched man that I am, who shall deliver me from this body of death?" My temper, naturally serene, now became chafed and irritated. I was dissatisfied with everybody, and most of all, with myself. In this state of mind I went to Oberlin, and fondly hoped that the preaching of Finney[15] and Mahan would bring me relief. So far from this, those wondrous sermons only raised my ideal of the life I *ought* to live, but left my *real life* more unsatisfactory than ever.

During the first part of my Sophomore year my mental distress was such that I sometimes wished I had never been born. In one of our society debates I used language toward my opponent which was harsh and sarcastic. He felt it keenly, for we had always been on friendly terms. And I too, charged it to the account of a temper, which of late, had become ungovernable.

After the debate I retired sullenly to my room and taking from my desk my book of Resolutions, I wrote with a heavy hand two resolutions like these:

Resolved, That *for one day* I will set a double guard at the door of my lips, and that I will thoroughly test my ability to live twenty-four hours without uttering one angry word.

"*Resolved, Further*, That should I find myself unable to keep so simple a resolution, directed against a single sin, then I will give up the struggle and drift with the tide."

As I finished this sentence, there was a knock at my door, and there entered the student I had abused by those sharp words. He expostulated with me for the sharp words I had used in the debate;

said he did not expect them from me. I asked, in sarcastic tones, did he ever know a man worsted in a debate, who thought he had been well treated. Alas! I saw in an instant I had already broken the resolution I had just written!

I was standing at my desk, and my hand was yet between the leaves of the book to keep the freshly written words from blotting. I now drew it out. My friend could get nothing more out of me and left me. When he had gone, I opened the book and lo! *the opposite page was blotted!* I threw down the book, saying, "Such resolutions may have helped Edwards, but with me they are of no account. They are broken reeds on which if one leans, it pierces his hand, and I will rely on them no more."

I omitted my usual evening prayer that night, and I lay down well nigh in despair. The next morning I rose up restless and reckless. My lessons were imperfectly prepared and carelessly recited. My patient instructors at length reproved me, but I answered back sullenly, defiantly. I was called before the Faculty; they talked with me, so kindly, but I gave them no promises of doing better. If they wished to expel me from college, do it, I did not care how soon. Why was I so reckless? Because I was the servant of sin. Satan was my master; what else could befall me, or what worse? Seeing how it was with me, they kindly resolved to bear with me, assured, as they afterward said, that God would ultimately lead me out and set my feet in a large place. He did so, and thus it came about:

I began now to reason from a new standpoint, and I said, "The man who is the slave of sin, has no business to preach the gospel. Unto the wicked, God said, What hast thou to do to declare my statutes? I cannot point men to Christ as a Saviour, when he is no Saviour to me. Should I do so, and they should turn to me and ask, 'Does He save you from sinning?' and I said 'No,' what faith would they have in me or my message? No; the idea of preaching must be abandoned.

"But if unfit to preach, clanking, as you do, the fetters of sinful habits, are you fit to go in with God's free people and sit down at the table of the Lord? What is the meaning of the act of eating that bread and drinking of that cup? Is it not a public profession that your spirit is fed and made strong by Christ, and that you are in covenant with Him? But you are not made strong morally by Christ. There is no evidence of his being in covenant with you. Your profession at the table is a false one, and you have no business there.

"Well, what of membership in the church? Your unhappy life, your inconsistencies, your downward tendencies will make your church membership a dishonor to the church and void of benefit to you." I must leave the church.

"Well, what of religious duties, prayer, for example? Is prayer without faith acceptable? 'Whatsoever is not of faith is sin.' When I pray for help to overcome temptation, I have no confidence that my prayer will be answered. I must then, give up prayer and drift with the tide, for prayer does not help me. It may help others, but in my case, it is like medicine to one moribund, in whom the constitutional basis has fallen out, and the medicine, however good in ordinary cases, cannot help him. 'Can the Ethiopian change his skin, or the leopard change his spots? then may those accustomed to do evil, learn to do well.' "

It was hard to give up prayer. But I saw no good to arise from it in such a case as mine. And here, a singular thought took possession of my mind. It was, that it was *not a decent treatment of God*, after all he had done for me, to turn my back upon his altars, to visit them no more, *without one word of acknowledgment* of my obligation to Him for all the past. Would it be honorable thus to leave an earthly benefactor, the words of gratitude unspoken? No, no; I would not leave my Maker thus. Once more I would visit His altars, and there I would enumerate such of His special favors to me as I could call to mind; I would thank Him for them, and express my regret they had not availed to redeem and sanctify a nature so perverse as mine. This done, I would leave the throne of grace forever!

For some weeks I lived without prayer, yet I was reluctant to come to *that last prayer!* I would take my time for it, and I made some preparation for it. As there occurred to my mind special mercies and blessings of God to me, I jotted them down upon a sheet of paper. A page was filled; then another, and I was surprised at their number and magnitude, too.

After much delay I came to an afternoon of leisure and I said, This is as good a time as any. So I locked my door, drew down the curtains, and spread out the sheet before me, containing the list of mercies I was to enumerate in this my last prayer. Finding my fickle, emotional nature greatly moved by the thought of this being my last and farewell visit to my Father's house, I remember to have asked the Lord to quench forever these vain emotions in my heart. For they had arisen in like manner a thousand times before, incited within a temporary hope of victory and improvement, only to be followed by an enslavement more absolute than ever. And I hated my rising feelings, because long experience had shown they were as unstable as water. I now took up the first item, my birth in a Christian land. What

a privilege, what a blessing; then for life in this age of revivals and
of light, this nineteenth century; I thanked Him for a praying mother
and sister, each so self-forgetful and so earnest for my salvation; for
my faithful Sabbath school teacher; for my early pastor; for my conversion, and helps so many thus far received in seeking an education.
From these side helps I turned to God himself, my best and infinitely
greatest friend. Had he not made me with his own loving hands? Had
he not endowed me with an endless being? Had he not given me
faculties capable of infinite expansion? Was it not in his heart to make
me His loving child, an heir of God and a joint heir of Jesus Christ?
"Lost by my sin, did he not give his Son for my ranson?" In my
perversity and fickleness what patience had followed me, even till now,
and was He not even at this moment waiting to be gracious? About
to break away from his arms in my despair, did I not hear Him say,
"How can I give thee up, Ephraim? How shall I set thee as Admah!
How make thee as Zeboim! My heart is turned within me!" The path
to the throne of grace had been deeply trodden by me, and how
could I now leave it to return no more? While I lingered the question
arose, Cannot an infinite God save a case so desperate as mine? Of
course he could were he disposed to do so, and do it as easily as the
ocean can float a feather on its heaving bosom. Oh! If he were only
willing! But is he not? And, if not, what is the meaning of this array
of mercies I have just recounted? What, too, mean the great promises
of the Bible to the worst of sinners, the most desperate conditions?
Did Jesus ever come across a case of disease so desperate that he could
not cure the patient when he besought his help? No, *there is a way* in
which I could be saved *if only I could find it*. Will he not take my hand
and lead me to it. "There is a path the vulture's eye hath not seen,
and the lion's whelp has not trodden." I will ask him to take my
hand and lead me to it, I know his loving heart cannot reject me,
nor throw back my outstretched palm. Hope now began to spring up
in my heart. My conception was that there was *an experience, a baptism
of the Spirit, over yonder*, which once received would so vitalize my
spiritual nature that thenceforth the flesh would be suppressed, and
victory would be easy and uniform. But not so did I find relief. But,
nevertheless, with this idea dominant, I asked the Lord to take me
and lead me to the great blessing, victory over sin. I arose, adjusted
my room and started off, leaning wholly on Christ's arm. The bell
rang for supper, and I asked the lord to go with me there, and keep
me till I returned. I hoped, also, some word dropped there would
prove a key to the great treasure. I returned and thanked him for
keeping me during that short period; then I asked him to keep me

till morning; then to help me prepare for recitation, and so on from one stage to another through the day, and so on till two weeks had passed, all the time *looking ahead for some special experience* from which I could date my emancipation, my entrance upon the liberty of the sons of God. One day a very devout student overtook me in one of my walks, and linking his arm in mine said, "Brother B., I have observed a wondrous change in you during the last two weeks. Tell me! Has not the Lord been doing wondrous things for you? And if he has I will bless his name forever." I told him how God was *leading me forward toward the great blessing* and how wonderously he was keeping me from my besetting sins. Then he said, "Why! Brother, *you have got the blessing now.* For what is it you are seeking but victory over sin, and that he has been giving you for two weeks past." Then I saw that "This is the victory that overcometh the world, even our faith." I had returned to my first love, I was now as then, no more leaning on circumstances, Christian society, resolutions, etc., to help me, but wholly *on Christ*, and now, as then, I was kept by the power of God. I remember that when hope began to dawn afresh, I said, "If the Lord shall keep me and give me victory over sin, then shall I know that he can keep others too, whatever their estate. I will go to the drunkard, who has broken his pledge a hundred times, and will say to him, 'As sure as you live, Christ will keep you if you will cast yourself upon him and follow his leading. *I know it, for he has kept me!*' "

Fifty years have come and gone since the scene thus described at length, transpired. But the lesson I then learned of human weakness, and the inadequacy of all human helps in the strife against sin, has never been forgotten. On the other hand the power of Christ to keep the soul that leans wholly on him, has grown upon the writer, and becomes the theme that always encourages and inspires. And in preaching Christ, my heart is always strong, when I tell weak and sinful men of a Christ, "Who is able to save unto the uttermost, all who come unto God by him." How could I doubt it, after all he has done for me? "I will go in the strength of the Lord God. I will make mention of his name, and of his only."

CHAPTER
6

AN EVENTFUL JOURNEY

Not many months after the great change above narrated I went East to my old home in Cheshire, Conn., and this is why I made the journey, how I made it, and the results. The reason for making the journey was that I longed to tell my brethren at home of *Christ as a Saviour from sinning*, and to warn them against leaning upon moral surroundings, or anything else save help from on high to keep them from backsliding, lukewarmness and sin. I wanted also to tell them that it was a great mistake, and a sad one, to suppose that the joy and peace of the convert could not continue, but in the nature of things must fade and pass away.

While praying over the matter I received a letter from a Miss Benham, a sister in the church in Cheshire, in regard to her brother Welcome. She was very anxious for his conversion; she asked me to pray for him; perhaps to write him. She wished I could see him. He had often spoken of me and said he liked to hear Mr. Stevens and me pray and speak. He believed they were real Christians.

My heart became enlisted in the young man, and as I prayed for him the conviction fastened itself upon me that should I go home he would be converted, and perhaps become a preacher of the Gospel. So in the early autumn I started for home. This was in 1837.

I left Oberlin with but seven dollars in my pocket, and the journey exceeded 800 miles. I hoped to get some money in Cleveland. I walked from Oberlin to Dover, some twenty-five miles, the first day. The tavern where I stopped over night was full, and I had to sleep upon a bench in the barroom. In the course of the evening I called upon the pastor of the Congregational Church. He inquired about Oberlin, and about the new doctrine of Christian perfection[16] now being taught there. In the course of our conversation on the subject I related to him my experience and the life of faith I was now living. He was deeply affected, and touching my arm significantly, as he left the room, I followed him. He led me to the barn and said, "Brother, that blessing you have received, I want and I must have it. I cannot live without it." We bowed together in prayer, and I think it was Jacob's wrestling with the angel once more repeated on earth as it has been a thousand times before! I think it very likely the minister repeated the words, "I will not let thee go, except thou bless me." I am quite certain that prayer-meeting will never be forgotten by him or me. Years after I heard of him as a man of power, and looking back *to that night* as the crisis in his religious life.

I resumed my walk the next morning, thanking God and taking courage.

At Cleveland I got no help, so I paid two dollars out of the seven I had for a deck passage to Buffalo, and proceeded. I told the purser on the boat I was short of money; could he furnish me some work to pay in part for my passage? He said, in substance, Make yourself generally helpful and I will pay you what is right. I did so, and when I reached Buffalo he paid me, if I recollect aright, some shillings more than my fare.

At Buffalo I took the canal route, walking on the towpath all day, and at night I stepped aboard a passing canal boat and took a berth. The next morning found me some thirty miles further on my way, and my fare was only forty-five cents, or one and one-half cents a mile. I then stepped ashore and resumed my walk, eating some crackers, etc., as I walked along. Taking a cross cut through Marcellus I was taken down at that place with bilious fever. It had been coming on for several days, and when I reached Marcellus I was completely prostrated with it, and could proceed no further.

The tavern where I stopped was quite full, and the landlord was quite reluctant to take in a sick man. He advised me to go to the minister's house. Not knowing where else to go I went. I introduced myself as a student from Oberlin on my way to my home in Connecticut. "Did he know of a family in his church where I could be housed and cared for till this attack had subsided, since there was no room for me in the tavern?" He could not tell me of one; though many of his people were rich and dwelt in large houses, they were reluctant to entertain strangers, especially if sick. As for himself his house was full, would be glad to entertain me but could not. I took it all pleasantly and said I had no doubt I should, in any event, fare as well as the Master, and what could a servant ask more. So I left, thanking him for his sympathy and kind wishes and words, asked him to have no solicitude about me for I knew One who possessed all power in heaven and in earth, would never leave me nor forsake me. I could with difficulty walk or even sit up, but I staggered down the steps, bound for the hotel again. Before I had proceeded many steps

I heard a female voice say something very earnestly to the minister and he opened the door and called me back, saying that his wife insisted that she could make room for me. I said "No, let me look elsewhere; I know ministers' families are overtaxed by calls of ministers, agents and all sorts of people in distress, etc." But as I was declining the woman herself came down the steps, and insisted on my staying with them, and when she added that if I did not she would be deeply grieved, I consented.

Well! I went in, was taken up stairs and was soon on a sick bed. After a severe turn of vomiting and two or three hours of rest, I was able to talk. Ever and anon the good woman flitted in and out of the chamber, ministering to my necessities. Occasionally this ministering angel sat down a few minutes by the bedside and fanned my fevered brow. Sick as I was my heart was full of the joy of God, and the peace which flows like a river. And a heart full always seeks suitable expression. She became deeply interested; she went and called her husband, and they both sat down by me, and we talked of the great salvation. Each day and indeed each hour drew our hearts more closely together. We did not talk much about names, or theories, we talked about *things*. My sickness was short. I was soon able to pursue my journey. But how endeared to me was that family? They insisted on my staying longer, and when I left they both wept and parted with me as if I were a brother after the flesh, and more, also, than that. Dear friends, I have forgotten their names, not their hospitality and their love. When I reach the heavenly mansions I shall inquire where they are and visit them and talk over that short visit, "when I was a stranger and they took me in, sick and in want and they ministered unto me."

Pursuing my way on the canal line, as I began, I reached Albany with just fifty cents in my purse. I found there was an opposition line of stages, running between Albany and Hartford, Conn. I went to one of the offices and found the fare between the two places was two dollars. I should need the fifty cents I had to buy a little food on my way. Could they trust me for the fare? I would send it up to their office in Hartford, when I reached home. The agent thought not; I could wait till the proprietor of the stage line came in. When he came he looked over the list of passengers and said, "There is room for him, so take him along, I guess he is honest."

The next evening, just before sundown, when near Farmington I got off the stage to take the road to Cheshire through Farmington. The sun set as I was entering the village, and I turned into the first tavern. Taking out the ten cents, all I had left, I said to the landlord, "My name is Bristol, I am on my way from Ohio to Cheshire, and I

am *so near* out of money, but I want supper and lodging, and perhaps
breakfast, and when I get home I will send you the money to pay for
these accommodations." He looked at me searchingly and turning
away, said his place was not an hospital. He did not keep a free lunch
and lodging house! No tavern could do business and live in that way,
etc. I went out upon the piazza and looked up the street and down
the street, doubtful which way to go, when I heard a female voice
calling the landlord back into the kitchen. Directly he came out and
asked, "Did you say your name was Bristol, and that you were from
Cheshire?" "Yes, sir." "Do you know one Gid, or Gideon Bristol
there?" "Yes, sir, he is my father." "Your father! Your father!" "Yes."
"And you want supper and lodging? Of course you can have it, and
the best that this house can afford too! Your father has stopped at
this house half a hundred times! He is one of my best friends, and
no boy of his ever asks a meal and lodging here and gets turned away!
Not much! Here Bridget! Get this young man the best supper this
house can furnish, and a good room too!" And then he went away
muttering other things to himself doubtless, to the same effect. So I
fared sumptuously that night, and after breakfast the next morning
I went on my way homeward. Thus I found that sometimes it is a
good thing to be the son of your father!

HOME AGAIN

The Saturday evening after reaching home, I attended the prayer-
meeting held in the vestibule of the Congregational Church. I was
called upon to speak and in doing so told my brethren how I began
my religious life among them, leaning wholly upon Christ and looking
constantly to him for help in every time of need. How wondrously I
was upheld. Also, how I began gradually to lean upon my surroundings. How from that point I began to decline in spirituality and in
power to combat my besetting sins and temptation in general. I told
them how obstinately I clung to these vain helpers, till at last, utterly
disheartened and despairing of help from man or from myself, I cast
myself upon Christ as I did in the beginning, and said: "Thou canst
save, and thou alone." That when I came to this, the same relief which
took me up and carried me in arms divine, when a lad of fifteen, now
reappeared and carried me as on eagle wings. I threw away my book
of resolutions, I gave up all reliance on favorable Christian society to
save me. I looked solely to Jesus. This one thing I did. It was now
six months since this return to my first love and to my first faith.
That the bliss of those days of first love had returned and greatly
increased—Jordan overflowed all its banks. That I knew of no reason

why it might not last a lifetime, yes, and forever and ever! I closed by saying: "Come, brethren beloved, let us take the hand of Jesus and let us go up higher."

I was listened to with deep interest, and I believe with entire candor. As the meeting broke up, quite a number pressed my hand and said: "That is what I want, pray for me." The pastor, Rev. Erastus Colton, thanked me for those words of cheer and words of love, and prayed that they might do us all good. His wife too was very cordial in her greeting and was not in the least afraid to ask: "Is there not something in the Gospel for me I have not as yet attained unto?" Mr. A. A. Stevens, the most intimate and deeply loved friend I ever had, then a member of Yale College, was at home on a vacation. I told him the interest I felt in Welcome Benham and my belief that he would be converted and make a useful man. He at once entered into full sympathy with me in the matter. As the best way of getting hold of him, we agreed to appoint a religious meeting on Cheshire street. His devout sister also entered into our plans, and agreed to induce Welcome to attend the meeting. The next Sabbath notice was given out in church, that "brothers Stevens and Bristol would hold a religious meeting on Cheshire street on such an evening. Doubtless the people in that neighborhood, and especially the young people, would be glad to hear our College brethren talk of the great salvation." Steven and I were much together and before the meeting had agreed upon the topic on which we would speak. It was to be the goodness of God to us all, and his worthiness to be loved, served and trusted. The evening came and the house was full. After singing and prayer, I rose to speak on the theme agreed upon — the goodness of God. In opening, incidentally I remarked that men *treated God as if* he was a hard master demanding a service exceedingly hard to render, so hard that they would run risks awful to contemplate, rather than render it. This led to other thoughts in the direction of human hostility to God and his government. On and on I was led till I had drawn a portrait of man's depravity, ingratitude and guiltiness, such as I had never conceived of before. It was a portrait fit for devils lost, rather than for men living in a world of mercy and salvation. I sat down astonished at the strange direction my thoughts had taken, and not less at the results at which they had arrived. Yet I felt that I had spoken with the manifest help of God, and as led by his Spirit. I was reminded of a sermon in a similar strain, preached by the Elder Edwards[17] at North Hampton, so awful in its arraignment of human rebellion, that one of his deacons rose up in the midst of it and cried out, "Oh Mr. Edwards! Mr. Edwards! is not God a *God of mercy?*"

Mr. Stevens followed me, fully intending when he rose to turn the thoughts of the people to the theme agreed upon — the goodness and mercy of God. But he must needs connect his remarks with mine, but a slight addenda to its thoughts. So he opened by saying, it was indeed true now, as before the flood, that the wickedness of man was great upon earth. He had thought of other ways in which it revealed itself. He mentioned one, then another, then another, and on and on he proceeded, describing graphically the downward road, till at last he too sat down, like myself, not having said one word on the theme agreed upon! How silent that house was when he ceased to speak! I called upon a deacon to pray. He declined. Upon others — all wished to be excused. We had to close the meeting ourselves. As we were about to disperse I said if the people will come together one week from this evening we will gladly meet with them. A few shook hands with us, but the majority scattered immediately for their homes, scarcely exchanging a word with each other. When we had got by ourselves, Stevens grasped my arm nervously and asked? "What on earth led you off upon that awful theme?" "Sure enough!" said I, "I don't know! I cannot account for it! But why did not you, who had ample time for reflection, correct the matter, by contrasting the love of God with man's alienation, ingratitude and sin? You had a grand opportunity." "Yes, yes," said he, "why did I not? I intended to do so, but I got my foot into the rut and I could not get it out. But why did you appoint another meeting?" said he. "Not one of them will come again! They are mad as hornets!" Well! I did not like to have the meeting close so. I wanted another chance to retrieve the situation. Besides, Welcome Benham *must be converted*. We felt so badly about the turn the meeting had taken, that we turned aside into a grove and asked the Lord to pardon our blunders and help us to regain the next evening the lost ground.

One week from that time we were on our way to the Cheshire street schoolhouse. Our expectation of seeing a good congregation was slight. Indeed, we doubted whether the house would be lighted at all. We believed we had offended the people greatly. Coming in sight of the schoolhouse, we saw no light, and concluded our fears were realized. But as we drew nigh, we saw the house was full; all the seats and benches and desks and even the windows were occupied, so was the entry way and all the standing room, and a crowd was gathered around the door!

What could it mean? We felt that God was there; that "This is none other than the house of God and the gate of Heaven." With difficulty we crowded our way within. A hymn sung, a prayer, and I began to speak. My theme was—if I remember rightly—"Seeking Jesus; how to seek him, and the certainty of finding him, if we seek him with decent earnestness and perseverance."

To illustrate this, I told the story of the African who went to England under a load of conscious guilt, seeking "The Christian's God who paid the debt." It is a simple story, and ordinarily when told, is not very impressive. But not so when told this night. The people were greatly moved by it. The whole house was in tears. Partially suppressed sighs were heard all through the house, by persons endeavoring to hold down their emotions. Before I had finished what I had prepared to say, I saw clearly the crisis had come, and called upon Brother Stevens to pray; and what a prayer that was! The healing Jesus had come into the room, and while he prayed, was wiping away penitential tears, and saying to one and another, "Son, daughter, thy sins are forgiven thee."

As he ended a hand reached through the crowd and rested on my shoulder. I turned, and lo! it was the hand of Commodore Andrew Foote, son of Ex-Governor Foote and brother of my beloved Sabbath school teacher, heretofore spoken of. He it was, who afterward became so famous as the conqueror of the Rebel forces on the Mississippi and branches, with his gunboats. He had that day come home on a short furlough, and hearing that Brother Stevens and I were to hold a meeting that night on Cheshire street, had ridden four miles to meet us and attend the meeting. I drew him into the little vacant spot where Brother Stevens and I stood, and said,—

"Here is our dear Brother Andrew Foote, fresh from the ocean. We will hear what he thinks of this great salvation." He began by saying: "After the clear exhibition of the way to find Jesus, and after that prayer which carried us all up to the very altar of mercy, what can I say but this: Let us, each for himself, lay fast hold on eternal life," and after this manner went on.

Dear man! I have never seen him since—one of the noblest men who ever trod the quarter-deck. Long since he died of a wound from a rebel cannon-ball received at Fort Donelson.

When he ceased to speak, we closed the meeting. But how loth the people were to part. Some twenty persons, it was estimated, that night, in that house, found the pearl of great price, and sold all and bought it. Welcome Benham was interviewed and before we let him go he asked us to pray for him and promised to pray for himself. And now, the people would scarcely let us go home. We must stay and visit the inquirers and the converts, and the people generally, and we did so.

Incidentally I mentioned, in the course of our stay there, to a leading person, how badly we felt, after our terrible arraignment of the people at the first meeting. He looked surprised, and said no one looked at it in that light, or as at all objectionable in manner or in matter, and that the reason why the deacon and others would not pray, was, "We all felt so guilty our mouths were stopped."

From Cheshire street, the work of grace spread all over the township, and as the result, I believe a hundred or more, united with the Congregational Church.

Among these was Welcome Benham, who soon went to Oberlin to commence a course of studies, and though prevented from finishing it on account of failing health, nevertheless has exerted a constant and extended influence in favor of the cause he then espoused. He now lives in Meriden, Connecticut; has long stood at the head of the Young Men's Christian Association there, and has been about as wholly devoted to the cause, as if he were set apart as a preacher of the gospel.

CHAPTER 7

RETURN TO OBERLIN

My work seemed to be done; the object for which I had revisited my native place accomplished, and I felt that I must retrace my steps and resume my studies at Oberlin, so as to overtake my class and be able to go on with them in the Spring term. So I announced to my friends that on such a day I expected to start on my return to Oberlin.

My mother asked, "Where is the money coming from" I replied, that the Lord had plenty of it, and if it was his will I should return, the money would be coming in due time. My dear friend, William Law, questioned me very closely as to the grounds of my faith in God's help *in financial matters*; thought it bordered closely on presumption, but did not know but what I was right, after all. He made me promise to take tea with him and his family the evening before I left.

On the previous Sunday, as I shook hands and said good-bye to numerous friends I was to see no more, quite a number left in my hand a piece of money; some, half-a-dollar; some, a dollar, and some, as high as five dollars. Blessed money, too, it was—all the gift of love, all enwreathed with prayer, and all blessed of the Lord! Shall I ever forget, or cease to love the hearts and hands which gave them? Where, now, in such an hour, was the momentary flurry which jostled our love some two years before, when I took my stand on the Anti-Slavery question? All gone, and gone forever! Even so—the great bones of contention, around which great sections of the church have striven, have many of them already moldered away and will yet become as the fine dust of the balance, as the eons of eternity come on.

According to agreement, I took tea with Brother Law and his family. He asked me how much I lacked of the amount necessary to return to college, and commence the new term, and when he knew, went to his drawer and came back, bringing the sum, which he put into my hand and sent me away with tears in his eyes and blessings upon his lips. On that last interview with that good man, he thanked me for having converted him to the temperance cause, some years before. And thus it was:

HOW MY FRIEND WAS CONVERTED TO TOTAL ABSTINENCE

In one of my vacations he had employed me to work on his farm. One day as I was gathering his winter apples, he came out into the orchard, and said, "There is some trouble over at the cider mill. Mr. Mallory, who is making the cider, is drunk, and is making a fool of himself generally. He cannot get the blocking on. Will you go over and set things up right and finish the job?" I did not like to displease so good a man and so kind a friend, so I started for the mill, keeping up in the meantime a vigorous discussion within, whether it was right for me, a Christian and a temperance man, to employ the strength the Lord had given me in making cider. This was not for vinegar; it was to be used for drinking purposes, the most of it long after it had fermented and become charged with intoxicating properties. Was it not pulling down, in one part of the day, a cause I was trying to build up in the other?

I came to the mill. There was Mallory, staggering about and swearing, monarch of all he surveyed. A few years before he was the boss wrestler of the township, but now, cider chiefly, had so shorn off his locks, that I easily managed him—set him down in a corner and bade him stay there and keep quiet. But my whole nature revolted against the whole drunkard-making business. After putting on a part of the blocking, I desisted—left the mill and went back. In doing so I fully expected to lose the favor and help of the best friend I had in Cheshire. He was a somewhat positive man, and was said to be rather impatient of contradiction. His influence was great in the community, and who would stand by me should Mr. Law turn against me? He had, up to this time, contended for the moderate use of wine and cider, and both these were usually on his dining table. The temperance people felt keenly his influence, but had not been able to bring him over to their views.

When I had reached the house, I said, "Mr. Law, I cannot tell you how much it grieves me to disoblige a man who has done so much for me as you have, or to lose the favor of one I so highly respect, but I suppose I must do so, or forfeit my peace of conscience and my sense of duty. Mr. Law, I cannot conscientiously put up that cider apple cheese. That cider will help to make drunkards like Mallory. I don't believe it is right for me to make it."

Mr. Law dropped his head and quickly said, "Well! well! I will go, and you can go to gathering the winter apples." I believed I had

deeply offended him. It did look absurd, a young man in his teens
sitting in judgment on a venerable man of sixty, and on his cider
making, and for that, his drinking too. And I said to-night after tea
I shall get a lecture, then my wages, and then my discharge papers.
But I kept praying, first for Mr. Law and then for myself, that the
Lord would control his thoughts and also guide my mind in judgment
and my lips in speech. At tea scarce a word was said. I ate a little,
asked to be excused and rose to go out. "Please step into the parlor,"
said Mr. Law, I wish to speak with you a moment." I went in and
waited. He came in and after a brief silence he said, "I wish you
would tell me why you could not work in the cider mill this afternoon."
I began by telling him what a curse cider had been among a number
of my kindred and dear neighbors, either making sots of them by
itself, or creating a hankering after stronger stimulants which at length
slew them, both body and soul. Could I help perpetuate and extend
this curse of curses? No, not by one day's work with hands Christ had
redeemed and set to work in the opposite direction. My feeling was
so deep I could proceed no further. Meanwhile Mr. Law had been
diligently plying his handkerchief to his eyes and cheeks. At length
he said in broken sentences, "My young friend, you are right, I am
glad you quit the old mill. It never looked so nasty as it did to me
to-day and I could not put on the blocking till I had promised the
Lord I would never put up another unless for vinegar." He could
scarcely say enough to express his approval of my course. He knew
well what it cost me. From that time he was doubly my friend. Thence
onward cider and wine were excluded from his table, and many were
the occasions when he told, to the delight of the temperance people,
the story of his conversion to the total abstinence principle. This
was the man who filled out the purse necessary to carry me back to
Oberlin College.

So having thus received help from God I went back to Oberlin,
with a heart full of gratitude and wonder as I looked over those four
months of journeying, and of visit to my native town. It seemed to
me then and it seems to me now, to border well nigh on the miraculous.

The students were nearly all away teaching school during the
long winter vacation. I looked up my studies where I left off, and
when the spring term commenced I was able to resume studies with
my class.

Nothing special occurred during my Junior year, save that I was
wonderfully provided for financially. Strange it was, but true, that
when I came to need money or books, or clothing, somehow they
came. And I noticed, too, that God held them back just long enough

to enable me to appreciate their value, and thus properly estimate the love of the giver. And I used often to wonder if the commandment to pray and to pray often, did not also arise in part from the yearnings of the great paternal heart for converse with his children.

A SPECIAL PROVIDENCE

I ought not here to omit the mention of a *special providence*, supplying a special need of so marked a character that I was compelled to say, *"This is the finger of God."*

I had borrowed five dollars of a Mr. Penfield, a student. One day he came to me in haste and said, "My people are sick and I must start for home this noon, and shall need that five dollars to pay my fare." I went at once to get it, but I could neither get it where it was due me nor borrow it. Just then money had become very scarce in Oberlin. The bell rang for twelve o'clock, the stage threw of its mails at the postoffice and was rushing to the hotel to change horses, then to rush back, take its mail and go on. I was returning to Tappan Hall and saw Mr. Penfield in the south door waiting for his money. What should I say to him? That the Lord had failed me this time? What a disappointment to him, and what influence would that failure have on my faith and his? But I saw a man running toward the Hall who reached it simultaneously with myself. Before I had time to speak to Penfield the stranger cried out, "Is a man by the name of Bristol here?" "That is my name," I said, "and I am the only one of that name in college." "Well," said he, handing me five dollars, "I suppose this belongs to you." "Who gave it you?" "Don't know, just as I left Cleveland a gentleman handed me this and said, 'Give it to a man in Oberlin by name of Bristol.' That is all I know about it," and he turned and ran back to the postoffice. I handed it over to Penfield, and went to my room to thank God for the gift, and also for this helper of my faith.

Years after, in passing through Cleveland, I met a lawyer by name of Sterling, and he asked, "Did you, some two years ago, receive five dollars from me?" I said I had no recollection of it, but told him of receiving five dollars of a stranger as narrated above. "Do tell!" said he, "I sent that five dollars and it has troubled me more than any five I ever lost or thought I lost. Thus it was: I was standing by the Weddle House as the stage was starting off one morning, gazing upon the passengers filling up the coach. As the driver was gathering up his lines a passenger thrust his head out of the window and asked, 'Does this coach pass through Oberlin?' 'Yes,' said the driver. At once I drew out my purse, and handing the stranger five dollars said, 'Give this to a student by name of Bristol there, they will all know him,' the driver cracked his whip and the stage was off. I was confounded at what I had done, and said of myself, 'What a fool I was to give that five dollars to a total stranger! He will forget the name, and if he don't he will have no time to look up Mr. Bristol; the stage only stops to change horses. Ten to one he will keep it. Surely I am a fool.' A hundred times I said this of my action, and wondered at its precipitancy. It seemed as if for the instant another will had control of my hand and my purse. So you received it after all, and just when you needed it, too," and he went away in deep meditation. Of course such singular interpositions are rare, but do not some such occur in every life, enough to startle us out of our materialism, with the conviction, "Thou God seest me"?

Thus I was provided for during my entire course of studies, academic, collegiate and theological, and when I graduated I owed no man anythng but love, save Messrs. Smith & Dove, and entering the ministry was to cancel my notes to them. While upon the topic I may add here that this divine care over, and provision for, my physical and financial necessities, has not abated one whit since I left the seminary, in 1842, till this year of grace, A.D., 1887, a period of forty-five years.

My life has been spent mainly upon the frontier; my salaries have been small, not averaging, probably, over $500 a year. My family has been larger than the average. Six boys and three girls have been brought up in my house and fed at my table. Yet our wants have been reasonably supplied. Our bread has been given us and our water made sure. My note has always been good for its face, and my ability to pay unquestioned. It is true I have passed through financial straits, like others, but the vessel, though half filled with water, did not go down, for Christ was on board and she outrode the storm.

In addition to self-support the bounteous Lord has given me ability to do a little for others. This I accustomed to do even while in college. I kept up there the habit of giving a little to each passing call. I did this not only to help along the cause, but also to keep my heart warm toward it. "For where your treasure is there will your heart be also."

Brethren in the ministry, living hard by me and receiving salaries twice as large as mine, did not lay up half as much per year as I did, nor do I think they gave more than I did away. And so it came to pass, "He that gathered much had nothing over, and he that gathered little had no lack." And here I am, at the ripe age of seventy-three, about as well off financially as I desire to be on my own account. And it is quite a comfort to an old man to be situated that he is not obliged to look to children or friends for pecuniary support when the working days of life are over. Better still it is to have a little laid aside to keep up one's habit of giving till the Master calls him home. To me it seems quite desirable that young clergymen should adopt the principle of laying up something every year, if possible, against a rainy day; possibly only their marriage fees. This, in time, and other small sums which can be added to them, will, in the course of thirty or forty years, amount to a quite respectable sum. The fact that many ministers whose friends have turned every way to help them to an education fail to lay up anything after entering the ministry, and when worn out are obliged to fall back helpless upon kind friends and parishioners, brings the profession into sad reproach. It is on this account that many a man says, "Let my son be anything rather than a penniless minister." And many a mother, "Let my daughter marry a respectable man of any profession rather than a minister." We do not object to a minister being poor if that necessity is laid upon him either because he won't work or will not be economical. A lecture on this subject, viz., the duty of being economical and laying aside something yearly, if possible, to meet the wants of age and coming infirmities, would be quite in place if delivered to a class of theological students just before going out to their fields of labor. Is there any class of professional men so improvident as ministers? How many there are who receive large salaries, yet never lay up a cent, but spend all as they go along.

THREATENED WITH CONSUMPTION

In the last part of my Senior year I had a severe attack of lung fever. It left me with a cough so settled and exhaustive that my physician said I had quick consumption. He advised my leaving college and hastening home. Reluctantly I came to the same conclusion, and prepared to return to Connecticut, expecting to die soon after I got there, and be buried by the sepulchers of my fathers. How affectionately our dear President Mahan and the other professors took me to their homes to stay with them a few days before I bade them a final farewell. The students, too, gathered closely around me as I was about to leave. But most of all my dear classmates clave to me as with one heart, and could not speak the word farewell. One of them, dear Hiram Hopkins, went with me to Elyria, and as we parted he held my hand in both of his and said, "Good-bye, good-bye, brother beloved, it is not likely I shall ever see you in this world again. It looks as if the Master was soon to call you home. We grieve that we shall not have your help in preaching the gospel, and we know that it is this that gives this parting its special pain to you. But, brother, whensoever we rise to preach the gospel, we will think that there is one less to bear the message, and it shall stimulate us to greater earnestness and zeal."

Five years thereafter I stood upon *his* grave in Plattsburg, N. Y., and read the inscription on his tombstone, myself a preacher, and this dear classmate lying in the grave so low.

President Mahan went with me as far as Cleveland, and his words of cheer and words of love were among the most stimulating and hope-inspiring I ever heard.

At Buffalo I took passage on a canal boat. The boat was crowded and when night came all the berths were occupied so that none was left for me, and I was obliged to sit up all night. There was a little more downright piggishness in their treatment of a sick man than is characteristic of Americans. Howbeit, God meant it for good.

Not sleeping during the night I escaped those night sweats which had followed me since my recovery from the lung fever, and which were daily reducing my strength and my flesh. The next day I was better and stronger. The night following I sat up again. No sweating that night to speak of, and so on till I reached my home in Connecticut. Here I soon got rid of my cough and other consumptive indications. I have the impression that I lost the use of one lobe of the lungs in part during this sickness, as my voice was never afterward as strong as before. I resumed my studies under the tutorship of our pastor, Rev. Erastus Colton, and so kept along with the studies of my class, that when they graduated I received my diploma with them.

CHAPTER

8

A YEAR IN NEW HAVEN THEOLOGICAL SEMINARY

I n the fall of the year I entered the New Haven Theological Seminary.[18] During the year of my stay there, a series of articles appeared in the "religious Herald" of Hartford, against Oberlin. In announcing their forthcoming, the editor assured his readers that now at length, we were about to learn something definite and reliable about Oberlin, as the writer of the promised articles was a clergyman of repute, and a ripe scholar. I forbear to give the writer's name, as he is truly a good man, and has I am told, long since become a strong friend of Oberlin. When the first article appeared, it seemed to me so faulty and vulnerable, that I ventured a reply. I signed my article — "A Member of the Theological Seminary of New Haven." It was published with editorial commendations of its candor and Christian spirit. The many corrections I made in the statements of my opponent, led the editor to remark, "The writer is evidently well versed in the history of Oberlin." But no one surmised who the writer was. The next article was still more vulnerable and the reply so complete, that Rev. H. G. Ludlow, one of the New Haven pastors, said to me, "That student has completely vindicated Oberlin. Professor —— had better stop writing." So the discussion went on, till the editor said in effect, that as no case had been made out against Oberlin, or was likely to be, he thought the discussion had best be closed. The authorship of these letters being traced to my door, not a little discussion arose between me and the other students over the Oberlin doctrines, experiences and practices. As New Haven was New School[19] in its theology, and as Oberlin in its doctrines was but an inevitable resultant of its cardinal principles, my classmates found great difficulty in escaping conclusions I was daily forcing upon them by inexorable logic. We began to congregate a little before the lecture hours to discuss those questions. Finally we gathered half an hour previous, such was the interest felt, and warmly we debated the matter. Few took sides

with Oberlin, but scarcely any two could agree upon an argument in
opposition to it. At length a public discussion of the question was
loudly called for. Four speakers were selected to open the debate, and
Dr. Taylor[20] was to close with a lecture on the subject. Myself and
another were to speak for Oberlin—a Mr. Griswold and another to
present the other side. Mr. Griswold was a man I greatly respected.
He was in the Senior class and soon to graduate and go on a mission
to Africa. He was a fine scholar, a powerful reasoner, an impressive
public speaker, and there was not a student in the seminary of more
promise than he, if I except Joseph P. Thompson, or "Tabernacle
Thompson," as he was afterward called. I went at once to Griswold's
room and said: "This debate about the Oberlin ideal, or the possibilities of the Christian life will be mainly between you and me. Our
partners have little heart in the matter. I propose that you and I spend
some evenings privately canvassing the matter. That we clear away
the rubbish, ascertain the points of agreements and differences and
reduce them to a minimum, and on these spend our strength when
the debate comes off." He consented. We prayed together and a
number of evenings of very candid and careful discussion followed.
In one of them I related my experience. It affected him deeply. Nearer
and nearer we came together. The evening before the debate was to
come off I called. He said, "Bristol, I cannot speak to-morrow evening!" "But you must," I said: "I cannot do without you." "No!" said
he, "I dare not go. Should I go and utter honestly my real convictions,
as they are now, I should defend what our professors and the churches
generally regard as 'Oberlin heresy.' So wide a departure from the
opinions of men I so deeply respect, should not be hastily made. If,
on the other hand, I array against Oberlin all the arguments I can
think of, the most of which I know to be fallacious, I fear the results
on myself and others. I fear I shall grieve the Holy Spirit by so doing."
I said no more, for I deeply respected his honesty and conscientious-
ness. The discussion came off and was followed by a lecture read by
Dr. Taylor. but it had little relevancy to the Oberlin doctrine of
Christian holiness. It was prepared years before, to meet a phase of
the subject which had little in common with that held at Oberlin or
presented by me that evening. When the vote was taken, four hands
were raised for Oberlin and three against it. The general feeling was
that both the lecture and the arguments used against Finney's views
and those of Oberlin were very unsatisfactory. Hence all save a few
refused to vote. The Doctor was chagrined, and said with spirit: "If
you wish the papers to publish, that at a debate on the subject of
Oberlin Perfectionism Oberlin was sustained, then refuse to vote; if

not, then say so by raising your hands." Under this pressure, a large majority voted against Oberlin.

TWO SINGULAR CONVERSIONS

In one of the vacations, Bro. Stevens and I went up to Cheshire and while there attended some neighborhood meetings. In one of them, held in the southwest part of the town, owing to the prospect of rain, there were but four persons present, besides myself and Mr. Stevens. Of these two were members of the church. The other two were sisters, daughters of a well-to-do farmer, but who was a pronounced infidel. As there were so few present, I proposed that each tell his experience in the narrow way. Stevens and I each told how it had gone with us since our conversion. No one else took any part. We walked home in the darkness and drizzling rain some four miles, feeling that we had labored in vain and spent our strength for nought. Not so, for the next day these two girls rode five miles under deep conviction of sin, to ask our pastor what they must do to be saved. Nor was it long before they were active in the Master's vineyard. "Blessed are they that sow beside all waters!" The remembrance of the results of that discouraging meeting went with me for many a day.

RETURNING TO OBERLIN

At the close of my Junior year I concluded to return to Oberlin and there finish my theological studies. I did this because of the superior religious privileges enjoyed there, where one breathed the atmosphere of nearly a perpetual revival, and also because being one with them in theological belief and reformatory measures, I felt it my duty to share with them the burden of reproach their position brought upon them. So I went back and entered the Middle year.

LICENSED AND PREACHING IN CENTRAL OHIO

When the winter vacation commenced, the Oberlin Theological Faculty received a letter from the Congregational Church Association of Central Ohio, asking that two young men, under-graduates, should be recommended to them for the purpose of assisting in the series of revival meetings, to be held in their bounds under the leadership of Rev. John T. Avery, a noted and successful evangelist. The Faculty recommended myself and a classmate, Mr. Samuel D. Cochran.

We went down to Mansfield, where the Association held its annual meeting. We were examined and licensed. I was appointed to preach the sermon. My text was, "Ye cannot serve God and Mammon;" and the central thought, "It is impossible to walk astride the line which divides the service of God from that of Satan," or the only acceptable state, that in which *we intend to walk in all* the commandments and ordinances of the Lord. It awakened some discussion, but the majority acquiesced in it.

We were at once set to work in Mt. Vernon, Knox county, visiting from house to house, and holding schoolhouse conference meetings. Mr. Avery, in the meantime, was preaching daily to a large congregation in the Congregational church in that city. An extensive revival attended, us usual, Mr. Avery's meetings. The work spread abroad, and Brother Cochran and I followed it up, into surrounding townships. In one of them, that of Liberty, it was especially powerful. The whole population was moved, and great numbers were converted; but there were many adversaries.

LIFE THREATENED

It was a rude backwoods settlement, and we were often assailed by other weapons than arguments. I did most of the visiting — that being my forte, while Mr. Cochran did most of the preaching, he being much the abler, in that line. I visited nearly all the time by day, and in the evening conducted the prayer-meeting before and after sermon. God's power was manifest and many hardened men and women bowed before Him, who in the days of His flesh, cast out devils, and healed all manner of disease among the people.

One morning before I had risen, the man at whose house I was staying, came to my room and said, "A boy at the door has a message for you."

When I went out, a rough looking boy of some thirteen years, accosted me thus:

"My pa says he will shoot you, if you come to his house."

"Where does your father live?" I asked.

"Over there;" he said, pointing to a log house on another street.

Making sure of the house, I said in my blandest tones, — "Yes, tell your father I will try to be there by nine o'clock."

For a moment the boy seemed dazed with astonishment; then swelling with wrath, said, — "He will put a ball through you; he will."

"Yes, yes;" I said, as pleasantly as if invited to a wedding, "tell him I will try to be there by nine o'clock."

This so disgusted the boy that he would have nothing more to say to me, and went off muttering something I could not hear.

My host overheard the boy's message and besought me not to go, as the man was a desperate fellow that did little else than hunt and shed blood.

Breakfast over, I started across lots through the snow for the man's house. When some eighty rods distant, I saw the man, rifle in hand, standing between his log house and straw barn, and made for him with quickened pace. I suspect the agility with which I vaulted over a high rail fence, rather startled him, for he immediately shied behind a straw stack. But I was soon there; looked into the barn, went around the stack, seeking my man, but he was nowhere to be found. But I observed some tracks in the snow, leading directly back into the woods. I turned back to the log house, and there sat a sad faced and forlorn looking woman, scantily clad and surrounded by half-a-dozen children as poorly clad as she was. I shook hands with her and addressed her kindly, as if an old acquaintance. I recognized her as one who had come forward an evening before to ask for the prayers.of God's people. I suspect *that* was the cause of her husband's wrath. I made no allusion to his message, but begun at once to talk with her about the great curse of sin, and of Christ as our deliverer; of his great love for us; his readiness to receive, and his patience with those who enter his hospital, and seek his help. Soon she began to look up—she began to hope. Her fear of her husband was gone. Had she not seen him flee when no man pursued? Where were his threatenings to shoot and to kill? Surely he was not omnipotent.

Well, after talking to her as a brother, and leading her to the Saviour, we knelt in prayer and she professedly gave her heart to the dear Redeemer.

But that boy, who brought the message! There he sat in the chimney corner, silent and wrathful. His eyes glared at me occasionally, like those of a young wolf. While I was praying, he started out of the house, and as there was an axe close to the door, it occurred to me that he might seize it and split my head open while we prayed. So I had to keep one eye half open, contrary to my custom, and watched while I prayed. But he did not come back. Like his father he hid, and I saw him no more.

From this house I went to the next, and there I saw my man of the rifle with two other men. I at once introduced myself in a pleasant and lively way, and soon we were upon the great topic of religion. They all took part in the conversation, and became greatly interested. They wanted I should talk with a neighbor about it, and we all went to see him. It was almost as good as an inquiry meeting, and before we closed, they all knelt and I prayed with them. When I left they all promised to attend the meetings and to give the great matter their first attention. If my memory seves me, two at least of these soon gave evidence of regeneration.

On another occasion, in another part of the township, I called at a house in the depth of the forest. The woman was under deep conviction, and felt herself the chief of sinners. Before I left her burden rolled off, and she felt that her sins, which were many, were forgiven her. I asked for her husband. She said he was off still further in the forest, clearing a piece of land; but she begged me not to seek him, as he was terribly angry about this revival; refused to let her go to meeting, and she was afraid he would kill me. Soon after leaving the house, I heard the crash of a tree falling, away in the forest. It occurred to me, the man was there; so I left the path and went in the direction of the sound, and soon saw him chopping off the butt log of a large tree. I had seen him at a meeting and recognized him by his long hair and beard. The top limbs had been broken by the fall, and I got upon the body and walked down the trunk toward him. He stared at me sternly. Advancing, I asked pleasantly, "Is this Mr. So-and-so?" "Yes," he answered gruffly, as if he would say, "What business is that of yours? Are you come hither to torment me before the time?"

But I shook hands with him, told him who I was, that I just called at his house, and then I asked if he had cut down the great tree that morning. "He must be a No. 1 chopper, let me try his axe." Reluctantly he handed it to me and I plied it vigorously, cutting down the half he had begun. This put me on a sympathetic plane with him. I could swing an axe; I knew the heart of a chopper. Of course I did not feel above him, I praised his work and his judgment in the selection of an axe. By this time we were on good terms, his confidence was won, and then we sat down on the log and I talked to him of the Great Redeemer, of the Christian's life, his deathbed, his heaven above, his endless life over yonder.

The stalwart and bronzed faced chopper bowed his head and wept. "Alas," he said, "I am too great a sinner, there is no hope for me." But I told him of One who came to save the chief of sinners, and who could save unto the uttermost all who would come unto God by Him. And when I left him he promised to attend the meeting, that he would try, at least, to find the Saviour, and that he would not hinder his wife in her endeavor to lead a Christian life. With a warm shake of the hand and tears in his eyes I parted with him in the forest.

As I went on my way how vividly came before me the story in the Gospels, of the Master's meeting with the maniac of Gadara. "Coming out of the tombs, exceeding fierce, so that no man might pass by that way, and who cried out, 'What have I to do with this Jesus, thou Son of God most high; art thou come to torment me before the time?' " Yet before Jesus left him he was changed into another man, and besought Jesus that he might be with him.[21]

Not to elongate the narration of incidents in these revival labors, I will but add that the number of converts in these schoolhouse meetings was so large that, in addition to those who joined other churches, there was formed a Congregational Church of respectable size, and a house of worship was erected by them the following year.

The winter vacation being now over my classmate and I returned to Oberlin, greatly enriched in joyful experiences, but poorer in purse and in wardrobe than when we left for Mansfield. The people where we labored were poor, largely recent emigrants, and all they had was locked up in land, and money was very scarce. We did not blame them at all. We had received at the Lord's hand, a reward far above silver or gold.

The financial prospects for the opening long term of nine months were dark. But, as I went forward ways of earning money opened before me, and when the nine months had gone by, in looking back, I was reminded of our Lord's question to his disciples, and their reply, viz.: "When I sent you without purse or scrip, lacked you anything? and they answered, *Nothing*."

9

FRANKLIN, PORTAGE COUNTY, OHIO

At the end of the Middle year I was invited to spend the winter in Franklin, preaching to the Congregational Church there. The church was quite demoralized by causes I need not mention, and was in a sadly backslidden condition. Arriving there early in the week I quickly took in the situation. The first sermon was from the text, "Come, and let us return to the Lord, for he hath torn and he will heal us. He hath smitten and he will bind us up. After two days will he revive us, and the third day we shall live in his sight." The appropriateness of this text to their condition, and the tender and earnest application that followed, won me a place at once in their confidence and respect.

There was not a word of scolding, not an attempt to show off a little smartness by some keen sarcastic expressions. They were addressed by one who spoke as if he realized he himself was encompassed by infirmities.

I at once commenced a course of visitation from house to house, usually closing up a visit through a school district with an evening lecture in the schoolhouse. One of these lectures was in a school district where Campbellites, or Disciples,[22] predominated. Those who know them well, as they were in those days, will not be surprised that the text I selected as specially appropriate, was this: "They have healed the hurt of the daughter of my people slightly, saying Peace, peace, when there is no peace."

There was a large turnout, and the house was filled. The discourse ran somewhat thus: 1st. the hurt of God's creation is sin, the refusal to obey God. 2d. the *quack prescriptions* palmed off upon sinners by devils and their human agents to cure the dread disease. 3d. Repentance, faith in Christ, and regeneration by the Holy Spirit, the only and the sovereign remedy.

Of course I did not speak very commendatorily of the doctrine that merely intellectual belief in the historic Christ, outward morality and water baptism was a settlement of the matter between the soul and God. But I denounced it as healing the hurt slightly, leaving the dread cancer as lively as ever, doing its work of death.

When about to dismiss the congregation, a tall man arose and asked if I was not going to allow some one to reply to my remarks. I said this was not a meeting called for a debate, but for a lecture on a religious topic. He answered, that most people nowadays believed in free discusion. It was plain that the young man who has spoken to us to-night does not believe in it. Well! he did not blame "the young man" for being averse to a discussion, after such a discourse as he had given us this evening. Could he have fifteen minutes, he would overthrow every one of his positions and not leave a grease spot of them. Up to this time I had kept my eyes on the floor and I presume they thought "the young man" was frightened. I now looked up and advancing a little said: "I am not acquainted with this Goliath of Gath or some other place, who boasts that he can do such great things, but I know that as a rule, such boasters as he and provokers of strife and debate, are the last men in the world to make good their pretensions. I propose to test this man and see if he does not come under that rule. I definitely accept your challenge and ask the people to stay by and listen candidly till this debate is over, and see whether he is able to overthrow all the positions taken in the discourse this evening. And now sir, I will sit down and give you the fifteen minutes you ask for and five minutes more. And don't wander off upon other topics, but stick to your points and show this people that *sin is not the great hurt* of God's people. That the quack medicines I denounced are good and will cure the evil, and lastly, that repentance and faith in Christ and regeneration by the Holy Ghost are not the only remedy." I sat down, watch in hand, and gave the time. Campbellites have improved immensely since then but in those days they were intensely fond of discussion and some of them responded *"Good, good!"*

The tall man rose, bowed low, squared off into speaking attitude and began a wordy preamble which lasted perhaps five minutes. When I called him to order and said, "Unless you can confine your remarks to the points under discussion, I propose that we adjourn," he asked me to re-state the points of my discourse. I did so in terse language and promptly. He then took up the first: "Sin *the hurt* of God's people." Several times he repeated it in tones designed to make it ridiculous. Said there are many other evils, poverty, sickness, etc., etc., magnified these, and treated sin as less than they. His time up I replied that "sin antedated human existence and woe. It had a horrid history before Adam's fall. Before man there was a devil and his angels! whence come they? They fell from lofty places! They were once holy angels,

but by sin they fell! were cast out of heaven and hell was made for
the devil and his angels. If sin is a trifle, look up to the heaven they
lost by it and down into the hell it prepared for them. What did sin
to our first parents? Drove them from Eden, thenceforth in shame
and sorrow to tread a thorny road till death came to their relief! Pass
on and behold it corrupting the whole race till it repented God that
he had made man, because every imagination of the thoughts of man's
heart was evil and only evil, continually. Go take your stand on Ararat
and look over the waste of waters whose black waves roll over the
whole habitable world, drowning all its millions, with the exception
of one family! What was it for? What was it *for*? Was it brought on
by a trifle? What does this awful scene indicate is God's opinion about
sin? Is it to be sneered at? To be made the subject of a joke like those
you tried to pass off upon us? Nobody laughed at your stale words!
They were ashamed of you—you, a preacher of the Gospel, speaking
of sin as a small evil. What do you mean by it?" Some one cried out
"Time" and I sat down. I was getting well aroused. I suspect the
congregation would have left, a part at least, had not the rain begun
to fall in torrents. Most of the speech the tall man made in reply was
of the nature of an apology for an apparent attempt to make men
laugh at certain forms of sin. Of course he made no headway in
refuting any of the positions I had taken in the discourse. His time
up, I resumed my portrayal of the dark history of sin. We looked with
Abraham over burning Sodom, Adma, Zeboim and Gomorrah. Then
at the plagues of Egypt and the catastrophe of the Red Sea! Then at
the destruction of the seven nations of Canaan, and so on till we came
to Calvary's Cross and looked up into the marred visage of the great
Sufferer there! And as we stood there we asked what was it brought
him here? Was it a trifle? What means that rending veil? What the
sun's veiled face? What the rending rocks and earthquake? What the
most plaintive cry earth ever heard—"Eloi! Eloi! Lama! Sabac-
thani!"—"My God! My God! why has thou forsaken me?"[23] What
does all this express as to God's view of sin? Again I resumed my
seat. My opponent said he thought the debate had better close. I
asked him if he had nothing more to say to make good his assertion
that he could overthrow every one of my positions. Which one of
them had he invalidated in the least? He said he had nothing more
to say. So I resumed the topic I was last upon, and spoke some fifteen
minutes. The rain ceased and the meeting closed, whereupon there
was an outburst of indignant voices pouring a torrent of hot words
on the head of my tall antagonist. I got out of the din as soon as
possible and left for home. But as I passed out I heard one say to

him, "I am ashamed of you! You disgraced us all! But you got a good thrashing and I am glad of it." Another said, "The next time you provoke a fight with a stranger, you first find out who he is." When a rod or so from the house, I heard a female voice over all the rest, crying out in a high key. "You called him *the young man*. Who is *the young man now?*" But I was soon out of hearing, hastening homeward through the mud. The good Deacon Burt, with whom I boarded, laughed all the way home.

That debate helped me not a little. The story of the debate spread all over town and I noticed that the principal men of the town treated me as if I had suddenly grown several years older. Everybody seemed to know me after that, and new faces began to appear in church. The large Disciple Church in Franklin sent me an invitation to preach them a sermon. But I declined, deeming it mainly complimentary and designed to show me their hearty disapproval of the coarse attack of their conceited and pugnacious elder.

ANTI-SLAVERY CONTROVERSY

Not very long after this debate with one outside our church there arose a discussion in our own house over the question of slavery. And this is what precipitated it. We had in our church a man who was wont to make himself very prominent in all its public affairs. This was true, also, in town matters. Col. Holden must always have his say and usually *his way* as well.

It happened in one of my discourses on the ever increasing difficulties in the way of escape from a sinful life that I illustrated it by an incident taken from slave life in the South. It was that of a slave in Kentucky. He longed for liberty and often looked across the Ohio River and said, "One day I will be there." One day he broke away from his master, got across the river, but was re-captured and taken back. His master soon sold him farther South to a planter down in Tennessee. He again tried to escape but the bloodhounds tracked him to his hiding place; manacled he was driven back and sent into North Alabama. Next he was sold to a Louisiana planter, taken to a rice field in sight of the Gulf of Mexico, and there all hope of freedom went out in his soul. So it is with sinful man; he is going south every day and the sunshine of hope is becoming more and more dim, every day of his life. I have no doubt there was that in my manner and tones while giving the illustration which showed that I had no special love for the peculiar institution or of respect for its apologists and advocates. As the congregation rose to receive the benediction, Col. Holden asked the congregation to be seated as he had something to say. I remember his words: "We like our young minister very well," he began. "He preaches us good sermons, and I am glad to see the church is filling up. But I am sorry he has introduced politics into his sermon to-day. I hope the audience will continue to come and I will assure them they will not be troubled with it any more."

When he sat down I said the audience would bear me witness, that I had only used slavery, civil slavery, "as an illustration of moral slavery. That the Bible did the same when it spoke of the slavery of sin. That I had no idea that the people of Franklin were so much in love with Southern slavery that they would not allow a preacher to touch it, even with a ten foot pole. Had I dreamed I was in the midst of such a pro-slavery people as Col. Holden represents you to be, I would have preached upon it long ago. But I don't believe he represents you rightly. But, perhaps, there are some, a few, who are of his way of thinking. I now give notice that on the next Sabbath you may expect two sermons outright upon the subject of American slavery, its enormous wickedness, and our duties in relation to it. You will be dismissed."

Great was the excitement as the congregation moved out of church. The majority seemed to regard Col. Holden as having needlessly provoked a discussion: "Why could he not hold still?" — "There was nothing offensive in the illustration." "Sorry he is going to preach on the subject." "Well, I am going to hear him any way," etc., etc.

I did little visiting that week, but gave myself wholly to preparing two sermons, exposing the nature and wickedness of slavery, the woes it inflicts on both master and slave, and the extent of our responsibility for it here in the North. I knew the brick church would be crowded, and very likely this would be my last opportunity to address them on the subject, for I fully expected to receive my walking papers at once after preaching two out-and-out Abolition sermons. So I asked the Lord to enable me to crowd as much truth as possible into those two discourses. By Saturday night I was like a bottle ready to burst with fermenting wine. I longed for the Sabbath to come. I slept little Saturday night and had no appetite for food Sabbath morning, but I felt within strong as a lion, and I longed for the coming battle.

When I entered the church, I could scarcely hold in, but I put on a curbed bit and spoke as slow and deliberate and unexcited as I could, especially at the first, till my audience gradually became heated up with me, and then I poured out my arguments without stint. And I did not stand on the defensive; I became the attacking party, and assailed the horrid monster as I would drive a pack of wolves from my fold of lambs. When I came to speak of the attempt of corrupt politicians to come into God's sanctuary, and there dictate to God's anointed embassadors what they would say, and what not, in regard to the sale and enslavement of His redeemed children, I think Col. Holden thought he was in the prisoner's box, indeed. When I sat down, of one thing I felt sure, no one had any doubt where I stood on the great question. The afternoon discourse was more mild. On some account I felt that the enemy's center was broken, and now I had little else to do, save gather in the broken fragments. A notice was handed me and I read a call for an important meeting of the church on Tuesday of that week. I went home with a song in my heart and often unbidden rising to my lips.

I had done my duty. I had stood up for Jesus and his poor; I had not shunned to declare the whole counsel of God. I had done it in full view of probable loss of reputation, and of place and salary, too. What mattered it, so long as Christ was mine? And I rejoiced that I was counted worthy to suffer shame for His name. I ate a hearty supper, sung half the evening and lay down to a night of peaceful rest.

The next day and the following I packed my trunk, ready to depart on the morrow. Tuesday evening Deacon Burt came home with a smile on his face and said, — "The church has resolved, unanimously, save Col. Holden and family, to stand by you. So, unpack your trunk and feel that you dwell among your own people."

This was a surprise to me; so I unpacked my trunk and entered with fresh vigor upon my work. Quite a number of conversions occurred during the winter; the church was edified and became united and harmonious. When the spring came, I was obliged to return to Oberlin and resume my studies. But though the ride was long, over forty miles, I went down often during the summer and spent a Sabbath with them. It was understood I was to be their minister after I had graduated from the Seminary. Accordingly, after my graduation and marriage, I took up my residence with them. With much warmth of affection that little church gathered around me. My salary was small, about $400, I think. I should, properly, have received from the Home Missionary Society $200 more, but its agents were afraid of Oberlin, and even the Congregational Association, to which our church belonged, refused to accept me as one of its members, solely because I came from Oberlin.[24] I was understood to sympathize with its doctrines. Well, it was somewhat hard upon me and a hundred others then, but God enabled us to wait patiently and live it down, and to-day it is no reproach to a man in all those regions, that he is a friend of Oberlin, or has studied in its halls. Despite my small salary, I began early to lay aside a little from time to time, especially my marriage fees, and many a discussion my wife and I had over a five dollar bill, whether we should use it for some present comfort, or send it to our banker to keep for some rainy day.

THE COW-HIDING WHICH DID NOT COME OFF

Near the close of my second year of preaching in Franklin, a serio-comic affair came off to which I am loth to allude. At a Sabbath school celebration, a lad had fallen into the factory pond made by a dam across the Cuyahoga River, and before he could be rescued, was drowned. I arrived on the scene too late to save him, but the efforts I made to rescue his body, led his grateful parents, who were Epis-copalians, to demand of the rector that I should preach the funeral sermon. As I entered the vestibule, I met a number of the principal men of the town and shook hands with them, but one, Dr. Crittenden, or "Dr. Crit," as he was called, drew back his hand, and refused, scornfully, to recognize me. He had previously been excommunicated from our church and had laid it up against me. I was not specially annoyed, but smiled and passed on to shake hands with others, in a way which said, "It is of no consequence whatever; there are enough more who will take this hand."

The funeral over, it occurred to me to call upon the doctor and explain to him that I had nothing against him personally. That in the matter of his excommunication I had only done as fidelity to our common oath required, etc., etc. So I called and found the doctor in council with several of the prominent men of the town who had witnessed the rude treatment of me in the church. As nearly as I could afterward learn he had called them together to tell them his grievances, and fixed purpose to flog me to vindicate his insulted honor. Just at this point, who should appear upon the scene but the man himself! Now the redoubtable doctor was short of stature, but made up for it with high-heeled boots and a tall stove-pipe hat. On several occasions he had sought to supplement his muscular strength by flourishing a pistol. Nor was he slow, at times, to hurl at his foes big words portentous and terrible. Now a few people were really afraid of him. Well! I knocked just at the moment when his wrath had reached its perihelion. As he opened the door a sensible pallor came over his face, but recovering his self-possession, he haughtily waved me in, but conducted me into the opposite parlor, then back into another room and finally into his harness and saddle room, where hung an array of whips, rawhide, and other material, etc., etc. What all this meant I could not divine! I fancied he wished to get me out of hearing of the men in the parlor so that he might not be overheard as he apologized for his conduct in the church. Judge of my surprise, when he took down a rawhide, stood back upon his heels and stretching himself above his natural height, said in gruff tones: "Mr. Bristol, I have resolved to cowhide you!" So suddenly this came upon me, and so ludicrous it was, that I burst into a roar of laughter which perfectly disconcerted him! So loud it was that they heard it in the other room. Laying my right hand on the nape of his neck, I shook all the strength out of him in a moment and his courage, too! He did not even attempt to strike me. "Is this," said I, "the purpose for which you have led me back here? *You* cowhide me! Why you little whiffet, I can throw you out of that window, and I will do it if you attempt to strike me! I could break every bone in your little body in five minutes!" Now this last, though I said it, was only part true; of course I was a little excited and indulged in some hyperbole. Well, the poor fellow was scared nearly out of his wits, not able even to speak, so I left him standing there and went back laughing at the unspeakable ridiculousness of the situation! This was too good a morsel for village gossip and sport to keep, and his counselors scattered in every direction and told the story of the doctor's attempt to cowhide the minister! Now I relate this not at all to defend it or commend it, but to relate one of those ludicrous experiences which sometimes occur in even ministers' lives, and which we cannot help but remember, and remembering, narrate and laugh over them. A good hearty laugh hurts no man, and in order to laugh there must be a cause.

The winter following was one of revival in my field and I followed it up from one neighborhood to another till I brought up in Hudson, where "Western Reserve College" was situated. Our meeting was held in the Methodist chapel and the Methodist minister and I alternated in preaching. A large number were hopefully converted and among them quite a number of students who came to make sport, but went back to pray. So important did this field at Hudson appear, that the Congregationalists, who favored the Oberlin view, began to build a church edifice and extended to me an invitation to become their pastor. Much as I loved the people and church in Franklin,[25] I was inclined to accept the call. Before the change was fully consummated I received another important call.

10

AGENCY FOR OBERLIN COLLEGE

The trustees and faculty of Oberlin College voted me a call to a soliciting agency for the college. Its finances were in a sad condition. For near two years the salaries of the professors had been unpaid. They had been obliged to run up heavy bills for food and clothing at the stores, hoping that money would come, but it did not. Nearly all its old stand-by friends in the East, such as Arthur and Lewis Tappan, Chapin of Providence and Sears of Boston, had been overthrown or greatly crippled by the great financial cyclone which had swept over the nation.[26] What should they do? To run up store bills on trust much longer, was neither right for the professors or safe for the merchants. Yet the institution was crowded with students and the spirit of the Lord was working wonders there! But the prospect of raising money was truly dismal. There were two reasons for this: First, the financial distress and almost general bankruptcy of the county. Second, the immense prejudice against Oberlin. To go out as its advocate and agent asking money, had just then a most forbidding aspect. I declined the call because I had little confidence in my ability to persuade men to give money, and also because I was enthusiastic in my attachment to the work of preaching the Gospel. Some letters passed between us, I still declining. At last there came a letter signed by President Mahan, Professor Finney and all the other professors, saying, "If you still refuse to act as our agent, and no one else competent undertakes it, within —— days, we *shall each and all resign our places* and give up the enterprise in despair." This was too much for me, and I wrote back at once: "Dear Brethren and Fathers! stay where you are and abide at your posts. Help will come I know. I will go and do what I can. Oberlin is worth a thousand lives like mine." So I left the dear flocks of my love, moved my family to Oberlin and went out as their agent. The salary I was to receive was $400 a year and that was about a fair specimen of what the professors were getting at that time. Working my way East, I gathered money slowly, for nearly all our friends were poor. By degrees I gathered experience and facility in my work. I adopted the principle of never urging a man to give. I only asked the privilege of laying before him the story of Oberlin, what it is doing, and its necessities. This done I simply added, "If you believe the Lord would have you give something to sustain such a cause, I am here to receive and transmit it." I never tried to pry into men's business or judge what was their duty. This put me on pleasant terms with people, and if they did not give they thanked me for my call. I was careful also not to intrude upon hours assigned to business, especially in the case of men of large affairs. Receiving an introduction to such, I usually asked if he could afford me half an hour within the week or so, in which I could lay before him an important matter. The time designated, I took my leave. And when it came I usually had his undivided attention, and I got the matter fully before him. Usually I was invited to take tea with the party after business hours and then when full and in pleasant mood, I seldom failed to get a liberal donation.

MONEY FROM A MISER

While in New York, some of my friends resolved to have some sport at my expense. So one of them, H. C. Bowen, him of the *Independent*,[27] wrote a letter introducing me to a rich miser who lived in South Brooklyn. Entirely unsuspicious of their design I took the letter of introduction to the miser's office. He received me coldly, read the letter, asked what the business was. Pleasantly I declined telling him, and only asked could he designate a quarter of an hour of leisure during the week, when I could lay it before him? He handed me his card and said, "Take tea with me at my villa, such an evening, in South Brooklyn." I bowed myself out of his office. I was there promptly at the appointed time. A servant took my card, and I was invited in. I found him walking through his grounds viewing his flowers and shrubs. I praised his rare taste in laying off his grounds, admired his shrubs and flowers, and did not allude to the object of my coming till we were called to tea. The conversation was pleasant. I spoke of a namesake of his in Ohio noted for his benevolence; was he a relative of his? Tea over he took his cigar and began to smoke—offered me one—"Excuse me, I never smoke." Now for my errand. In about twenty minutes I told the story of Oberlin, its 500 students going out every winter to teach school, etc., etc., the immense good that school was doing, the small salaries of the professors, etc., etc. He was interested, and remarked when I closed, "That is a good thing, we ought to support it." Took a pen and gave me a check for $300! Some days afterward I met Mr. Bowen on Wall street and he asked, "Did you call on Mr. ——— in South Brooklyn?" Yes! He smiled and asked, "Did you get anything?" I showed him the check. He took it and calling aloud to one broker and another showed it and they laughed and shouted over it, for they said they never heard of his giving anything before. There is policy in war and in peace too. I did not collect a great deal of money, but what I did gather was promptly sent right where it was needed. The institution still held on its way and after two years I resigned, and other agents much more efficient, I think than myself, took my place, and I returned to my favorite pursuit.

CHAPTER

11

THE FITCHBURG PASTORATE

I n the course of my agency I had become acquainted with the
Trinitarian Congregational Church[28] at Fitchburg, Massachusetts,
and when my work for Oberlin was done, I accepted a call from it.
Here I labored two years. The church was anti-slavery, and that was
everywhere spoken against. Its members had come out of the old
church on account of its subserviency to the pro-slavery sentiment of
the county. Of course the new church was unpopular. So too, was its
minister, for the same reason, and because he came from Oberlin. I
did not accomplish much while there; it was a time of trial both to
me and to the church. There are periods when the tide sets strongly
against us, and we can do but little save to hold our own and keep
from drifting back, and losing ground. Such a time was that I spent
at Fitchburg. A few were added to the church, but no revival movement blessed my brief pastorate of two years. Before I had left Fitchburg, I had received a call for a year's service in the Sullivan Street
church in New York City. I went directly there and found an active
and energetic church with which I worked most pleasantly during the
year. We enjoyed during that year a constant revival, more or less
persons professing conversion nearly every week, and some uniting
with us on confession of faith at each monthly communion.

FORMATION OF THE FREE SOIL PARTY

It was during my stay in New York that there occurred the celebrated
"*Buffalo Convention.*" This was a gathering of diverse elements, consisting of Whigs and Democrats who were dissatisfied with the subserviency of their respective parties to pro-slavery domination, and
the Liberty Party, at the head of which stood James G. Birney.[29] All
these elements gathered in one great and enthusiastic convention at
Buffalo, and there formed the Free Soil Party. It nominated Martin
Van Buren for the Presidency and Charles Francis Adams for the
Vice-Presidency. I was a delegate from New York City to that convention. It was a wonderful meeting, and I believe the Spirit of God

was there inspiring the speakers, many of whom were old-line wire-pulling politicians—Cretes and Arabians—we heard them all speaking the Abolition language and uttering sentiments of liberty which astonished us all and none more than the speakers themselves. Often, after a speech fervent in its advocacy of liberty to all, we old Abolitionists cried out, amazed, "*Is Saul also among the prophets?*"[30]

After much speaking and long conference, a platform was drawn up, acceptable to all parties, Whigs, Democrats and Liberty Party men, and they all were merged into one party whose central principle was, liberty to all, white and black, and uncompromising hostility to pro-slavery propagandism in America. The name given by one of the speakers, and accepted by the convention, was the "*Free Soil Party*," the meaning of which was, that the soil of our country, not yet having passed under State control, should be sacred to freedom; no feet of slave ever to be suffered to tread upon it. When the organization was complete, congratulatory speeches became the order of the day. In one of them, a Democratic lawyer by the name of White, used this language in regard to the party. He had been speaking of the shameful truckling to slavery by both the old parties, Whig and Democratic, and showing where the Whig party, under pressure from the South, had sacrificed the great doctrines on which it was founded, and which alone gave it a right to live; and also, where the Democrats had done the same, and even worse, and where it received its fatal stabs, and thenceforward staggered, moribund, to its grave; then the orator, turning toward the seats occupied by members of the "Old Liberty Party," asked, "What shall I say of the *Liberty Party*, the party of Birney and Tappan and Leavitt[31]—a party, small in numbers, bitterly persecuted, misrepresented and ostracised, yet ever true as the needle to the pole to the great principles of righteousness, justice and truth; what shall I say of it? What can I say, but what the Great book says of Enoch, who lived before the flood, 'Having walked with God 300 years, was not suffered to see death, *but was translated!*' " As he said this the vast audience rose to their feet and shouted as I never heard men before.

ISAIAH RYNDERS

Returning from this convention, and going down the Hudson River on steamboat, I had an encounter with that prince of roughs and shoulder strikers who so long held New York in terror—Isaiah Rynders.[32] Rynders was then and had long been in the employ of the Tammany Hall Democrats. He had gathered a club of a hundred pugilists and assassins from the purlieus of the great city, and these he had trained for such scenes of violence as from time to time should further the domination of his party over the city. Rynders paid his men liberally from funds received from the Tammany officials, who in turn indemnified themselves by the stealings for which that party became so notorious during the reign of Boss Tweed, his predecessors and successors, for many years. For a long time prior to the trip I am speaking of, "Ike" had held a rod in terrorem over the heads of New York Whigs, and indeed, over all decent and peace-loving citizens.

Especially was this true on election days, and at the primaries which precede them. It was then that this Democratic devil was as busy and active as a weasel in a brood of chickens, darting from precinct to precinct, consulting with the leaders, giving peremptory orders to his lieutenants and voters. Short and sharp were his orders, and woe to the Irishman or Dutchman who hesitated about obeying the imperial mandate. He knew the politics of every ward in the city, and how many Democratic votes must be had to carry it. *And he knew how to get them, too.* In one, *terror* would keep from the polls a sufficient number of timid Whigs. In another, *stuffing the ballot-boxes* was feasible. A third could be best carried by practicing the rule prescribed by one of their authorities, viz., "Vote early, vote late, *and very often!*" But of all these none suited the genius of "Ike" so well as the *reign of teror!* There he was at home. He loved to see men tremble when he and his club came nigh. I will give a sample which I once heard from his own lips. At a city election a great crowd of near a thousand men were waiting for a chance to vote. It was in a Whig ward. But Isaiah came and distributed his assassins among them, and he shall tell the rest: "Mounting a box," said he, "which overlooked the crowd, I shouted, '*I am Isaiah Rynders!* My club is here, scattered among you! We know you! Five hundred of you are from Philadelphia — brought here to vote the Whig ticket! Damn you! if you don't leave these polls in five minutes, *we will dirk every mother's son of you!*' " etc., etc., and he added, with a grin of pleasure, "In five minutes five hundred men left the polls." Of course, these were peaceable citizens, and went home without voting, for fear of assassination.

About a year prior to the encounter I am about to relate, an anti-Slavery convention was being held in the Broadway Tabernacle,[33] New York. Scarcely had the meeting been organized, when in pushed this rascal, followed by his henchmen. He mounted the platform, and swore no white man should speak in that meeting! Garrison attempted it, but was summarily put down and silenced. A New York City minister rose to speak, but Rynders marched to his seat, and rubbing his fist

under his nose, said, "Not one word from you! Sit down!" and he did
so. A negro tried to speak, and he allowed him, saying this was "a
nigger meeting!" No one else was tolerated. The police were either
in league with him, or feared to interfere. The Abolitionists well knew
it was in vain to appeal to them for help. Complaints had been lodged
against him many times before, but the leading Democrats of the city
would go his bail, and the courts would so shuffle his case that either
no trial would come off, or no fine be inflicted, or other punishment.
So this contemptible tyrant was allowed to break up an anti-slavery
convention in New York, and scatter its members.

The writer was not himself present at that Tabernacle Convention; but when he heard of it there was enkindled within a curiosity
to see this New York autocrat, and perhaps feel of his muscles and
learn "what meat this Caesar lived upon, that he had grown so great!"
The opportunity occurred on this trip down the Hudson. There were
on board the steamer, Mr. Lewis Tappan, the New York merchant
and anti-slavery man, and also a noted New York jurist and politician,
Hon. Joshua Spencer of Utica. The two men fell into a discussion on
the slavery question. Mr. Spencer admitted the duty of Congress to
abolish the slave trade in the District of Columbia. Mr. Tappan wrote
out a petition to Congress to do this, and asked Mr. Spencer to sign
it. Before he had time to do so, Rynders drew up his Empire Club,
and swore he would throw any one overboard who should sign that
petition! For five minutes he swore great oaths and cursed the Abolitionists. Neither the captain of the boat or the passengers dared to
question his right to rule the ship. Meantime I was measuring him
with my eye from head to foot, and my conclusion was that he had
ruled the country about long enough — that I would be willing to be
put into the North River, *provided I could take him along with me!* I had
no doubt of my ability, once in the water with him to extricate myself
from him and swim to either shore. So edging my way up to the table,
I took the pen and signed my name. In a moment the Plug Uglies
were upon me. Leaving my cloak in their hands, I sprang like a cat
upon their leader, exclaiming as I did so, "I have got you now, you
old Jacobin!" Before he knew it he was stretched out and sprawling,
the other side of me and back again, and this way and that, he was
thrown about, before his company could help him, and when they
did, he was weak as a rabbit, and scared half to death!

Meanwhile he was trying to get away from me, and his club were
helping him, but I held fast to him, and when they pulled him they
dragged me. They rained blows upon me, perhaps fifty of them, but
they did not hurt me materially. We became so crowded together that

neither of us could do anything, and I began to call out, "Let him fight his own battles!" "If he can't handle me he is not fit to be your leader!" "Does it take a hundred of you to handle one man?" "He says he will throw me into the river, let him try it if he dare!" etc., etc. Others too, began to gather courage and cry out, "Fair play!" "One at a time!" etc., etc. As the club held back a little I started with him for the side of the ship, but he seized a post we were passing with both hands, and I could not pull him away, so I let him go after talking rather plainly to him and his gang. I found this man of terror weaker than common men. But with the frenzy of strength and energy which came over me, I could have handled with ease more than one at a time like him. On the way down as I passed him he was careful to keep near the center of the boat. If any one should ask what I would have done with him could I have got him to the side of the boat, I answer I should assuredly have thrown him over the rail, and have gone with him! Whether I should have helped him, as Cassius did Brutus, to reach the shore, I do not know, but I imagine I should have exacted some rather humbling promises first. Should any one say this was not a very ministerial performance, this rough grapple with such a brute, well, I may concede it. But may it not have been *manly* after such provocation to stand up for human rights, and with might and main to shake the conceit out of this Democratic bulldozer? There are diseases no mild medicine will cure. Brute force for brutes, and "*a rod for a fool's back!*" What ultimate effect this had on Rynders I know not. But I never heard of his heading a riot afterward. He was quietly retired soon after to a place in the custom house at a small salary, and has long since passed out of mind. I may add here, that the occasion of his being on the boat, he and his club, was that he was returning to New York from a visit to the Legislature then in session at Albany, where he had been sent by the Tammany authorities, to *overawe and control the vote of the city representatives* there on certain questions before the Legislature. After I had been in New York the year for which I had been hired, the former pastor, my classmate, Rev. S. D. Cochran, revisited the city. A part of the church wished to re-engage him as pastor, and a part desired my continuance with them. To avoid a division of the church I refused to stay, and left.

AGENCY FOR THE AMERICAN MISSIONARY ASSOCIATION

I at once received an appointment to an agency for the American Missionary Association.[34] The first place I visited to present the cause in public addresses, was Meriden, Conn. My first address was in the church ministered to by my brother-in-law, Rev. A. A. Stevens. Rev.

Mr. Perkins, the pastor of the larger church down near the railroad, would only give me the evening hour. I did not like this, because at that service few save young people attended, and this was not the class from which much money for the cause was to be expected. But I did the best I could. Mr. Perkins treated me quite coldly and after the service lectured me for the space of near two hours, in a manner most humiliating, not to say exasperating. No mortal man ever wounded me so deeply by his criticisms as did Mr. Perkins that night. I was tired out and made no reply. I felt like David when Shimei threw stones and cursed him, "Let him curse, for the Lord hath bidden him." About eleven o'clock I left the lecture room, he neither asking me to go home with him, or knowing where I was to lay my weary head. The next morning I wrote to the New York Committee that I must resign, that I had not the nerve to endure such assaults as these. Great was the indignation of Professor Whipple[35] and Mr. Tappan at Mr. Perkins. But I could not be persuaded to act further as their agent. Soon after I received a call from the Free Church of Andover,[36] Mass., and accepted it. Singular it was to go back to the place from which I had been expelled fourteen years before on account of anti-slavery, and find myself pastor of a large anti-slavery church and in fair standing with the other ministers of the place. More singular still it was to see occasionally in my congregation, Principal Taylor, "Uncle Sam," who was one who voted me away, now cordial and expressing his pleasure to meet me again and hear me preach! He thought "Mr. Bristol had changed greatly!" Well, I hope he had. But I thought "Uncle Sam," as the boys called him, was fairly entitled to the same compliment.

GETTING EVEN WITH REV. PERKINS

While at Andover a great convention of New England Abolitionists was called in the Melodeon Hall in Boston. I was a delegate. The second day of the convention Mr. Tappan came to me and said: "You must make a speech this afternoon." I inquired who the regular speakers were to be. Among others he mentioned Rev. Mr. Perkins of Meriden. "What is he to speak upon?" He replied, " 'The servitude recognized and regulated by Moses.' By the way," said he, "that is the very theme for you, and if you will speak upon it I will call upon you first." There was a twinkle in his eye and a smile on his cheek. "All right," said I, "call on me." A vast and inspiring audience was assembled and in the course of the afternoon the president called out, "Rev. S. Bristol of Andover will now address you." I took the platform and announced my subject, "The Old Testament and human rights." The audience was with me in full sympathy from first to last, and the house shook with applause when I left the stage! "Mr. Perkins of Meriden," was now called on for a speech. Slowly he rose, walked up the aisle in deep meditation, his eyes fixed upon the floor! Slowly he mounted the rostrum, paced the whole length of the stage, then came back, and looking up, said: "It has been my lot often to address audiences like this, and sometimes under embarrassment. But never was I so nonplussed as I am to-day. The speaker who has just addressed you so ably has taken my speech out of my mouth and carried it off bodily! Not only has he taken my subject, but has brought forth every principal argument I had intended to use, and not content with that, he has anticipated me in my illustrations also, and in fact, has left me nothing to say on the subject! I feel like saying there is nothing more to be said on that topic, and taking my seat! But perhaps I can say something on the subject of West India Emancipation." So he went off upon that, but he made no headway. The audience saw it and many beginning to leave, he flatted out and sat down. Now there were two men who thoroughly enjoyed Mr. Perkins' humiliation. One was Mr. Tappan and the other Professor Whipple. After the adjournment Mr. Perkins came to me and congratulated me on the speech I had made. I shook hands with him and bowed myself away, in a manner which seemed to say: "Good-bye, let the past be forgotten; *we are even now!*" And I have never had one hard feeling toward him since. What is it the old proverb says about *"Time having its revenges?"*

At Andover I preached only a little over a year. I did not accomplish much. The church held its own and the congregation was kept together for a more auspicious day. But the long term of excitement, the strain of mind and nerve during the nine years of preparatory studies, followed by nearly as many more fighting the battles of reform and preaching the Gospel, had begun to tell seriously on a constitution naturally vigorous and hardy beyond the common lot. I had become excessively nervous. Insomnia had become chronic. Determination of blood to the brain had set in, and physicians unanimously advised my giving up preaching and pastoral work for some years at least. I would have gone West, taken up a homestead and worked upon it, but I had not means sufficient for that and support a family consisting of a wife and three children.

CHAPTER

12

A TRIP TO CALIFORNIA

After much reflection and prayer over the matter I decided to go to California. So I sent to my friend Mr. Pelton of Ohio, for the money I had deposited with him from time to time, and he sent me some over six hundred dollars. Dividing this with my wife, I took passage on the steamship Empire City, and sailed from New York to Chagres, on the Isthmus of Panama. I was very sick on my passage, but recovered soon after reaching land. We were poled up the Chagres River in dug-outs by natives, and the rest of the way to the Pacific we walked and had our baggage packed on mules. Wonderful was this land of perpetual summer to me! There was not one tree or shrub or species of grass I had ever seen before! Yet I was surprised at the poverty which in many respects prevailed. The people were poor, very poor, and looked upon us "Americanos" they called us, as all of us rich! In general their crops were poor, cane excepted. The pastures were very poor and our Northern hay brought fabulous prices. The vast tangled forests were utterly destitute of such berries as raspberries, blackberries, strawberries, and even such a thing as our wild plum was nowhere found in a state of nature. No such building timber as ours in the temperate climes was found in all their wood-covered country. On the Isthmus we were obliged to wait sixty days for the "Sarah Sands" which was to take us to San Francisco. These sixty days I improved in acquainting myself as thoroughly as possible with the country, its people, its animals, its birds, its reptiles, its plants, and its prospects. To this end I made journeys in different directions from Panama and carried a gun, for the double purpose of self-defense and of capturing game for the market. In this latter object I was so successful that I was able to hire a man to accompany me and carry my game and market it. I was able to pay him three dollars a day and have as much left for myself. In these excursions some rather thrilling incidents occurred, two or three of which may be worth relating.

STEPPING ON AN ALLIGATOR

On a visit to the site of old Panama, a ruin now overgrown with cactus and large trees, I undertook to cross the narrow entrance where the sea rushed in at full tide and filled an inland bay perhaps a mile in diameter. My game carrier chose to go around, while I undertook to wade across. The tide was out and the mud soft and deep. When about half way across, I came to a small pond surrounding a rock. The water was very much riled, I judged by fish. Near the rock the water was nearly waist deep. I got upon the rock and rested awhile. As I let myself down on the opposite side, a foot or so beneath the surface, I stepped upon what seemed a slab, or a water-soaked log. It gave way gradually as I bore my weight upon it. Instantly I was hoisted some ten or twelve feet and thrown upon the top of the rock! The water was dashed all over the rock, and out of the pond rushed an alligator from twelve to fifteen feet long, and the time he made through the mud-flat to the sea was surprising! My companion who was near by on the farther side and saw the whole, remarked that he had seen pictures of men riding on the backs of crocodiles across the Nile. He had hitherto regarded them as fiction. Now he believed it a reality. Had he not seen it with his own eyes? But was it not enough to make one's hair stand on end after that to be obliged to let myself again down into that murky water and wade to the other shore? But I had to do it, for the tide was coming in and would bring around that rock hundreds of hungry alligators and sharks, and perhaps a crocodile too!

ANOTHER ENCOUNTER

At another time as I was following down the course of a partially dried up rivulet, shooting game which visited its occasional pools, I suddenly found myself within five feet of a large alligator. His jaws were partially open, revealing his great ugly teeth, his eye was fixed upon me, his neck partially bent as if in the act of springing upon me, and his feet spread out and ready for a leap! I had mistaken him for a log till now I was upon him. I stopped short and taking an ounce ball from my pocket, dropped it into one of the barrels and as it rolled down I quickly turned the muzzle down and fired. I think the discharge was simultaneous with the contact of the ball with the load. The ball struck an indentation back of the eye and penetrated the brain. His head dropped and I sprang back and none too quickly, for almost instantly he struck with his tail the ground where I stood, breaking into oven-wood the drift limbs scattered over the ground.

I believe one of those blows would have broken in pieces a good strong cart-wheel. The alligator, like all amphibious animals, dies slowly. For an hour I stood by this dying creature studying his anatomy, examining his feet, teeth, hide, etc., etc. Following down the stream I came to a number of Spanish women washing clothes. I asked for a drink of water and told them how I had just killed an alligator. They at first shook their heads incredulously. But as I described the paroxysms of the dying animal, they began to believe, and delegated two of their number to go and see if it was so. With difficulty I allured them along from one point to another, going before them, till at last they saw it raising a dust and beating the ground, and then they ran back, crying, "Aligate! Aligate!" and soon the whole company was there singing and shouting! And they blessed the "Americano" patting him on the shoulder, and even kissing his gun. And they caught up their babes and pressed them to their bosoms and said of the dying reptile, "He will no more eat the pickaninny." From that time onward "the Americano" was in high esteem when he came through their settlement, and their cabin doors flew open wide as he passed by, and every favor was shown him he could reasonably ask.

A CROCODILE

While on the Isthmus, I heard several times of a huge alligator, some twenty-five or thirty feet long, which had been seen some dozen miles up the Rio Grande River. At first I was incredulous, but by and by it became confirmed by the testimony of men whose candor I could not question, and I determined to go and see for myself. Two trips I made, but could not find him. Returning from a third trip in a large dug-out, I saw ahead what seemed a large log floating in the river. Fearing we should run afoul of it, I said to the steersman, "Look out for that log!" "I see it," he said. Looking again a moment after, I cried out, "Take care, you will upset us!" "I am trying to keep clear of it, but *it will* keep before us!" he replied. Just then I saw it was no log, but a crocodile which was making for us. I brought my gun down but he dashed under the boat and struck it a blow so violent that it threw me into the bottom of the boat. Had our boat been made of boards like a whale boat, I believe he would have stove in her bottom. After flourishing around us a few moments and making the water boil like a pot, he disappeared, and we saw him no more, *"unum sufficit."* I did not get a fair view of this crocodile, but I believe he was twenty-five feet long.

ENCOUNTER WITH AN ALLIGATOR

FOLLOWED BY A PUMA

FOLLOWED UP BY A PUMA

But another and more serious encounter while on the Isthmus, was
with a land animal, the puma, or South American lion, as he is called.
This animal is very common on the Isthmus, and is by far the most
powerful of all their beasts of prey. It is very bold, having next to no
fear of man. In the early days of emigration to California it often
deliberately trotted through some of the outside streets of Panama,
regardless of dogs and men. It is not much of a lion in appearance.
It has many more of the characteristics of the tiger, but is much less
fierce than that animal. I encountered several of them in my excursions, but as I usually had a shotgun only and revolver, I neither ran
from them or gave them chase. Like the Priest and Levite, I "passed
by on the *other side*."[37] Had they shown a decided disposition to try
titles, I should have done the best I could with the weapons I had.
My plan was to reserve fire till in close quarters, and then aim at an
eye. For I found that nothing so completely confuses and demoralizes
man or beast as to put out or wound an eye. There was one occasion,
however, when I was so persistently followed up by one of these
animals, with such obvious advantage on his side, that I did my best
to get away from him. I was returning from a hunting trip to the
mouth of the Rio Grande, when I saw a fox-squirrel crossing the trail.
I followed him quite a distance, as he sprang from limb to limb,
clambering over the trees. He led me off into a large flock of Isthmus
grouse. They flew up all around me, and I shot them on the wing.
It was impossible to see them on the ground, for the whole forest
was overgrown by a giant species of fern as high as one's shoulders,
and completely shading the ground. When I had killed half a dozen
or so of these grouse I called aloud to my game-carrier to come and
take the game. I supposed him near; I had heard his footsteps some
ten or twelve rods off, following me about. Receiving no reply, I
continued to shoot till overloaded with game. I called again and again.
While loading both the barrels of my gun I heard what I took to be
his footsteps, slowly approaching in the leaves. I urged him to come
faster, and then he stopped short! Again I called, and wondered he
did not answer nor come! It was not like him—what could it mean?
While I was thinking of the matter I heard another step in the dry
leaves! then another, then another—each of them slow, long, cautious
and measured cat-like steps, such as that animal makes in stealing
upon game! *It was a puma!* It must be a large one, and a bold one,
too! For he had heard the report of my gun ten or fifteen times, not
a dozen rods distant! Perhaps he had drunk human blood and eaten

the flesh of man, and was now hankering for mine! Could I have had open ground, where I could see him, I should have known better what to do. Alas! the all overshadowing fern tops completely hid him from my view, and it would do so if not one rod distant! I now called louder than ever to my game carrier, and again and again, but no response came back. He had not followed me at all, but had lain down beside the trail and gone to sleep, and not finding me when he awoke, proceeded on to Panama. I felt in my pocket for my hunting knife. Alas! it was not there — I had lost it! I searched for balls, but my game carrier had them, with some extra ammunition!

Which way was the trail? I had turned round and round so many times, I was quite at a loss to know which way to get out of the dark forest. Looking northward, it seemed lighter than in any other direction. Perhaps there was a clearing there! I would make for it. So, with a yell of defiance at my slowly approaching foe, I started off at a rapid pace. A half-mile or so, I came to a lower level of land — a tropical swamp, overgrown with low bushes, some five to fifteen feet high, and all overgrown and laden down with vines and creeping shrubs, which formed windrows which succeeded each other like the waves of the sea. Meanwhile, the puma, too, had quickened his pace, and trotting after me had kept his distance, but stopped again when I stopped. Looking over the swamp, I fancied there was a clear spot in the center, and I determined to reach it if possible. I crowded through the brush and clambered over the windrows. At each difficult one I turned and yelled defiance at the puma, and then vigorously clambered over, often becoming so entangled in the network that, had the puma attacked me there, he would have had an easy time of it. Alas! the farther I proceeded, the higher rose these windrows! Seeing a tree some thirty feet high on my right, I sought to reach it. Could I do so, I would climb into its branches, then let the beast come — I would blow out his eyes, and then kill him at my leisure. Reaching the tree after a great struggle, to my dismay, I found it *a tropical thorn tree!* — a species of black or red locust. The thorns were *from six to twelve inches long, and as sharp as a needle!* they were as large around at the butt as one's little finger. And they guarded every part of the tree — the trunk and all the branches, *and they pointed backward and downward,* so that to climb the tree was an utter impossibility! And now it seemed to me my time had come! How many things had combined against me! Well! I must die some time; might not this be as good a time as any — might it not even be the best? Why should I fear death in any form? I knew that my Redeemer lived. Still, I did not relish death at the hand, or, rather, the paw, of a beast. Had not

God, away back in the days of Noah, given us a command to kill the beast which takes the life of man? "At the hand of every beast will I require the blood of man." Did not Paul speak of fighting with beasts at Ephesus? And if this was literal truth, he doubltless did it with a will, and effectually. Well, I too will fight this beast as a religious duty, and with faith in Divine help, too!

I was beside a windrow some twelve feet high. It was fifteen feet through it, and the puma was now on the other side—he was within leaping distance. Would he crawl through, or with a strong bound come leaping over? With fingers on the trigger of my gun, I stood there a long time, occasionally kicking against the bush, and yelling defiance! But he was very cool—he was in no hurry! I could hear his step, and even the wagging of his tail against the leaves! Suddenly a shadow came over my face, which startled me! It was made by a distant mountain behind which the *sun was just then sinking!* The tropical twilight is very short, and well I knew that in twenty-five minutes darkness would set in, and the puma would have his own way, for what could I do in the darkness? What I did must be done quickly. I resolved to settle the matter at once. I would crawl through the windrow to where the animal was, and blow his brains out, or die like a man! So, tearing aside some vines and pushing my gun forward of me, and lying on the ground, I wormed my way among the vines, perhaps half-way through. My attention was arrested by a vine hanging before me, which, evidently, *had been cut off by a knife!* Some one had been here before, and cut that vine—probably a Mexican, with his broad blade, or *machete.* Then I saw another, and another, and soon I got the direction in which some Mexican, a year before, had cut a path, through which he could crawl through this jungle. I followed up the lead, occasionally kicking the brush behind, and sending back a yell of defiance. So I scrambled on, perhaps fifteen rods, when I came into a wider trail, where I could stand up and run. By and by I came into a cattle path. It was growing dark, but I ran with a lightness of foot which surprised me; I seemed scarcely to touch the ground. The owls flew from the bushes as I passed them, and I imagined I could hear the puma bounding along but a few rods behind! Then I saw lights ahead, and more and more, and before nine o'clock I had reached the suburbs of Panama, and had found my tent and deserting game carrier, too!

While on the Isthmus I tried much to find an anaconda, but though I often heard of their being seen by others, I was never able to find one, nor any other snake of much size in all my journeyings. We staid at Panama some sixty days, waiting for the "Sarah Sands"

to come around the Horn and take us to San Francisco. Well, she
came at length, but proved a very poor sailor. Her bottom was covered
with barnacles, and she had 1,200 passengers and was so top-heavy
that she rocked fearfully, even in calm weather. For nearly two months
we plodded our weary way up the coast, all the while living on salted
beef and hard tack. Scurvy began to appear, and other forms of
sickness, and, added to all, our coal gave out when 500 miles from
San Francisco! We put in near shore and anchored. We tore up a great
cattle corral and rafted the timber to the ship; got well out to sea,
but had to put back and anchor again, and the captain determined
to send a messenger up by land to Monterey, the then coaling station
of California, for a lighter to come down with coal.

NARROW ESCAPE FROM A WRECK

Coming in toward shore in the dense fog of early morning, the ship
came near being wrecked on a reef of rock, a mile or so off the shore
of San Simeon. It was singularly averted. I was at the time afflicted
with three large boils, one on my hip, another on my back, and the
third on the top of my head. And because of the great crowd which
thronged the deck by day and by night, I obtained permission to sling
up a hammock, just under the awning which covered the deck, and
over the heads of those on deck, who often surged against my boils
and hurt me terribly. It was about four o'clock in the morning, and
we were under full head-way, when I was startled by what seemed to
be the barking of a pack of bull dogs close at hand. The murmur
and bustle on deck prevented those below from hearing it. Looking
over the side of my hammock, I saw the mate passing below and cried
out, "Captain Thatcher, we are close in ashore, I hear the dogs bark!"
Glancing up he answered roughly, "The devil you do!" But I called
out the more energetically, "I tell you captain, we are close in shore,
I know it." Seeing now who it was, he cried out to the man at the
wheel to "about ship." He did so, and as the great ship swung around
she almost brushed against a long reef of jagged rocks, *covered with
seals and sea lions*, whose barking at our near approach I mistook for
bull dogs. Had we proceeded three minutes longer as we were going,
our ship and her 1,200 passengers would have been dashed in pieces
on that reef! Few if any would have been saved, for it was near a mile
from shore and all the way the water was white with foam, surging
and dashing against innumerable rocks! For once I was profoundly
grateful for an affliction of boils! But did Captian Thatcher ever thank
the writer for his timely and energetic warning? Not he! It would have
compromised his dignity! It would have been an admission of the

possible fallibility of the pope of the sea. Few of our passengers ever knew how near that night we approached the eternal shore. Dropping down the coast a short distance we came to anchor in what is now the roadstead of "San Simeon," some twenty or thirty miles up the coast above San Luis Obispo.

UP THE COAST OF CALIFORNIA BY LAND

Not willing to stay by the ship till a messenger could be sent to Monterey for coal, and a lighter come down to our aid, I formed a company of eight to leave the ship there and make the *land trip to the mines*. The Captain gave us twenty dollars in money, each, and what provisions we could carry. The first night we were out came near being one of sad catastrophe. We camped on a hillside covered with wild oats, beside a spring. I had killed some game on our way and the savory smell of the roast had spread far and wide on the evening air, and I remarked to my messmates, that we would have a visit from a bear before morning. It was arranged that I should sleep in the door or front of the tent, my gun within reach, to be ready for any emergency. Being chosen captain, a sense of responsibility in leading a company through an unknown country, kept me largely from sleep that night. I had been awake as I thought, a couple of hours, when I heard a rustle in the wild oats near the spring, some three rods distant. I quietly rose up and cocked my gun. But first I would count the occupants of our tent and be sure that all our men were there. I counted in the moonlight seven beside myself. Crawling out I discovered what seemed a bear sitting on his haunches by the spring! Taking deliberate aim at what seemed his head, I drew upon the trigger, but as I did so, the thought flashed over my mind, "What you are aiming at *may not be the animal's head!* Should it be some other part, and you only wound him, you will have a lively time here!" So I let off my finger, and was astonished that the gun did not go off, for I had distinctly felt the give of the spring! I waited a moment for some movement which should reveal which was head and which not. A well recognized "ahem!" froze my heart with horror! It was my friend Elliott, who had risen unknown to me, lifted the tent cloth and passed out to the spring. I must have fallen into a momentary sleep, and awoke without being aware of it. And the way I was mislead in counting was this, an additional man had left the ship and overtaken us and turned in with us that night, and I had forgotten it. Several months after I told Elliott of this and he turned pale and said, "Had you pulled an ounce harder on that trigger, that would have been the end of me."

A PARADISE OF WILD ANIMALS

This was a very paradise for wild game, and the next morning, with its first opening light, I sallied forth in quest of something savory for our breakfast. I had not gone half a mile, wading through the rank wild oats, before I started up a huge elk. A few rods he bounded, and then turned and stared wildly at me! How grand he looked in the morning fog—his horns branching abroad at least ten feet high, and half as wide! He was quite within shooting distance, but I hesitated to fire upon so magnificent a beast. But, as he turned to run, I let fly a charge of some twenty revolver balls into his shoulder. He was doubtless badly wounded, but was able to run a short distance. The dense fog prevented my seeing which way he went. Following carefully his trail some twenty rods, I came upon the great, broad, slouchy tracks of an old grizzly bear! He had passed only a few moments before, for the stones he trod upon bore the wet imprints of his toes and claws. I had never seen a grizzly, and I left the trail of my wounded elk and followed the bear. That this was foolhardy in the extreme I now freely admit. Subsequent acquaintance with that animal has forced upon me the conclusion that no man has any business with a grizzly unless well armed with a Spencer rifle, nor even then, unless he has several well-trained dogs to hold the bear at bay or distract his attention while the hunter pours into his tough carcass half a dozen or more ounce balls. And even then it is not a bad precaution to have in view a tree to whose friendly arms he can flee, if worse comes to worst. Well, recklessly I pursued the bear. Soon his steps turned down into a ravine densely filled with live oaks. Slowly I ventured down, and tracked his wet steps up the ravine, after looking out for a tree into which I would spring, should he suddenly turn upon me. His droppings, warm and smoking, made my heart beat quick, for surely I was just upon him. Just then a great flock of quail came dashing into the ravine. So thick they were, I could kill at a single shot a good meal for all my mess. What should I do? "a bird in the hand is worth two in the bush." Quail meat is better than bearsteak. Besides, the bear may dispute my title to it. So I let fly among the quail, and though badly torn by my revolver balls, I bagged a good mess for breakfast, and returned to camp in time to help dress and cook them.

Speaking of the game which in that day abounded in that part of California, I may add that on another occasion, a few days before we took this trip, going out to hunt with a companion, we saw a deer, perhaps eighty rods off. My companion said, "You go and shoot him, as you are the best shot." I skulked around the hills to get at him, but I saw a couple not much farther off, so I went for them. Just as I was about to shoot, I saw on my right hand a very fine, large buck, so I crawled in the oats to get at him. As I slowly rose up to shoot, my attention was arrested by the broad horns of an elk lying in the shade of an oak, not twenty rods distant. Leaving the buck, I crawled up the hill to shoot the elk, as I had never killed one. Before I reached a good shooting point, my companion fired at a passing herd of elk, and a general stampede took place, and deer and elk and wild cattle were seen running in several directions. A wild cow and her calf came near me, and I shot the calf and wounded, but did not get, the cow. On another occasion still, I counted at one time over fifty deer and antelope in full view.

Resuming our journey along the cattle trails, pursuing in general a northerly direction from San Simeon, in about one week's time we came upon the Salinas River some twenty miles above the old Catholic Mission of Soledad, or Solitude.

CROSSING THE DESERT OF SOLEDAD

We staid all night at a ranch house occupied by a man who could speak some English. In the morning we inquired about the trail we should take to reach the Mission—we had observed there were two trails deeply worn into the ground, one leading to the left, and the other to the right. The ranchman said take the right-hand trail.

"Is there any water on the route?"

"Not a drop, till you reach Soledad."

"Is there any on the right-hand trail?

"No." There had been no rain in this part of the country for three years, and it had become a desert of moving sands.

We started out, and soon came into the moving sands. As far as the eye could reach, all was a waste of sand—a desert, such as we had never crossed. Our water supply was sadly inadequate, and we concluded it would be rashness to venture on as we were, so we turned back to get a larger supply. We had but a single camp kettle, holding two quarts. Alas! we could get nothing—not even a gourd-shell! While we lingered I asked an old, impoverished Indian about the route, and when I made him understand our inquiry about the best trail, he pointed to that on the left hand. I asked, "Is there any water on it?"

"Mucho aqua" (much water).

And when I asked, "*Rio?*" (river) he replied, "Poketo aqua" (little water).

This seemed a contradiction, and the ranchman said he was an old fool, but his evident sincerity led me to think there might be something in it.

Filling our camp kettle we started out again and looked off upon the sandy plain before us, twenty miles long, and ten or twelve wide! Coming to the sandy border, we debated the question of the direction we should take over the desert — that leading toward the hills on the right, or those which bounded the valley on the left. A majority of one voted to take the left, that recommended by the Indian. This we did, because there was *one chance* of finding water there, while that chance was wanting for the other route. The question decided, we plunged directly into the desert. Not a shrub was there, or weed, or one blade of grass, not a bird, or rabbit, or squirrel, or animal, save perhaps now and then a horned lizard or a snake. All traces of trail were buried out of sight and our only director was the general trend of the adjacent barren mountains. We had not proceeded far before a sad accident befel us which came nigh costing our lives. One of our company, Mr. M. S. Robinson, had been intrusted with the carrying of our precious water. Stumbling, he fell prostrate. All our water was spilt, save perhaps a pint which we used at once, serving only to moisten our dry lips and parched throats. Our friend Robinson had a special facility in this line. He could "find an occasion of stumbling," like others I wot of, in very small obstacles. And when once under headway, he seldom failed to improve it, even if it took an incline of a full rod to reach the ground! On one occasion, as I was laughing at one of his feats in this line, he gravely said, "I fall *upon principle!*" "No doubt," I replied, "the *principle of gravitation!*" "No," said he, "what I mean is that when I begin to stumble, I could save myself, but it would wrench me so to do it that I find it easier to go ahead and fall as easily as I can." To return from this digression, taking our last sip of water, we bowed toward the driving hot wind and pressed forward, the flying flakes of sand cutting our cheeks at every step, and obliging us nearly to close our eyes.

THE MIRAGE

One of our company looking off toward the hills some four miles distant, descried what he took to be a lake of sparkling water. With a hoarse outcry and a wild gesture he called our attention to it. We turned fron our course and hastened toward the blessed lake. On and on we trudged for a couple of miles, when I perceived that the lake had risen from the valley and was now well up, hanging on the side of a hill, a position impossible for real water. It was not water, it was only a deceptive pretence, it was the mirage! I ran to the foremost and seizing him by the shoulder, I whispered in his ear, "Mirage! Mirage!" He looked a moment in blank despair. The others coming up, stopped and gazed and were convinced, and then we all turned slowly and sorrowfully away and retraced our steps. Not one word was said. Our mouths and throats were so dry we could not articulate. At length there appeared in the distance before us the tops of some cottonwood trees, and we hastened toward one of them. We hoped to find some water there, at least a little shelter from the blazing sun. At length we reached it, but it afforded us but little shade and no water. But we pawed holes in the sand and buried our feet in them. I distributed some raisins and perhaps prunes (dried) and trying to masticate them, the saliva began to flow, the throat was lubricated and we could talk once more. This was about two o'clock in the afternoon and we were now only about half way across the desert. It was not the mere time we had spent without water which affected us so much, it was the burning sand, *the dry sirocco* which drank up every particle of moisture it could find about us. My companions were usually very kind to me and always polite in their speech, but now they began to upbraid me for leading them into this desert, from which it was doubtful if any of us should escape. In vain I replied that a majority voted to take it. That for aught we knew the other route might be as bad as this. That all agreed there was no water there. Every argument failing, and fearing I too should lose control of my temper if I reasoned longer with them, I rose up and started off saying, "I am going to yonder tree. If I find water I will wave my hat."

I had proceeded a dozen rods or so when there rose gradually before me, first the banks of a creek, then the further edge of a stream of water, then a rivulet some three rods wide and twelve rods long! Yonder it came, booming up out of the broiling sands, and yonder, in the opposite direction, it sank away and disappeared from sight! All around were the glistening, burning sands! Could this be the mirage again in a new form? But there were boulders in the stream! Then I heard the music of rippling waters running over the tiny falls! Scarcely daring to believe I ran to the bank, dipped my hand into the cool stream and dashed a handful into my mouth! Oh, it was water! water! real water!! and then swinging my hat wildly around my head, I cried out in a clear voice: "Water! Water!! Ho! every one that thirsts, come ye to the waters!" The wind wrenched my hat from my hand and it went bounding over the plain, but nearly in the direction of my comrades. At my shrill call they all sprang to their feet and ran, some to intercept my rolling hat, and some for the water! When they reached it I had all I could do to restrain them from overdraughts which might be fatal. I urged them all first to wash their faces and heads and then drink only a handful at a time. Some of them laid down in the stream with all their clothes on, but in half an hour every thread was dry. Resting here half an hour, wading about in the water and admiring the blessed stream, we came to understand what the old Indian meant when he said of it, "Mucho aqua," much water, and "Poketo aqua," little water. It was indeed ample in amount but little and short as a river. Thoroughly refreshed we left the blessed stream and renewed our journey. Before ten o'clock that night we had reached the mission grounds of Soledad[38] and were housed in one of the adobe stalls where had lived and died whole generations of Indian Catholic converts. This was Saturday night. The rest of the Sabbath which drew on, was timely and refreshing. Monday morning at break of day we left the Mission, and wending our way through the fog, across the Salinas River, we proceeded down the valley on the north side. As the fog lifted, an immense valley spread out before us, perhaps twenty miles wide and fifty long. It was covered with grass and flowers and occasional trees. Vast herds of semi-wild cattle and horses were gathered in clusters on the plains. Not being accustomed to see men in our costume and with such packs on their backs as we prospective miners carried, they set up a wild looing, and soon they came running toward us till not less than 5,000 horned bullocks and cows, on either side, gathered in solid phalanx, and pawed the ground and tore it up with their horns. Some of the old bullocks were formidable indeed. Several times I drew my rifle upon one of them, but hesitated about firing till he came a little nearer. Finally they gradually drew off, the great bullocks being the last to give way and retire. Taking a right-hand trail we crossed the Gabilan Mountains and came down upon the little village of San Juan. There, crossing the San Benito River, we went up to Gilroy. There was immense excitement there at theat time, on account of the discovery of a quicksilver mine, the "New Almaden." This mine has been worked ever since, now some thirty-seven years, and has produced millions of dollars worth of quicksilver, and is perhaps, the richest quicksilver mine in the world.

From Gilroy we went to San Jose, and thence to Martinas, a new town opposite Benicia, on the south side of the Sacramento River. Here we staid a week, because we could not get a boat to take us over. While there we were offered fifty dollars a ton for simply cutting oat hay and stacking it in the field. Perhaps we could have accepted the offer, but there was not a scythe in Sacramento, Benicia, or even in San Francisco, which could be bought for less than fifty dollars!

So, declining the tempting offer, we were taken over to Benicia the following Sabbath, in a ferryboat. I pointed out a good camping-place, just back of the government fort, where I intended to spend the Sabbath, but my companions, sorely disappointed by our week's delay the other side of the river, were minded to push on toward the mines—Sabbath or no Sabbath, and while I tarried a little to get a supply of bread, they rushed by the camping-place designated, and were soon hidden from view among the hills around which the trail to Marysville led us.

I was badly encumbered with my load of supplies, blankets, etc., but put spurs to my horse to overtake them and see what this meant. I had run my horse five miles before they were overhauled. I asked what this meant, and they replied that, so far, they had listened to me, and had kept the Sabbath—now, in fairness, I ought to yield to their wishes; that they were in a hurry to reach the mines, make some money, and go back to their friends and families.

Why did they not let me know that at Benicia? Then they could have gone on and I would have staid there? "Well, you have broken the Sabbath already, why not keep on?" We had quite a parlay over the matter, and then we separated; five went on and three of us spread our blankets under an oak, sang hymns, read the Bible, and kept the Lord's day according to the Commandment. Proceeding on the next morning, just before noon we reached a fork in the trail, one diverging off the the right led to Sacramento, the other led to Marysville and the Northern mines, our destination. I perceived at once that our Sabbath breaking campanions had taken the wrong trail and were now well on their way toward Sacramento. Pursuing our way, after several days of travel we reached Marysville, but our friends were not there. And we waited for them three full days, when at length they came up on a steamboat. And a ragged and sorry looking set they were, and about as thoroughly ashamed of themselves as men well could be. They apologized frankly and humbly, and said that was the last of their Sabbath breaking in California. My only reply was that we had a pleasant time, and inexpensive, had been there on a rest for three days. Had got valuable information about the mines and had purchased all the supplies we could take along, even to the rocker, and all we had to do was to start off for Foster's Bar. Nor did I ever allude to it afterward. And this silence I believe had a better effect upon them than any lecture I could have given them. Loading ourselves down with about seventy pounds each, we wended our weary

way toward Foster's Bar, stopping once in a quarter of a mile to shift
our galling load or rest a while. In two days we reached Foster's Bar,
some thirty miles from Marysville, and what a scene of busy and
excited labor presented itself! A hundred men at work, as for dear
life. Some in the river, some on the bank, shoveling gravel into buckets,
carrying it to the rockers, rocking out the gold, occasionally lifting
the apron to see how fast the gold was gathering at the rifle, etc.,
etc. The Juba River was broad here, spreding out over a large gravelly
flat called a bar, on which the gold washed down from above had
been accumulating for centuries. This was our first sight of gold-
mining. Inquiring of the men how much they were taking out per
hand a day, the general answer was, from twelve to twenty dollars a
day. Some answered rather curtly, "Congress wages!" e.g., eight dollars
a day!

GOODYEAR'S BAR

The next day we went over the mountains and came down upon the
Juba again at Goodyear's bar. It was like Jordan, a hard road to travel.
And when we came down upon the river, having carried our heavy
loads of from sixty to eighty pounds each, over twenty-five miles that
day, we were none of us in a very happy mood. We were all footsore,
our joints all ached, we were fagged out, hungry, *"ragged and saucy!"*
Scarce a word had been spoken for the last five miles. But all of us
kept up a "terrible thinking!" If any of our company were wont to
swear, I fear they would have given vent to their feelings in that way,
could they have found any words in the language equal to the situation.
But at last in the dusky twilight we reached the bar and each threw
off his load and threw himself also upon the ground. Turning to me
they said in censorious tones, "Well, Captain, what are you going to
do now?" They had eaten no dinner that day save a cracker or two,
for the good reason we had none to eat, and were out of money all
around. I replied, "Cheer up, boys! build up a good rousing fire! We
will have a good supper, then a good sleep and to-morrow we will try
the gold digging!" Some one grunted forth his scornful *"Humph?"*
We had observed a lighted tent not far off, into which persons were
going, and we took it to be a store. So leaving my messmates to make
the fire, I stumbled over the logs and went to it. Two men were
waiting on customers, dealing out supplies at enormous prices, and
weighing out gold dust and nuggets in tiny scales. One of them I took
to be the proprietor. Approaching him as soon as he was at leisure,
I said, "My name is Bristol; I am one of a company of seven persons.
We are fresh from the States. We are all strapped, out of money, out

of provisions, and as you see, nearly out of clothing. We have come here to mine, and we want some provisions, such as flour, bacon, coffee, sugar, salt, rice, etc., and besides this we want ten dollars in money to pay for some freight now coming down the mountain." "Do you know anybody here?" he asked. "Not a soul," I answered. He quietly took out his memorandum book and said, "What name?" then how much flour, bacon, etc., gave the list to his clerk to fill out for me, then—"How much money?" and gave me a ten dollar gold piece, and quietly went to other customers. I gathered up my arms full of provisions and was soon at the fire my companions were slowly building. When I laid them down before them, their faces lighted up, and each lent a hand to hurry up the supper. But before we were through, the train of packed mules came down bearing our freight, and when I paid the ten dollars due, they asked, "How did you get that?" I answered, "I asked for it!" Three months after this, in settling a large bill with this same trader, I expressed to him my surprise that at my first interview he had trusted me so largely and so readily! He laughed and said, "I am seldom deceived in men, and after the frank and straightforward statement you made, I knew I was dealing with a square man and I would have trusted you to almost any amount."

MINING

The next day we crossed the river on an immense pine tree which had fallen across the stream. It was probably from 150 to 200 feet long and as we went across one at a time it swayed up and down in the middle perhaps five or six feet, and it made one's head swim to look down into water ten or twelve feet deep, rushing beneath us like a mill stream. Some of us lay down and crawled over it. Passing a brush house, a couple of fellows just crawling out of their blankets hailed us, "Hallo! just from God's country?" "Yes!" "Well! call in, we want to inquire about things." We stopped and after awhile they proposed to show us some specimens of the gold they were taking from their mines near by. One of them named Eaton said, "Stuart, where did you put it?" He fumbled about in the blankets and drew forth a shot bag partly filled with gold and we took it out in handfuls. It was mostly in lumps about as large as lead-drops, or the size of kernels of corn, and bright and beautiful. They showed us favorable locations near them not yet taken up, and we went to work with a will. In a couple of hours we had found a specimen worth about three dollars, very much in shape of a heart. One of my partners who had a lady-love in the States said, "I want that to send to the 'girl I left behind me.' I wish to send it as a token of the heart which in the mines still is hers, and as a pledge that the gold I get shall all be hers." Of course I could not resist such an appeal. I might add, however, that my friend, after sending this and sundry other sums to his fair correspondent and affianced, returned a couple of years after only to find his bird of Paradise had flown and was fondly nestling with another. He wrote me that he was "terribly disgusted!" Very likely. We had reached the mines about the first of June and we wrought on with the usual varying success of miners, but averaging about six or eight dollars a day, for the months of June, July, August, September and October.

ROUGH TREATMENT

About the first of November, having worked out our claims, we went up the river to Downeyville. On my way there, as we passed Coyotaville, a tall man, sitting by a rocker, hailed me. He proved to be one Dr. Welber, whose acquaintance I had made on the "Sarah Sands," on our way up from Panama. And here occurred an encounter with a rough, of which I hesitate to write lest the reader should regard my action as savoring too much of the "Fighting Parson," and as being quite unministerial if not unchristian. However, as it was more ludicrous than serious, I will give it for all it is worth, and as it occurred. While conversing with Dr. Welber, the owner of the adjoining claim came over the heap of boulders piled up between the two claims, and the Doctor introduced me to him. In doing so Dr. Welber remarked that I had preached some excellent sermons to them on the ship. As he said this I noticed a look of alarm upon Dr. W.'s face; also a broad and surprised smile on the face of the other.

"A minister!" said he, "A minister!!" Dr. Welber said, in an undertone, "You let him alone; he is a friend of mine." "Not much!" was the reply, "will we let him alone!" "It is all my fault," continued Welber, "I called him down here; but you will catch a Tartar if you go to bothering him."

But our new acquaintance was not to be foiled by any such considerations. He despised ministers and church members. He would have some fun at their expense. A ludicrous story to tell at the saloon, not once nor twice. He had "struck it rich." He stood high among the miners at the bar. He, too, like Welber, was a doctor, from Illinois. He was the one who organized a club on the bar, one of whose resolutions was *to treat to a dose of mud any clergyman who should chance to come upon their bar!* Well, he mounted the pile of boulders, and swinging his hat, he cried out: "Hear ye! Hear ye! O yes! Every miner quit his work! Hurry here! There is fun ahead! Big fun! Come one! Come all!" Instantly, from up the river and down, the rockers ceased their rattle and the miners came vaulting over the piles of boulders, and in five minutes some thirty to fifty were on hand, and more coming.

I suppose I could have got away by hard running if I had started quick enough. But I have a constitutional reluctance to using my legs in that way unless the danger is quite extreme; so I had treated the matter as of little moment, and continued to talk with Dr. Welber. As the crowd gathered, Dr. Welber begged them to spare me as his friend; but they wanted fun. Like the pugnacious Irishman, they were "spoil-

ing for a round or two," and they would not hear, but bade their
captain *put them through!* He seized my collar and said: Enough of this
gab! Dry up, Parson! I will show you how we do it!" So saying he gave
me a violent jerk which brought my right hand against his neck,—
my left hand was resting on a windlass post—very naturally it grasped
a handful of his shirt-collar and vest, and perhaps some of the flabby
flesh adjacent. There came over me a strange spasm of impulsive
energy, giving me about thrice my ordinary strength, and without
taking my left hand off the windlass, his feet left the ground, and
half way around the windlass he landed upon his back in a puddle of
water! What a shout went up from every miner's mouth—save one!
His hold upon me was not broken, and he sprang up. Seeing that I
was in for it I let go of the post and took hold with both hands, in
wrestler's style, knocked his feet from under him and laid him on his
back again! Jerking him up again I threw him from me, ten feet
distant, against a pile of rocks! I intended this should end it, but the
wicked eye which looked at me as he was rising, instantly changed my
mind. I thought he might have a dirk or pistol and I resolved to shake
that out of him quick, so I sprang like a cat upon him, and, seizing
him by the pants and collar, I gave him such a shaking up as made
him limpy as a rag. "Will you behave?" I asked, energetically. Not
answering, I started with him for the river, some eight rods distant.
Once in a rod or so I repeated my question and emphasized it with
a fresh shaking up. Meanwhile the crowd followed making the welkin
ring with their laughter and shouting. When within a rod of the river
he cried out, "Enough, Parson!" and I threw him down, saying, "The
next minister comes along here do you treat him decently." Wishing
to get through the dirty job as soon as possible I now turned to the
largest man among them; but he gracefully stepped back, bowed, and
said, *"No, I thank you! You will pass!"*

As no one else seemed disposed to try his hand at "dirtying the
minister's coat," I tried to resume my conversation with Dr. Welber
as if nothing special had happened; but his mirth knew no bounds.
He laughed and fairly roared, and so did the rest, even the members
of the club. They were not malicious men. They wanted fun and they
had got it, and they cared little at whose expense. Dr. Welber soon
introduced me to the miners, each by name, and soon we got into a
lively conversation. They said they hoped I would not regard them
as the worst of men if they were a little rough, etc. I said I could
easily believe that, for I had seen several men before! They said they
"should judge so." Meanwhile my assailant, the Illinois doctor, sat on
a stone, looking as foolish and crestfallen as a picked goose.

And now the miners were eager to have me go to their tents and take dinner with them. They wanted me to stop on the Bar. They would help me to a good claim. And if I would preach to them the next Sabbath they would all turn out, would help in the singing, and they assured me the best order should be maintained, and that the resolution to put ministers through an initiatory course of sprouts should thence onward be considered as antiquated and annulled. Within two days I had bought a claim for over three thousand dollars, two thousand of which was loaned me by these same miners, without interest, and with no security save only my note and name.

The Illinois doctor did not feel like working that afternoon, so he went over to Downieville. But the story of his unsuccessful effort to dirty the minister's coat had preceded him. They piled the questions about it, and the jokes upon him so thick, that he had to treat men to let him off, and when he came back that night he said it had cost him one hundred dollars to pay for the drinks! Poor fellow, he soon sold his claim and left for another camp. The following Sabbath I preached to quite a congregation. As no house could hold us, our meeting was held out doors and I preached to them literally standing on a rock. Better order, or closer attention no man could wish to have, and so it was for the following four months, and till my claim was worked out and I went elsewhere. The same miners voted me afterward a share in a claim worth at the time a thousand dollars, and I do not think my vigorous self-defence narrated above, detracted in the least from my moral and religious influence.

THE BOXING MANIA SQUELCHED BY A NEGRO

A colored man by name of Isaac Isaacs accompanied me from New York to the mines, and as colored men had in those days "no rights which white men were bound to respect," I took him under my special charge, and as by miners' law in California he could not hold a claim, I took him as a partner and he worked on my claim. He was a man of gigantic proportions, of enormous strength, quick as a cat, and tough as a bear. Withal he was brimful of good nature, and above all, he was an honest Christian. He was the strongest man I ever saw. His arms were long and his great broad hands, when spread out, as they hung down, looked like a pair of spades. During the winter of my stay at Coyotaville, boxing became all the rage at the city of Downieville. In the course of the winter, a Kentuckian became the acknowledged champion of the ring. He was very proud of his position and boasted much. Some one suggested that Isaac, or "Bristol's negro" as he called him, was more than a match for him. This the boxer resented with scorn. "No nigger walked the green earth he could not whip. Had he not done it on his father's plantation in old Kentuck half a hundred times?" The dispute soon rose high, and the betting went up into large figures. One morning as I was about to go down the river on business, I saw a crowd of a hundred men coming toward my cabin from Downieville. When they came near I was introduced to this famous pugilist. He explained the situation politely and somewhat braggadocially, assuring me he *"would not hurt the nigger,"* he "only wanted to show how superior a white man was to a nigger!" I replied that we did not believe in boxing here in Coyotaville, and I could not suffer the brutal contest. That I had no special fear that he could hurt Isaac, but Isaac was a Christian and of course would not engage in the dangerous and useless contest. It aroused his mettle somewhat to hear me intimate that he could not hurt Isaac, and strutting back he uttered his scorn of the negro's strength and prowess, however large. I surveyed him from head to foot and saw clearly he was no match for Isaac, and briefly said, "No, the fisticuff must not come off here." They lingered around in scattered groups. No sooner had I left and gone over the hill and out of sight, than a rush was made for my cabin. Isaac was washing dishes. They bade him come out and have some rounds with the champion pugilist. He refused and then the boxer came up and said, "We have made a bet and I am going to lick you and get the money." Reluctantly Isaac went out, but said, "I have no chance with a white man. Should I beat him he would draw a pistol upon me." "No! no!" said the crowd, "we will see you have fair play." "Well, I believe in self defence," said Isaac, and then tried to put on the gloves. Alas! they were by far too small. They were thrown aside and Isaac squared himself for the trial, saying, "Come on, let us have it over quickly." Those who saw it said the sight of that negro was the most magnificent spectacle in that line they had ever witnessed. He showed the trained boxer that he was, having been taught in his youth in Philadelphia. As the boxer came up, his passes were easily neutralized by those long arms and those quick motions. The first pass made by Isaac planted a gentle knock on the boxer's nose! Then another, and another, till sixteen times in succession that gentle knock on the nose had been made, without having once been touched on the body by his antagonist! The sixteenth, however, was a little harder than the others, and was followed by a stream of blood! Isaac expressed his sorrow, but the boxer now boiling over with wrath at the jeers of the crowd, many of whom had been bruised by him, and finding he could not touch Isaac with his fists, kicked at his abdomen spitefully. The negro's quick hand seized

ROUGH TREATMENT

A NIGHT WITH THREE ROBBERS

the foot as it came toward him and throwing it into the air the man came down upon his head and shoulders. Rising up he drew his dirk knife and was about to rush upon Isaac when the crowd interfered and carried him off the ground and back to Downieville by force. Thenceforth and for years it was admitted that a negro stood at the head of the boxing gentry in those parts, and the demoralizing and brutal sport passed into well-deserved ignominy and neglect.

OAK RANCH AND RANCHING

The following spring I took up a vegetable ranch, over in the mountains, near the head of Goodyear's creek, some eight miles from Downieville, and at the base of Monte Cristo, and associated with me Dr. Welber, before spoken of. We called it "Oak Flat." I insisted upon *two explicit agreements* as indispensable to the partnership. One was the keeping of the Sabbath; the other that no liquor should be sold upon the premises. We planted a large garden and bought a number of milch cows. Soon we began to take horses to pasture, till we had two hundred at a time. Our charge was a dollar a week. Miners began to get their supplies from us, we could easily bring freight from Downieville by the pack mules which we sent there daily with kegs of milk. They also left with us their buckskin bags of gold dust. Within a few weeks a great amount of travel came past our door, and not a few were the controversies we had over the liquor question. We always kept, in the corner of our great fireplace, a huge coffee kettle and a teapot, steaming and ready for use, while a spring of pure cold water sparkled near the door. Nearly every day a squad of miners, or rather several of them, would ride up to our door and call for something to drink. My answer usually was in substance this: "Here is hot coffee, with milk and sugar to season it; or if you prefer it, there is a good cup of tea, hot and savory. If neither of these suit you, there is 'Adam's Ale,' conducted here from a mountain spring, pure and cold as that which impearled its way through the garden of Eden; but if you want the stuff which makes a man a fool, eats a hole through his stomach and his pocket too, impoverishes his family and sends him to a premature grave, *we don't keep it!*"

The boldness and emphasis with which this, or something like it, was said, sometimes quelled opposition, but not unfrequently some such words as these followed: "What do you keep a public house for, if you have no liquor?" "We don't. This is *a private* house and ranch; but if people come along here hungry and thirsty we give them such as we have. If they are disposed to pay for it, well; and if not, they never go from our house hungry. But we never send a man away *drunk!* And if any of you die in California of drunkenness, as many of you will, your friends shall never point the finger at us and say, *"You did it!"* "Well, if you keep a private house of course you have a right to do as you see fit. Let us try some of your coffee and see how it will taste once more with cream and sugar in it." After "a good square meal," as they usually called it, with vegetables fresh from the garden, they would generally say: "Well, we are glad to see your pluck and principle! Wish more had it. It would have been a fortune to many of us." And when they left, it was with a warm shake of the hand and a promise to call again. Sometimes a hardened wretch would swear at us and curse us, but I used to request them not to take God's name in vain, and if they must do it they must leave the house. One such case, and its interesting sequel, I will relate.

WON OVER TO TEMPERANCE, AND HOW

It was that of a man from Calais, Maine, by name of Cooper. He had been a tavern keeper in that State, and from all accounts had been his own best customer at the bar. Quarreling with the temperance movement there, and I believe with his wife also, he migrated to California, for some reason taking along with him his two boys, one aged twelve years, and the other nine. When he heard our response to his call for whiskey he flew into a rage, cursing temperance people and saying that he left Maine[39] to get away from them, and here they were, away off among the mountains of California! Poor, persecuted man; like Noah's dove, he found no rest for the sole of his foot! I had to laugh at his confession. This enraged him still more, and he became so boisterous, profane and insulting, that I told him he must stop swearing or leave the house. He went out and stood before our door, and opened his mouth wide to let out the big words of male-diction against temperance and all temperance men and temperance women, against the owners of this ranch, against the Church, the Bible, and perhaps his Maker too! Tired out at length, he built a fire before our door, and there he boiled his coffee and fried his bacon. The two boys looked at their father, as he raved and tore about, with an expression on their faces which showed clearly they were accustomed to such outbursts of passion, but that they could not appreciate the cause.

We took no notice of what he said, but kept about our work. We had that day made a hasty pudding, and with milk it was a rarity for miners in those days. Seeing the boys look wistfully at it I took out a couple of bowls of the mush and milk and set it down by them, with some kind words to them, which showed that I had not forgotten that I was once a boy myself. Sour and mad as their father was he had not the heart to forbid their touching it, so they turned from the greasy bacon and coffee, and eagerly went for the mush and milk. It did one good to see them eat. Their bowls empty, I filled them again. Their father became less noisy but did not thank us or appear to notice what we had done. As they packed up and moved on we bade the boys goodbye, and invited them to call again; we should have some watermelons by and by.

About three weeks after who should appear one Sabbath morning but this same Cooper of Maine, and his two boys! He was now quite pleasant; had come to buy a bowl of that mush and milk such as we gave the boys. Did not care if he took a bowl himself; it would remind him of home and old times. Ignoring all the past, we made haste to accommodate them. They ate and ate till satisfied. What was the pay? *Nothing for the boys!* We liked to see them; we had boys at home. They should always have a free seat at our table, come when they might. As for himself he might pay the usual price. Toward evening they went back, but we noticed as they went, it was with reluctant steps and many a lingering look behind. Two weeks from that Sunday they came again, came early, and Cooper said we had stolen the hearts of his boys and their stomachs too. They had been talking about Oak Flat Ranch about half the time! When should they go over again? How beautiful those peas and corn looked! And those melon vines, and squashes, and new potatoes, and how good that mush and milk would taste again! Well, it was hard fare for boys like them to have, bacon and coffee and beans served up to them three times a day with unvarying monotony! In fact, he sometimes himself hankered after fresh vegetables. An idea had struck him that possibly his oldest boy could be of some use to us, waiting on the table and watching the house when we were out. Could he pay for his board in this way and perhaps earn a little over, enough to encourage him to do his best? This was a new thought to us. We would think it over. Let him stay a week and try his hand. We would let him know when next he came. So he departed, leaving his oldest boy. We had two easy riding mules, very docile and we used them to pack kegs of milk over to Downieville. The boy took quite a fancy to them and before the week was out he had learned to take them to town walking down the steep mountain slopes and riding the rest of the way. When his father came the following Sabbath, we told him we liked the boy and had concluded we could give him *three dollas a day, for six days in the week.* Perhaps we could clothe him too, if he proved faithful. Cooper got up and stared at us. "*Three dollars a day and board!* That is *eighteen dollars a week, and seventy-two dollars a month!* That is *more than I have taken from the mines* so far!" Yes, we thought we could afford it. He was a fine boy. It would pay to encourage such a boy. He will be a man by and by. But we stipulated that the *first* $200 of the boy's earnings he might *send to his mother* as a present from his own earnings. He readily assented. I believe there were tears in his eyes, and down deep in his heart I think repentings were kindling together. He went away happy, and when he reached the camp, I have no idea that he cursed the "bigoted Puritans of Oak Flat." But now, and all the following week the *younger* boy was pining for the ranch. "Why could not Mr. Bristol and Dr. Welber take him too?" He could work, could bring in the wood, sweep the floor, watch the house while his brother was gone to town, could feed the chickens as well as eat watermelons and mush and milk, green corn and peas! The next Sabbath Cooper and the younger boy came again. He told us of the boy's pleading during the week. Could we not use him so as to pay his board? We would try him a week. Saturday night he came and we made answer that we would give him his board *and a dollar a day* for six days, or twenty-six dollars a month! He was evidently trying to quit drinking. He was no more profane and low in his talk. He was cleaner in person, more rational and gentlemanly in demeanor. Every week he was sure to come to the ranch Saturday evening. At last he proposed to give up mining and come and work for us. We told him we could not hire a man who drank intoxicating liquors. He said he had considered that and would pledge himself that if we would employ him he would not drink a drop. So we hired him and he proved a faithful hand and a firm friend of ours till I left California. We paid him seven dollars a day or forty-two dollars a week and $182 month, and he and his two boys so laid up their money that after I left he purchased the ranch of Dr. Welber, sent money to Calais and brought to the ranch his wife and the other children. This was quite a change from the blaspheming saloonist who came down the mountain that day, and the industrious and sober rancher as I leave him now.

LIQUOR SOLD ON THE SLY

But the liquor pressure was a little too great for my partner, and especially for a side partner of his, a German, who worked more or less on the ranch. They at last yielded so far as to try the experiment of selling it on the sly. There was quite a demand for vinegar among our customers in the mines, and Dr. Welber bought some kegs of whiskey in town, and wished me to bring them to the ranch, as he wished to make some barrels of vinegar. Suspecting nothing, I did so, and soon observed less clamor for "the stuff" about the ranch. One Saturday night, as we were weighing out our gold, and giving to each his share, there stood by itself a yeast-can half full of gold dust. When we came to that, and it was weighed, and my half pushed across the table to me, I asked whence this came, and why kept by itself. The German answered, "So much we get mit that vinegar whiskey!" I looked straight at them while they tried to justify it. I pushed it back to their side saying, "It is the price of blood! I will have none of it. Doctor, I did not expect that of you," and rose up hastily and went out, deeply grieved and offended. What became of the money I know not. The subject was never alluded to afterward, and never again, while I was there, was one drop of liquor freighted to Oak Flat Ranch.

A NIGHT WITH ROBBERS

The Fourth of July was near at hand, and great preparations were made at Downieville to make the attractions as great as possible. Our hired men must all go, Cooper and his boys. Dr. Welber and I were to be left alone. But early in the morning Dr. Welber was called to Downieville on important business, so I was left alone through the day; but the Doctor promised to return by midafternoon. We had a large sum of money deposited with us by the miners who left their horses with us. One soon gets tired of carrying about his person a bag of gold dust weighing from five to twenty pounds. It galls his person and makes him sore and lame. We had a nice place to deposit it, where no one would think of looking for it, and there we hid our own and that of our friends, enjoining on each depositor to keep the matter a profound secret; but when many thousands had been received, we found to our dismay that the report had gone all over the country that immense sums were deposited by the miners at Oak Flat Ranch. It was freely talked about at all the gambling saloons. We were warned of our danger of being robbed. Persons were killed nearly every week, near us, for their money. Suspicious characters began to hang about our house, watching us by day and night, to discover, if possible, *where* we hid the treasure. We removed it from the house and hid it in five-gallon tin cans, which we buried among the squash vines. While there, hoeing and pulling up weeds, we could easily make a deposit unobserved. But to the Fourth of July.

Reaching Downieville, the Doctor found the important business was a proposition to buy out Oak Ranch and make of it a fashionable watering place, a pleasure resort for the city, the mines and gamblers. The company making this proposition was composed of the most desperate gamblers in Downieville. What would we take for it? Would

we sell out for $15,000? Dr. Welber demanded $20,000. Long they
debated the matter, and at last, late in the afternoon, compromised
upon $18,500. The money must all be paid down, and it took till
sunset to raise it all. And now the writings must be drawn up, and
at this they worked until nine or ten o'clock at night. Just here the
whole game was blocked by one of the party rising up and going out
with his money, saying he would conclude no bargain to-night, he
"was too full!" This broke up the conference. Then for the first time
it burst upon the Doctor's mind that this *was all a ruse!* a scheme to
keep him away from the ranch while confederates and employes were
sent to kill his partner, and rob the ranch! His agony knew no bounds.
He rushed to the stable for his horse, but when mounted it was so
dark and so difficult to keep and to ascend the steep mountain trail,
he found it impossible to proceed, and, after hours of effort, was
obliged to turn back and wait till morning. All night he paced the
room in agony, but started for home with the first ray of breaking
day. Meanwhile Oak Flat was the theater where the other part of this
drama was being enacted.

The Doctor did not come home by mid-afternoon, as he had
promised. Four o'clock and he is not here! Something has happened!
Has he not been waylaid and murdered? Very likely, and if so, Oak
Ranch is to be attacked and robbed to-night, and myself murdered!
The sun goes down on such meditations, and darkness comes on. I
cannot call upon a human being for help! There is not a soul within
seven miles! A cannon fired would arouse nobody! A fusilade kept up
all night around my house, and the buildings burnt to ashes, would
be known to no outsider until tomorrow! Well, I will trust in God and
do my best to defend myself and my neighbors' property. Nailing fast
a double pair of Oregon blankets over the windows, and lighting a
pine knot in the fireplace, I proceeded to overlook my means of
defence, to put on fresh caps and place them in easy reach if needed.
And this was the small armory I put in readiness: A Colt's navy
revolver, an Allen's six-shooter, a double-barrel shot gun, a double-
barrel pistol, a rifle, a musket, and a Mexican sword! Nearly all these
weapons had been left for my use by the miners depositing their gold.
These, all stacked in a dark corner, where the head of my bunk was,
could be quickly seized and used. A loose board near my pillow, which
I could remove at will, enabled me to look out and see what was
passing.

Nothing special occurred till near twelve o'clock, and I had laid
down in my bunk. But I heard the footsteps of several men approaching through the dry leaves. They stopped near the corner of

the house and held a parley in whispers. Then one of them came forward and tried the door. He did not knock but tried to force it open, but finding he could not, went round the house and tried the window, and then went and reported. Then all came to the door and knocked loudly. Instantly I was on my feet, unlocked the door, lifted the great latch and removed the huge crossbar, and swung open the door, and there I stood squarely before them, as good a mark as they could have wished! A navy hung swinging on one side and Allen's six shooter on the other! Before me stood three full whiskered men with hats pulled down over their eyes, all armed with revolvers, and each holding in his hands a short rifle! The boldness of my action in opening the door so promptly and standing so squarely before them, completely disconcerted them. "Good evening," said I, "come in; you are late this evening!" Mechanically they obeyed, and when inside I shut the door, latched it and put the great bar across. This bewildered them still more, and they peered back among the bunks to see if I had not helpers lying there. I had not a moment to lose, so stepping back into the dark corner among my fire arms, cocking my Colt's navy, I ordered them to *lie down!* to lie apart! The voice with which I spoke had a vim and terror about it which frightened them, and startled me too! Quickly they were on the floor. All fear was gone. I felt girt with supernatural strength, and I could scarce keep from dispatching them at once, for I believed they had murdered my partner. Not to prolong the account by details, thus I held them at bay *for four mortal hours, not allowing them to touch one another, or to turn over or move!* About four o'clock in the morning, a horseman rode up and cried "Hallo!" I opened the door and it was daylight. The horseman inquired the way to Canyon Creek, and as I went out to show him the trail, the three men filed out past me, and in single file went straight into a thicket and down toward Goodyear's Creek, paying no regard to trails or anything else, save to get out of sight! I stood and looked after them till they were out of sight, and then there went back into the cabin a man offering in his heart and from his lips, thanksgiving to God for the strange and wonderful protection! The supernatural strength and absolute fearlessness of those hours made me think of David's words when he said, "The Lord taught his hands to war and his fingers to fight, so that a bow of steel was broken in his hands." But now the day was coming on, and to work off the excitement I went to chopping on a log. About sunrise I heard a shout on the mountain top! It was the voice of my partner, Dr. Welber. He was frantic with joy at seeing me safe and coolly chopping wood and the ranch house still standing. All the way home he had urged his horse to the top of his speed. His fevered fancy had pictured the attack of the night, the fierce and well fought battle, his partner at length overcome by numbers, the ranch robbed and burned down, and the white bones of his comrade crumbling in the ashes! With what trepidation he approached a point on the trail whence he could look down upon the house and corral! "My heart," said he, "was in my throat as I drew near the spot! I don't believe I breathed for minutes!" Well, he came down shouting, embraced me, and cried. He told over the story of his detention as I have narrated it. We sat down on the log and then I told him mine, and again he embraced me and cried like a child. Some days afterward he said he would give a hundred dollars to know the conversation of those robbers, when they got to where they could talk over the experience of that night, when they were cowed down and held in mortal fear *by one man!* I suspect they mutually accused each other of cowardice and that each threw the blame of failure on the other! A man once asked me what I could have done had I been one of the three? I replied I would have done just as they did, for I had no doubt I should have been killed if I had not, and that was just what they were not prepared for. I will add here, that never after was one word said to the doctor about buying the ranch. The gamblers maintained a singular silence about it.

CHAPTER

14

GOING HOME TO THE STATES

And now the summer gone and the autumn nearly over, I began to turn my eyes homeward. I had got over my sick headache, slept well, had laid up some $3,000, and was as I wrote to my friends, hearty as a buck, tough as a bear and as strong as a lion. Before I started on this tour, I had promised the Lord that I would return to my work of preaching so soon as my general health was restored, and my nerves had recovered their balance again. But here was the temptation. We were making money rapidly, not less than from twenty to thirty dollars per day. "Stay," said my partner, "but a single year, and you will make all the money you will ever need." But I dared not trifle with a promise I had made to the Lord in time of trouble. So to the surprise of all I announced my determination to start for home as soon as I could arrange my affairs. It took a couple of weeks to take account of stock, sell off my share, and balance accounts. In spite of our efforts to conceal the purpose, it got out and spread abroad. It was reported that we had made a mule load of money, and a dozen suspicious characters hung around our ranch. They had no business there, but they would not leave, and one of them was kept in our house from morning till night.

It was plain what they were after, to see our gold and how much I carried away, and to rob me before I got home, probably before I was out of California. I told the Doctor *the boldest course was ever my best hand.* So one evening we brought out the hidden bags of gold, weighed out some fourteen pounds of gold, as my share. This we deposited in spaces about large enough to put one's finger, which ran up and down the front of a double lined buckskin vest. These spaces were made by seams about an inch apart up and down the front of the vest, so that when I put it on, the whole chest was covered and shielded by a layer of half an inch of gold! This was the heaviest vest I ever wore, and I did not take it off till I reached San Francisco. And no garment ever tired me like that! In fact, I wore it until I came

near New York. It was a grievous burden! But it was a partial shield
to the more vital parts.

In concluding my settlement with Dr. Welber a scene occurred
not usual in such transactions, which will well illustrate our general
dealings with each other. Two hundred dollars remained on the table
between us, which, according to Doctor Welber's figures, *belonged to
me;* according to mine belonged *to him.* This arose from our different
estimates of the cash value of certain notes I had consigned to him,
and which were by neither of us considered quite as good as their
face indicated. The Doctor pushed the $200 over to me and said,
"The notes are worth all I estimated them at, and that belongs to
you." I reviewed his estimates and compared them with mine, and
said, "Mine are the most reasonable," and pushed the money over to
him. He held his hand on the money a moment, argued his side and
pushed it back to me. I replied at length and pushed it back, and so
the money, $200, went back and forth, perhaps half a dozen times.

We were all absorbed in the matter, when one of the twenty
lookers on burst forth with the exclamation, "That is a scene I never
saw before and never expected to see in this world — two men, arguing
each against himself and in favor of his neighbor!" We looked up and
several of those rough men were in tears, and one had gone out
crying, to give vent to his feelings! I presume it stood out in strong
contrast with the treatment he had received in some financial settlement, perhaps with kindred and supposed friends. I don't know but
this was a good thing for me. For the next morning when I left, most
of those suspicious characters pressed my hand very warmly and seemed
really sorry to have me go! The matter of the $200 in dispute, was
finally settled, by my passing the money over to Welber and saying,
"If your estimate proves right, you may send me the money. If mine,
then you retain it."

I had agreed with one Langston, who ran an express to Sacramento, to go down with him, and to meet him at Goodyear's Bar,
and travel with him for mutual protection. The next morning I started.
But Cooper would go with me until I met the express train. We were
well armed, and had eight miles to travel, mostly through the woods.
When a mile or two from the cabin I saw a man in a thicket looking
up the trail; he disappeared, and we knew that danger was ahead.
Cooper and I separated some ten rods apart, and rode rapidly through
the thicket. Three or four armed men were there. We had evidently
come upon them before they expected us and being separated they
dared not fire upon one when the other was out of reach, and could
either return the fire or ride off for help. So we reached Goodyear's

Bar safely. I wore my usual rough miner's clothes to disguise my intent. But as we rode past the gambling saloons, I found how vain all my precautions had been, for the gamblers rushed out and said, "Hello! parson! made your pile and going home! Made lots of money, I hear!" So I had to say, "Yes! made a little, hope I shall get home with it! Good-bye, boys, take care of yourselves. Adios! and rode on.

The ride to Foster's Bar just at that time was very dangerous. Several miners had been robbed and killed on the route within a few days. And we of the express company, separated a few rods apart as we went through the more dangerous places. Thousands of men, rich in the spring, were now in the fall dead broke and desperate, on account of failures of river-bed claims whose workings had been immensely expensive, and which had proved worthless.

SAN FRANCISCO AND OAKLAND IN 1851

Arriving at San Francisco I called at once upon my friend, Mr. Penfield, formerly a deacon of my church in New York City, and now a merchant in San Francisco, and took rooms with him. Sauntering one day about the city we chanced to bring up on Telegraph Hill, and lay down upon the grass. The conversation beginning to flag, pointing toward the scattered clusters of oaks over in Oakland and the herds of cattle roaming among them, I said, "Penfield, *that* is Brooklyn. *This* is New York! Come here a few years hence and you shall see a ferry boat loaded with people going from that point on this side to that one over yonder on the other side. Another will ply across from yon point, to another one there. And a third will cross and recross, once in an hour, between them. The men of wealth and refinement will do business *there*, and there they will spend their money. City lots in Oakland will sell at fabulous prices, and if you and I were to get a boat to row us over there to-morrow, and buy out some of the ranchmen who own those cattle, in a few years we would be millionaires!" He smiled at my reverie and lazily said, "Very likely!" And then we went down to his store. I took my $3,000 from his safe, bought my ticket for New York, and the next day left for Panama! To-day, and long since that daydream has been a reality, and to human view, our neglect to make the purchase suggested, looks like an egregious blunder! But it may not have been such in the sight of Him who sees the ultimate and complete results of such an investment, its influence upon ourselves and our families, and upon others in this life and the life to come. It takes the balance sheets of eternity to tell what is true prosperity and what is not.

The steamer on which I had taken passage, was the Tennessee, and was commanded by one Capt. Totten, a United States officer. He was a fine officer, but in poor health. There were 1,200 passengers on board and we were terribly crowded.

Just outside the Golden Gate we took some cattle aboard to kill on the passage for fresh beef. I was amused at the mode of handling them. A herd of the semi-wild creatures was driven down to the shore and held at bay there by the Spanish horsemen. Some of them were crowded into the surf. A lasso from a man in a boat was thrown over the horns of one of them, he was hauled off into deep water, and the rowers towed him a mile or two to the side of the ship. An end of the lasso was thrown on board, and the steam-engine in a trice lifted him from the water and raising him thirty or forty feet by his horns, swung him into his stall on deck where he was to stay till the ship's butcher had need of him.

It was a singular sight, a huge bullock of 1,000 to 1,500 pounds thus swinging between heaven and earth, dangling by his horns and kicking and pawing in the air!

Thus getting our supply of beef, we proceeded on our way. The next day Capt. Totten called the passengers together and said, "I cannot do justice to this crowd of passengers without help. I propose to divide you into groups of one hundred each. There will be twelve such groups. Let each choose its Captain. Let that Captain have charge of his mess. Let him preside at their tables and note all their wants and communicate them to me, and through him I can see that justice is done to all his mess."

I was chosen Captain of the second mess of a hundred which was formed, and got along finely. We had some sick in my company, but none of them died on our way to Panama. One of them lay at death's door near a week and the way of his recovery was quite remarkable. I was watching with him one hot and sultry night, not expecting him to live till morning, when a cyclone accompanied with a water-spout, struck our ship. Tons of water fell upon the deck almost in solid mass, sweeping overboard hats and blankets, and every other light thing on deck. The ship careened and lurched as if she would capsize. My sick man, startled at the unexpected visitation, sprang to his feet and with a wild shriek leaped upon the rail and in an instant would have been overboard, had I not seized his clothes and with a jerk brought him back upon the deck. We both fell, I upon him with a force which might nearly have killed a well man! From that moment he began to recover, and was well, and on his way to meet his family in Iowa, when I parted with him. His gratitude was unbounded, and I had to promise him I would visit him and his family. A promise—

alas! I shall never fulfil in this world, as I have forgotten his name and place of residence. I returned him the gold and letters he had given me to bear to his wife in case of his death, and bade him a long farewell. That cyclone, that bath of water and that fearful fall were the things which broke the fever, startled into action the vital forces and saved him, so I believe.

A SAILOR'S VIOLENCE SUPPRESSED

Perhaps I may go back a little and relate what else happened over this sick man a few days before. It was a hot noon day, when I was fanning this man and wetting his forehead, that several sailors were passing through the crowd on deck, and crying, "Clear the way!" Of course I could not instantly move the sick man, but was trying to do so, when a tall, athletic sailor coming along, cursed him and kicked him in his side. I seized the sailor's heel and he fell back! He was the largest sailor on the ship, and their acknowledged bully. Indeed, he was a petty tyrant over the sailors, none of them daring to offend him.

The officers too, found hard work in managing him. Mortified by his fall, he sprang up and attacked me; I was up as quick as he; we grappled and he was floored. Seizing the middle fingers of both hands and turning them nearly out of joint, I held them in that condition, till he dared not stir, for fear of what else I might do with them. The sailors rushed to his help, but were pulled off by the passengers. An officer came and ordered me to let him up; I did so saying, Now you must take care of him. No sooner was he up than he flew at me again. Once more he fell upon the deck, and I was on the upper side, and again I pinioned him so that he could not possibly hurt me. Again the officer bade me let him up, but I refused, and sent for the Captain. To him I gave my reason for not obeying the under officer. I now let him up again, and he went off with the Captain.

The sailors were now all down upon *"that bloody landsman."* Meeting this same sailor a day after he said, "Your little pile will be of no use to you! When we land at Panama I will see that you don't cross that Isthmus!" I smiled and said, "Let me see your face on the Isthmus if you dare! If I get hold of you there, there will be no Capt. Totten to help you up when I have got you down!" Well, I suppose he meant to scare me, at least that was all I meant. I thought it best to let him know that I was not afraid of him, there or elsewhere.

AN ATTACK OF ROBBERS ON THE ISTHMUS

When we arrived at Panama, we heard that *two steamers*, one an opposition boat, were waiting to receive passengers on the Atlantic side. A meeting was held on board before we landed. A committee of three was chosen to hurry across, and secure passage for New York, on the best terms. I was one of them. Landing, we found some two thousand mules and horses and their owners waiting to carry us and our baggage.

Wells & Fargo's express alone, required *one hundred animals, to carry* across *their packages of gold*, containing $2,000,000 and each horse-load being $20,000, or 100 pounds in gold. The next day we started off, on our way to Cruces, the head of boat-transportation on the Chagres River.

My two companions began to run horses. Not wishing to be left behind I too, put spurs to my horse. The trail was woody nearly all the way, and we ran through a defile, at full speed, one horse a dozen rods ahead of mine, and the other as far behind.

A band of twenty robbers lay there concealed, ready to rob the train. We passed through unharmed, but they opened fire upon those who followed us, and robbed and wounded quite a number. It was a sad sight that night when they were brought into Cruces, bloody— gashed—penniless, and among strangers! Some of the mules laden with gold were captured, taken off into the forest, and their loads taken off. But the miners returned their fire and soon routed, pursued and captured several of them and recovered most of the booty. The fifty pound packages of gold could not be carried off very fast by a footman.

At Cruces I took passage down the river, and soon found I had fallen into about the most low-lived gang of dissolute fellows I ever fell in with. Finding they had a minister aboard they did their "level best" to annoy and disgust me. And we had a hot time of it. I believe I never before or since heard as much profanity or obscenity uttered in the same length of time. I stood my ground, and attacked them "hip and thigh," right hand and left, sometimes answering a fool according to his folly, and sometimes not deigning to answer.

On the way down, a tropical thunderstorm aided me greatly. It came upon us very suddenly, the wind nearly capsizing our boat, the rain falling in torrents and blinding the helmsman while the thunder and lightning were terrible. In five minutes we were all drenched through to the skin, and a sorry looking set we were. The most of them were terribly scared. When the rain-cloud passed, my hour of triumph had come; they were too wet and cold to joke and too badly scared to swear, and I talked to them very seriously. Before we reached Chagres, they had become very quiet and decent. Most of them openly admitted their conduct had been most reprehensible, that I was right, and they meant to turn over a new leaf when they reached the States. One of them took me aside and said, When we reach Chagres, let us room together in the hotel. I said, No, you had better room with your friend—a downright atheist, who with him had been the leaders of the crowd. No, he said, he could not trust him, or a man of his sentiments, for said he, "I have $5,000 in gold about me, and I dare not room with him." Well, I finally consented, and the week I spent in Chagres, before starting for New York, he was often gone half a day leaving his gold with me! Atheists and deists will always trust Christians as they will not each other.

Apropos, I may add here that I once overheard a tavern keeper, in the place where I had lived some years, running down the character of the Christians of the place. He said to his guests there was not one of these Christians he would trust with five dollars, without security. Just then I walked in and asked him to repeat it. He did so, and then I turned to the strangers and said, "Over a year ago this man came to me and said, 'I have $1,000 paid me in gold to-day. I dare not keep it at the tavern; wont you keep it for me till I call for it?' Well, reluctantly I consented, saying I would not be responsible for it, as I should take no pay for running the risk. Well, gentlemen, I kept it without giving him the slightest security and when he wanted it he came and found it all there and got it, too!" His guests laughed and he left for the other room.

To return to Chagres. On arriving we found the opposition steamer had taken fire and burned down, no doubt the work of an incendiary suborned by agents of the other boat. The price we had to pay for passage to New York amply illustrated the saying that "corporations have no souls!" On our way home our ship called at Kingston, Jamaica. Just off the harbor a pilot came aboard and as usual took charge of the helm and the ship, giving out his orders as captain. He was a mulatto, but very polite and civil. Some Southern bloods on board were greatly incensed at hearing a "*nigger*" as they called the mulatto, give out commands to white sailors, and they were very free with curses and words of scorn they heaped upon him. Our captain was a coward and did not summarily suppress it as he should have done. The pilot said nothing, but attended strictly to his business, bringing the ship into port. When he had laid her up beside the wharf and taken his fee, he turned to these bloods and said, "If you think either of you is a better man than I am, step down upon the wharf and we will settle the matter." This was too much for them, and they rushed upon him, half a dozen of them, struck him and kicked him down the gangway. In about five minutes, half a dozen policemen, all black as the ace of spades, came marching up the planks with the pilot, and seizing one and another of this Southern gentry, bore them and their defenders off to the calaboose. And there they had to lie and sweat and fight fleas for nearly a week, for it took that time for tardy English justice to get around to their case, which finally they did, fined them severely and let them and our ship go on our way. I wanted to get home, but I was quite content to stay for the sake of having these haughty oppressors for once punished for their insolence and pride. It was amusing to go daily and look through the grates, and see these young despots of the Southern plantation sitting demurely in the dingy calaboose, and doing the bidding of stalwart negroes wearing Her Majesty's uniform, and clothed with her authority!

On our way from Jamaica to New York we encountered a fearful storm. Nearly all of us were seasick. In the course of a stormy night, when the air was too foul to stay below, and on deck we were drenched with the rain, my buckskin vest and a belt of gold dust besides, became too oppressive to bear, so I took them off and rolling them up together I staggered down the stairs to the purser's office and left them in his keeping. In going there I had more than once stumbled over some person lying on the floor. When I got back it occurred to me that I had handed to the purser *but one* of my gold packages, and that probably the other had slipped from my hand in one of my falls or lurches, as I went down. But I was so sick and exhausted that I could not go and look for it, though it contained $800. But feeling better toward morning, as soon as it was light, I took a look where I had fallen, and there I found indeed a purse of gold, but it contained about $400 only, and it was not mine. I called aloud, "Who has lost a purse of gold?" The sleepers woke up and began feeling about themselves and one of them said he had lost one and described the one I had found, so I gave it to him but did not find mine. When we reached New York I called on the purser, paid him ten dollars and received my buckskin vest and found the $800 purse wrapped up in it!

From the time I left New York, one year and a half before, an impression had been upon me that I should not live to return and it held fast to me like a vampire till I stepped upon the dock, and then its hold was broken, and it vanished forever.

CHAPTER 15

PIONEER LABORS IN WISCONSIN

Hastening to my family in Massachusetts, I staid with them a couple of weeks and then started off on a tour through the States of Ohio, Michigan and Wisconsin, in search of a location. The place I wanted was one on the frontier, where a home missionary was needed and where I could invest the $2,500 brought from California in a homestead for myself and family; where I could work the blood off my brain after preaching, and keep my nerves in tone, and where also I could do something toward self-support. It seemed to me I was specially fitted for such a field by my sympathy with toiling and struggling humanity, the practical in distinction from the theoretical cast of my sermons, and by the necessity of much physical exercise, which in a minister will be tolerated on the frontier, and scarcely nowhere else but there.

Landing at Milwaukee, Wis., I stopped at the American House. Wishing to be by myself, to think over plans of further travel, I went into a small room whose walls were lined with cloaks and overcoats. I seated myself in a corner, and tipping the chair back against the walls, I drew the coats and cloaks over me. This nearly concealed my person. After a time a man came to the door, looked in, and turning around, said: "The coast is clear! No one here!" Three men came hastily in, and, locking the door, sat down around a table and began a lively talk over the late political contest in that State. After no small amount of cursing and swearing at random — volleys shot off in the air — they began asking each other how much they had made by selling their votes and influence to the different parties, Whigs, Democrats and Germans. One swore he had made five hundred dollars! another a thousand or so, while one, whom they called "Sat," swore that he got big money *from both parties*, but voted the Democratic ticket! Much they laughed over this feat, and slapped Sat freely on the shoulders, and called him "a devilish good fellow!" I had heard it all, and at this juncture the cloak was seen to move aside, and down came the chair upon all fours, with a thump, and *a man in it!*

With a smile on my face I walked up to their table and said to the astonished men, I have been quite interested in your conversation. From your own account you must be a scaly set of fellows, selling your votes and perjuring yourselves, and what not in that line; but which of you is that man '*Sat*' who deceived alike friends and foes?" One of them colored a little and said, "We have not been accustomed to be talked to in that style." "That is because we have not been accustomed to meet," I said. "Where are you from?" he asked. "Fresh from California," I replied, and at that they all quieted down, for in those days a Californian was deemed little less than a grizzly bear walking on two legs! I afterward lived within half a dozen miles of this same "*Sat*," or *Satterly Clark*, and often met him, and found my first impressions quite correct in his case.

SETTLEMENT IN DARTFORD, WIS.

Taking the stage, I fell in with the State Superintendent of Schools, a Professor Root. He invited me to visit his home at Dartford, Green Lake county, Wis., and spend the Sabbath, and I did so. A new Methodist church had just been built. I attended church in the morning and was invited to preach in the afternoon. As soon as I had entered the pulpit a home feeling came over me. It seemed to me that everybody there knew me and had confidence in me, and that I knew and loved them all. When I rose to preach, how silent was that house. Every word seemed to go to the heart. And when I prayed it seemed as if God were there too! The sermon was by no means select or a favorite with me, but to this day, though thirty-five years have gone since then, I remember the text and much of the sermon. I have heard some who were there say, not long since, it was so with them. The text was, "The Lord is my Shepherd, I shall not want." It was a parallelism of the model shepherd's treatment of his flock, and God's care and tender love toward his people; and I think when the people went home that day, the Lord seemed nearer and dearer to them than when they came to church. When the meeting closed there was a hasty call of the official board and leading citizens, and an earnest invitation was tendered me to cast in my lot with them, and the use of the house was offered me half the day each Sabbath.

On the following Sabbath day I preached to them again, and it was now settled in my mind that this was the field for me; so I negotiated with Prof. Root for his farm, and not long after I and my family were there, clearing my farm, visiting the people, and preaching the Gospel. I soon established three preaching places, in as many adjacent towns, where every Sabbath day I preached one sermon, about as fully crowded with Gospel meat as I could pack and press it. One was in Dartford, one in Green Lake Prairie, and the other in Metomon. My usual Sabbath day's journey to reach these places was fifteen miles, when I staid at the latter place over night; when I returned home the distance was nearly thirty miles. Other weekly meetings I held in schoolhouses, but the above were my regular appointments.

In process of time the schoolhouse gave place to the church edifice in each of these places. I greatly enjoyed my work. I loved the people, and they were not slow to return it. I rarely preached without feeling upheld by a hand unseen. The free use of the handkerchief about the eyes in my congregations showed that others, too, beside myself, felt the moving power. Somtimes men staid away because they could not keep from weeping when they came.

REVIVALS

Revivals of religion began to follow my preaching, and when commenced I was wont to follow them up, even to strange places. Sometimes I spent the whole winter in these revival labors, and besides doing a great deal of work in visiting and prayer-meetings, I sometimes preached nearly one hundred sermons in as many consecutive days. I was by no means particular under what denominational auspices I held these meetings. Thus often I preached through a revival meeting with the Baptists, then with Free Will Baptists,[40] then with Presbyterians and Methodists. Indeed, my own denomination complained much that I helped other denominations more than my own; but I went where the way seemed open, with a promise of most good; besides, I believed I had a special mission to bring all these churches a little nearer together, and to show to outsiders the essential unity of the whole household of faith. And so it came to pass that each of these denominations put in a special claim to me as being specially near to them. Some of these revivals were remarkable for the firm establishment upon the Rock of nearly all the professed converts. Thus, in one of them, in counting up the converts, we estimated that thirty-two gave satisfactory evidence that they had passed from death unto life. *Two years after,* in looking over the list, *there were thirty-six* of those inquirers whose conversion time had proved to be genuine.

After an absence of twenty years, in revisiting these fields I was surprised at the *number of ministers* who came out of those revivals and are now preaching the Gospel. From one out of the way place *five preachers came forth,* and from nearly all of them at least one. Thus and in such labors on the border I spent ten of the most active and successful years of my life![41] And, albeit there were serious drawbacks, they were among the happiest years of my life. Did not the Master say, "Your joy no man taketh from you"? My salary was small, seldom rising as high as $500 a year. I had a wife and three children to support. But what I lacked in salary I made up in economy, self-denial and toil on my farm. It was often a comfort to read Paul's words, *"These hands* have ministered to my necessities and those who were with me." And I took joyfully these extra labors and this stinted salary because God gave me what was better than gold, he gave me "souls for my hire and crowns for my rejoicing in the day of the Lord Jesus." This labor on my farm was much criticised by my brethren in the ministry, and especially by the agents of the Home Missionary Society. They even refused me a grant of $100 per annum to help me in my work, solely on the ground that I worked more or less upon my farm to eke out what was lacking for my support in the gifts of my people. Rev. Dexter Clary, long time agent of the great Home Missionary Society, admitted that the society had not in all the State of Wisconsin one home missionary who preached as much as I did, or as successfully, but said the society could not aid me unless I gave up work upon my farm. "What shall I do," I asked, "with nerves so unstrung that should I stop work, I must stop preaching also?" "Travel! travel!" he said. But I said that would not restore them as hard work will. Besides, where is the money coming from, and who, in the meantime, will take care of these precious flocks, many of whose members are tender lambs and need constant care? No, I cannot leave them, *and I will not!* "Well!" he said, "these are our printed rules!" and so they were. But in my view they ought to have been flexible enough to meet such a case as mine. Well, I told my friend Dr. Clary I believed the Lord had given me too much good sense to follow his advice, and too strong and tough muscles to make it absolutely necessary that the society should help me in order to continue my work. So we parted good friends, and I wrought on unaided, and lived and prospered. And now as I look back over the years and call up before me the fellow missionaries who wrought by my side, and who received aid from the Society, I cannot see but I fared about as well as they, my family lived as comfortably, and I gave as much as they to benevolent objects and laid up against a rainy day a little more than nine-tenths of them did. "He that gathered much had nothing over, and he that gathered little had no lack."

STRIKING INCIDENTS

During the ten or twelve years of revival labors on the frontier, not a few incidents of special interest occurred. Among them there rises up before me one in which *two dollars* played a conspicuous part.

A gentleman and his wife came to our place from Vermont. Soon after his arrival he visited me with a Mr. Brooks, a friend of his, in quest of a new milch cow. I showed him two or three I had to sell. He took a liking to one, for which I asked twenty-seven dollars. Would I not take twenty-five? No, I had rather keep her than part with her for less. He had heard my neighbor, Mr. Sherwood, had some fine cows for sale. Yes, he has I hear. They are blooded cows and I should think much nicer than mine, but I suspect his price is higher. And I advised him to go and see them and showed them a short way across lots to his house. They started but soon came back and took the cow. That night I felt somewhat troubled about *that cow trade*. Perhaps she was worth only twenty-five; besides, this man is a stranger, perhaps not specially well off, sold out at low prices, has had an expensive journey and now has to buy at high prices and feels poor! So it was with me; I know the heart of a stranger. I ought to have been specially lenient in his case. Well, I promised the Lord I would hand him back two dollars, turned over and went to sleep. Some days after, meeting him on the street, I handed him the two dollars and said, "Here are two dollars which belong to you." He took them mechanically and asked whence they came. I told him my thoughts after he left with the cow, and the promise I made to the Lord. He thrust back the money and protested against receiving it. Said the cow was better than I had recommended her to be. She was worth twenty-seven dollars. He would not take that sum for her. But I refused to take it back, saying I had given my word to the Lord and could not go back upon it. That night at the supper table he laid the two dollars before his wife and asked her to guess where it came from, and when she could not, he informed her and added, "I believe that man is a Christian if there are any, and I am going to hear him preach next Sabbath." So the next Sabbath they came. The meeting was in the town schoolhouse, and before we built our church. They listened attentively. Going home they talked about the sermon. It was excellent, only it was *too personal; it meant them.* Somebody had informed Mr. Bristol of their history, and that sermon was cut out so as to fit their case. But how did he know they were coming to the meeting? The next Sabbath they were there and joined in the singing. They were still more interested in the discourse than the Sabbath previous. The only fault was as before, *too personal*. He certainly meant us this time. Who had told him? Dora, or Azel, or Susan. It was too bad! They would give them a talking to for it. That week they saw Dora and she denied it. Had not spoken with Mr. Bristol in three weeks, except on the Sabbath at church. Then it was Susan sure. She was seen, but in her mild way said, No she had never informed the minister of their history nor any one else. Azel was seen. He smiled and said, "That is characteristic of our minister's preaching. People often go away saying, 'He told my history sure.' " So as they talked about it one evening, Mr. Williams remarked, "I have heard it said that when people are under conviction they imagine the preacher means them in all he says." And then there was a long solemn pause and the conviction came upon them, "God's spirit then *is striving with us*, we are under conviction! Now is our accepted time and this the day of salvation," and before the clock struck twelve they had bowed upon their knees, had opened the door and the Friend of sinners had come in and was supping with them and they with him! Meantime my heart had been greatly moved toward the strangers, and the next day I called upon them and they told the story as I have related it. Rapidly they grew in grace, united with our church, Mr. Williams became leader of our choir, superintendent of our Sabbath school and I believe deacon of our church. Sometimes I had calls from other places, but he used to pray that I might not leave till he was called away. The prayer was answered. Just before I left the Lord called him home. I was with him at his bedside the last half day of his life, saw him crossing the Jordan, and heard him say when well nigh over, "*I am happy!*" "And I say unto you, make to yourselves friends of the mammon of unrighteousness, that when ye fail they may receive you into everlasting habitations." Another incident full of interest to me, yet pathetic and sad in its outcome, occurred in connection with a revival meeting I held in Ripon, a thriving young city adjacent to the village of Dartford.

ALDERMAN BERLIN

One Alderman Berlin, whose home was in the township of Green Lake, and a well to do farmer, was living in Ripon at the time. Being of a literary turn of mind and fond of society he spent his winters in town, boarding at the best hotel. In his rooms were wont to gather, once or twice a week, men of like literary tastes, education and leisure—doctors, lawyers, etc. These meetings were largely for the discussion of topics of interest, and were concluded with wine drinking and feasting. Unfortunately Alderman Berlin was a disbeliever in the

Bible and all revealed religion. As our meeting progressed and not a few professed conversions occurred, some of them being men and women of note and influence, the matter was brought up in this literary circle. In the course of the talk about it, Alderman Berlin remarked that "*the philosophy of a revival*, or of these periodical religious excitements, had never been satisfactorily explained to him. He would like to understand it." Referring to the preacher, he said, "There is Rev. Bristol, carrying on these meetings; he is my neighbor; lives just across the lake. He is a man of education, well informed on all subjects, and a man of good common sense. How is it that he can be carried away with these excitements; and more than that, how can he do so much to promote them? It is a mystery! I propose we investigate it." "Agreed," they all replied; "let us go to the meetings and watch the whole process." So the following evening they all came to church.

Quite a sensation was produced as a score or so of them came filing into the church, led by Mr. Berlin. They gave good attention, and even staid after sermon till the inquiry meeting was half through, and then quietly withdrew, and repaired to their quarters in the hotel. A discussion followed, but the conclusion was that they had not got the clue yet. The discourse was sensible, and admitting that there was a God and that the Bible was His Revelation, the conclusions were irresistible. They would go again. The next night they came in a body and were among my most quiet and gentlemanly hearers. Returning to their rooms they admitted "that was *a very practical discourse!* Would all men live as the preacher exhorted them to do this would be a vastly better world than it is. Such preaching will hurt none of us." They were surprised at the absence of excitement. There was no effort to produce it. The appeals were all to man's conscience, his reason, his common sense. "Surely this is not the kind of revival so often described! Yet what effect that preaching had! How many were moved by it! We will go again." And again they came, and so on for several meetings, the judgment on each occasion being the same substantially.

It happened one evening, during the inquiry meeting, that I went into the back part of the church to encourage a timid inquirer to come forward to the consecration seats. The congregation was standing and singing. Mr. Berlin was in the aisle. I had no thought of asking him to go forward until, as I passed him, an impulse came over me to do so, and with it an appeal whose language I have never been able to recall. Like a flash it came and went, but such was its effect upon him that he took my arm and walked half way down the aisle. Then he held back and said, "This is a great step! Excuse me to-night!" "Mr. Berlin, do you want to be excused from pledging yourself to do anything which is right toward your Creator and your fellow men?" "Let me have till to-morrow night to think about it." "God has given you fifty years to think over the great matter. Have you the heart to ask for *more time* in so plain a matter?" "It is a great step for me to take." "Is there not more danger in *not taking* it?" "Yes, yes, I know it; but you must excuse me for to-night." "But will God excuse you? Will your conscience?"

Well, so we stood in the aisle and reasoned, my heart yearning after him, as once Paul stood and reasoned with trembling Felix, when he said, "Go thy way for this time; when I have a convenient season I will call for thee." He sank down into a side-slip, and slowly I went down the aisle, with longing looks behind, at the seat where my friend sat down. The meeting proceeded, and "they that were ready went into the marriage." The next morning, before the sun was up, a boy came to my boarding place, bearing a letter from Mr. Berlin, and thus it began:

"DEAR FRIEND: Can you forgive me for the sorrow I gave you by not complying with your request last evening? No act of my whole life has ever stung me so deeply! That request so kindly presented, so gently pressed, and prompted I well know by a deep interest in my eternal welfare, how could I refuse to comply? No one ever presented this great matter to me in such a rational light before. No one ever took my arm before and volunteered to go with me to the altars of the Lord, and I cannot forgive myself for the grief it gave you because I did not go," etc., etc. It closed with an invitation to call at his rooms that day. I did so. But his fertile mind had conceived *a plan of delay* from which I could not dissuade him. It was that in the coming summer, after the spring's work was done, he was to hire a man to take my place on my farm, and I was to spend a couple of weeks at his place, and there we would talk over the whole matter, and then he would settle it forever. In vain I argued against delay, its sinfulness and its dangers. He was persistent. He still attended the meetings, was very attentive, and even serious. The proposed discussion of the philosophy of a revival was dropped in the club. Our meeting closed. Over one hundred registered their names as having come over on the Lord's side. But my friend *Alderman Berlin's name was not there!* * * As the last snows of winter were leaving the hillsides and hollows, and I had returned to my home, a messenger drove up to my door with a livery team smoking with swift driving and said, *"Alderman Berlin is dying*, and wishes you to hasten to his bedside." I sprang into the carriage and went with him. When I arrived I found the room full of doctors and nurses and friends, and Mr. Berlin lying across the bed vomiting and purging incessantly, his eyes bloodshot and protruding from their sockets and inexpressible agony in his countenance! Oh, the look he gave me as I entered and took his trembling hand! He would have spoken but the vomiting prevented. I did not say one word and only looked upward as if to say, "Look to God my friend, for none can help you now but him." And then I went back to the window and leaning my brow upon the sash, silently prayed for my dying neighbor. Soon after his understanding failed him, and before twelve o'clock that night the body was dead and the spirit had returned to God who gave it! Where now were those friendly conferences on the great matter of personal religion he had planned to take place in the early summer, in the groves around his rural home? And what had become of those arrogant hopes? His family and friends wished me to preach his funeral sermon, and I did so. But it was a sad service, relieved only by the hope that on his dying bed, like the dying Israelite bitten by the serpent in the wilderness, he had looked to the cross and Him that hung thereon and been forgiven! And Felix said unto Paul, "Go thy way for this time. When I have a convenient season I will call for thee."[42]

THE BOW DRAWN AT VENTURE

Another incident more pleasant in its final result occurred during the progress of a meeting I held in Bluffton. In that revival nearly all the people in that vicinity were either converted or greatly moved. I visited in the daytime and preached in the evening. I was quite successful in visiting from house to house; but especially so in talking with the skeptically inclined. Somehow it became a current saying that in talking with Mr. Bristol it would not do for an infidel *to admit anything*; if he did, no matter what it was, Mr. Bristol would begin at that admission, and by inexorable logic compel the man to admit all the great truths of religion. In the course of a day's visiting, I called upon a family where the husband and wife had agreed that they *would admit nothing*. Mr. Bristol should not catch them. They received me with cold and formal politeness, and then squared off for resistance. After a few commonplace remarks, I observed that we were having some very interesting meetings. "*They say so*," was the reply. "Don't you believe it would be a great blessing in this community, if we should all from this time, begin to love the Lord with all our heart, and our neighbor as ourselves?" "Well, there are different opinions about this. We don't know." "You believe the Bible, don't you?" "Well, sometimes we think it may be true, and sometimes not. Many learned men don't believe it at all, and some do. We don't know who is right." "You believe there is a God, do you not, who made you, and all things so wondrously?" "Don't know what to think, when wiser people than we regard it as an unsettled question, whether these things came of themselves, or whether there was a God who made them—don't know! Half the world reject your God and believe in other Gods, and of the rest, many believe in no God at all. Who knows which is right?" "You believe that you exist, and that these two boys of yours *are real beings*, do you not?" "Well, maybe we exist, and maybe not; it is all guesswork after all!" By this time I saw clearly their intent to admit nothing, and not wishing to have my visit end thus, I remarked to the man, "You and I must be of about the same age." "What is your age?" he asked, and when I gave it he said, "I too was born in the same year. Was your father a minister?" he asked. "No, he was not even a professor, was your father?" "Yes," said he, "he was a Methodist presiding elder." I bade them pleasantly a good-afternoon, and went on my way with the prayer in my heart, that on some future occasion I might be more successful. When I was out of hearing the man remarked to his wife, "There, he did not catch us, did he?" She gave a cold and reluctant assent and sat pensive, looking out of the window, as if she felt that they had small cause for congratulation over a victory obtained at the expense of denying the Bible, the being of God and their own existence too, and that of their dear boys also! Had it come to this! And all to get rid of conversion, of Christ, and of Heaven! For a few moments they sat in silence and then the man went out to the barn, and thus he mused as he went: "That man and I are of the same age substantially, but what a difference there is between us! He is a Christian, a preacher of the Gospel, and the blessings of many ready to perish is coming upon him! But I—what have I done; not yet given my heart to God. Not one soul was ever led to Christ by me. Many have been kept away! No doubt my wife had long since been converted but I stood in the way. Even now I can see her heart is yearning after the pearl of great price. And those dear boys are held back from salvation by their father's words and example. My father has prayed much for me and have many others, but I have resisted them all, and to-day when the man of God called to win me to the Lord he loves, I braced myself against him and denied truths plainer than the sun in the heavens! I made myself a fool in his eyes and in mine own too! *I lied to him! Yes, that is the word, I lied!* He knew it, and God knew it, and I knew it also!" When he reached the stable the horses turned and looked wildly at him as if they feared the coming of a man so wicked! He tried to pray but could not say a word; his mouth was shut, the heavens were brass, as if God had risen up and shut the door and said, *"Not one word from you!"* He staggered back to the house and said, "Wife, get ready, you and the children. I am going to meeting to-night." And when I reached the schoolhouse where our meetings were held, there they were, husband, wife and their boys, all sitting on the lowest seat before the desk, all with faces covered with handkerchiefs, sobbing and waiting for some one to come to pray for them, whose words God would hear. before the close of that evening's meeting they were rejoicing in hope of the glory of God. At a subsequent experience meeting they told the story as I have rehearsed it. "And a certain man drew a bow at venture and it smote the king between the joints of the harness." "In the morning sow thy seed and in the evening withhold not thy hand for thou knowest not which shall prosper, whether this or that, or whether they both shall be alike good."

ATTEMPT TO BREAK UP A MEETING UNSUCCESSFUL

The best of order always attended my preaching; save only in one case was ever an attempt at disturbance made. A scandalous affair transpired near one of my places of preaching in Green Lake township. It had long and odious ventilation in the courts, and finally the unfortunate young woman in the affair, the victim of outrageous perfidy and treachery, was defeated, through the perjuries and combination of a large number of young roughs who abounded in that vicinity. the rascals escaped and gloried in their shame. About that time I preached a sermon there on the text, *"their feet shall slide in due time!"*[43]

I did not know that the principal perpetrator was there. Indeed, I did not know him. But he said and others, too, that in the warmth of my denunciation of such crimes as his, I turned toward him, shook my finger in his face and poured vials of wrath upon him without measure. That I said in effect, "Take care, young man! Your day is coming! Justice is on your track, and will take you to another court! There, there is no quibbling.

"Not a fact can be withheld. No false testimony will be heard. The pit will open before you and 'Your feet will slide in due time!' "

It did not even occur to me that he was there, or that I had offended any one. It was an imaginary young man I had in mind. The next time I went to preach there, I saw an immense crowd gathered about the house, horses and teams three or four times the usual number hitched to the trees and fences. Some influential and noted person must have died! Who could it be? This is a funeral gathering! What shall I preach? Slowly I drove up, gathering my thoughts about a funeral discourse. Hitching my horse several men came out to me, and told me the cause of the gathering, said the excitement was great, the roughs had taken possession of the house; that it was not safe for me to go in, etc. I smiled and said, If that was all, I would go in. And so I went in, followed by my friends and all who could find standing room there.

Omitting singing—a few words of prayer—I commenced my discourse, standing on the front edge of the platform, almost within reach of the foremost of the roughs. I don't think I looked or spoke as if I was much afraid of them. For some five minutes they were restive and then one blurted out, "That's a d—— d lie!" I paused, looked at him in the eye till he turned this way and that uneasily. Then I repeated the remark and went on a little and then another said, "That is a lie." I now said in strong voice, "It is evident there are persons here who have come to break up this meeting! To prevent us from worshiping God according to the dictates of our judgment and conscience. And I propose to stop right here and settle the question once for all—whether law and order reigns in this part of Green Lake, or whether a mob rules us. I am about to put the matter to vote, and I want you all to stand by your colors like men and women too. The law of the land, the law we have all pledged ourselves to support, guarantees to us the right of religious worship, and denounces punishments against those who disturb such worship. Do you mean to defend them? Will you allow a few roughs to trample on them here, and on you all? If I mistake not, you will not.

"I now ask all in this house, who *do not believe* in the right of religious worship guaranteed by the laws of Wisconsin and who *mean to-day to trample them under foot*, to raise their hands!" Three or four hands were raised, but quickly taken down. "Hold them up, young men," I said. "Don't take them down so quick. I want to show you to the people. They want to know who you are.

"Only three or four that sustain these disturbances of our meeting? If there is one more, lift your hand! For three or four is a contemptible minority in such a crowd as this!" No more hands being raised, I said, "Now I am going to call for the vote on the other side.

"Those who believe in the right of undisturbed religious worship, and in these State laws referred to, and are determined to maintain them, peaceably, if they can, and forcibly, if they must, will now rise to your feet and those standing lift your hands!" And at that the whole congregation rose, save only the three, and those standing, raised high their hands!

After the vote was taken, I admonished these young men to show a decent respect for that vote. I then recommenced my discourse, and went through without interruption.

My meetings there were never after disturbed. Going home that evening, three of these young men went before me and made a fence across the road! I saw the obstruction and them some twenty rods distant, and walked my horse slowly as I approached it. Seeing a low spot I drove over it and the wheels knocked down the rails and I passed on. Two stood on one side and one on the other, but they did not venture to attack me. I had one hand in an overcoat pocket, and possibly they thought it had hold of something there!

NARROW ESCAPE FROM DROWNING

Having an evening appointment across Green Lake, in the spring of the year, I attempted to cross over on the ice. Borrowing a pair of skates I endeavored to go straight across. Reaching the middle of the lake, I found a crack and open water some ten feet wide, extending nearly the whole length of the lake. I was obliged to go down to the inlet some three miles distant to get round it. This made me late. It began to grow dark as I went up near the south shore. I passed several air-holes, and fearing I should fall into one as I skated in the dark, I picked up a fish pole lying upon the ice and ran it forward of me. I was skating rapidly when suddenly my pole dropped off the ice into the water, and I whirled upon my skates and made for shore, and walked the rest of the way.

The next morning returning, I went to the place where the pole slipped from my hand and went down, and lo, the scratch of my skate within perhaps five inches of the slippery edge! Had I plunged in, I should probably have *come up under the ice!* and had I not, it would have been difficult to have got out with skates on, and had I succeeded in this latter, with my wet clothes on, I should probably have been frozen to death before I could have reached the nearest house, as it was bitterly cold that night. This instance of imminent peril does not stand alone in the history of my life. Twenty others or more, of like perils have been safely passed through. Yet I have never had a bone broken, or a limb disjointed.

"The Angel of the Lord encampeth round them that fear him, and delivereth them."

Living on the borders of Green Lake, one of the most beautiful sheets of water in Wisconsin, I had occasional visits from work-worn ministers, in need of a vacation, and whose slender salaries did not admit of travel or a resort to expensive watering places. Those visits and the privilege of hospitality I greatly enjoyed. Was it not a gentle way of ministering to the disciples of the Lord? But there was one drawback.

Staying with me over the Sabbath, they would naturally expect me to invite them to preach for me. They would consent though weary, lest they should seem ungrateful for the hospitality. On the other hand, I always had a sermon in mind, which I longed to preach to my people. "And the word of the Lord was as fire shut up in my bones." It was a great relief to preach these messages as I received them. Perhaps this resulted from having nearly all the time a state of revival in some one of my fields, inquiring souls to be led to Christ, and lambs of the flock to be fed and nourished. Under these circumstances, I had often to apologize for a seeming want of politeness in not inviting them to preach.

On one occasion a city pastor spent a Sabbath with me. Learning the condition of my people, he positively refused to preach, but went the Sabbath-day rounds with me. He was struck with the solemn attention given, and the teardrops which ran down many a cheek. When I went down from the pulpit they gathered around me and told of the struggles of so and so, the new hopes of another, the conviction of a third, etc., etc. Such a one wished to be prayed for.

Then we hastened on ten miles to the second service. Then five miles further to a five o'clock appointment in a large schoolhouse in a grove. Farm wagons were all around, and teams tied to the trees. The house was full and we had scarce room to sit down, for the platform and aisles were filled. I presume we looked tired, and so the whole audience broke forth in song-singing:

> "There is rest for the weary,
> There is rest for the weary,
> On the other side of Jordan,
> In the sweet fields of Eden,
> There is rest for the weary,
> There is rest for you."

This spontaneous exhibition of Christian sympathy greatly affected my visitor, and he wept. I was used to it. The country minister gets very close to the hearts of his people; no conventionalities hold him off at a distance.

On our way home my city brother seemed sad, and said little. I asked the cause. He replied, "I have been thinking of the *poor pay* I get for preaching."

Why, said I, I thought you had a fine salary, of ———— hundred dollars and promptly paid! "Ah, yes," he said "*in money!* But, brother, *money never can pay for the heart work* of preaching. Nothing pays for that but such pay as I have seen you receive to-day. We must have 'souls for our hire, or we get nothing!' "

Never after that did I repine because my salary was small, or envy the large stipend of the city minister, while the joy of seeing souls converted was mine, and though poor I seemed to be making many rich. To the young man about to enter the ministry, and choose his field, I commend this remark of the city clergyman, that nothing pays for preaching the gospel but salvation and life attending the Word.

The labors in the midst of which these scenes transpired stretched over a period of ten years or thereabouts. They cover the prime of my life. Unnoted and unknown it was to the general public. But souls were there, and their Redeemer, too! Not large were my audiences, but we had audience with God. My salary was meager, but yet my bread was given and my water made sure, and the discipline of faith and patience there was beyond all price! And here again let me say to young men looking for fields of clerical labor — don't be afraid of frontier work — of going as Paul did, where Christ was not preached, or where, as the colored sage expressed it, "Der am little money and much Debil." Nor hesitate to sit down in a low place till another bid thee go up higher. I once heard President Mahan say, "I thank the Lord he will let me work *anywhere.*"

During these ten years *twenty-one distinct revival* meetings were held by me — where I did the preaching. In these from ten to 100 or more were hopefully born of the Spirit in each of them. While in California and praying for a restoration of nervous health and vigor, I often fixed upon *ten years*, and asked that God would give me that length of time for gospel work! Singularly, as this period became well nigh spent, the old brain trouble began to return in force. Sleep departed from me. Nervous action became spasmodic and unreliable. The long winter campaign through which I wrought in season and out of season — not counting my life dear to myself — had at last broken down sadly the mental machinery.

Some changes must be resorted to. A call coming from Elmwood, Ill., I went down there and preached a couple of years. Each winter we had a revival in our church, and one of the winters I aided Bro. J.M. Williams — my old classmate — in a revival of marked power in his church in Farmington, Ill. But I was scarcely myself there. The troubles of nerve and brain were constant and increasing, and called for a halt. So I resigned and went back to Wisconsin, and to my old home.

16

ACROSS THE PLAINS TO OREGON

A few months of rest at Dartford did me little good. I suffered from sick headache about one-third of the time, and the average of sleep was not more than one night in three. I needed not only physical exercise but change—something to get the mind out of the old ruts, the grooves it had worn so deep. Then came the happy thought of *a trip across the plains*, with covered wagon drawn by oxen or horses, and plodding along for six months, with little opportunity for reading books or mental exercise, and an abundance of calls for muscular employment. Very opportune for my plans was the discovery of the "Salmon River mines."[44] Quite a number of neighbors were eager to form a company and go together over the plains. Some time in March, I think it was, that three four-horse wagons, covered with white canvas, filed through the streets of Ripon, each having a complement of four men, all well known and substantial citizens, and bound for the Pacific coast. A large crowd gathered around us to bid us good-bye and pour upon us showers of good wishes and hopes of success and a safe return. Some one of the crowd wrote in large letters on the wagon I was in, "Capt. Bristol's Train." I don't know who it was, but our good-natured company of twelve accepted the suggestion, and so called me Captain after that. My messmates were Deacon Bainan, McKinnon, and Principal Walcott, the latter long time the head of the Ripon Academy and embryo college. Our course from Ripon to the great midland plains was via Madison, Galena, Des Moines and Omaha.

At Council Bluffs[45] we laid in our supplies for a journey of two thousand miles, and which was to occupy the following six months and more. From Omaha we proceeded up the Platte River, on the north side. Several other emigrant teams falling in with us we organized a company. I was unanimously chosen Captain. I did not relish the office, on account of its care and responsibility, for I wanted rest and freedom from care; but I accepted, chiefly because it would enable me to secure *the keeping of the Sabbath.*

Encamping on the Loup Fork one evening we heard a din of doleful voices, proceeding from the tepees, or tents of buffalo hides, occupied by a band of *Pawnees* near by. Our sympathies were excited, and a man and I went over to see what was the matter. Some of them could talk English, and they told us with artless simplicity, how that some weeks before they heard that a band of adjacent Sioux Indians had gone on a buffalo hunt, leaving large numbers of ponies, their wives and children, in a defenceless condition. This was too good an opportunity to rob and to kill to be neglected; so a band of their young braves, like young eagles, made haste for the prey. Alas for Indian sagacity and rapacity in this case! The young Pawnees met the Sioux on the border, were defeated, some of them slain, and the remainder put to ignominious flight! Hence these tears, these ululations which had aroused our pity. My companion and I went back to our camp much less inclined to weep than when on our way to visit them. Years afterward—some eight or ten—when Miss "Bright Eyes," the Pawnee Indian girl,[46] was moving Boston audiences by her tales of wrongs done by white people to long-suffering Pawnees and other Indian tribes, this scene came up very vividly before me.

FROM FORT LARAMIE TO FORT HALL

Arrived at Fort Laramie I resigned my captaincy and another was chosen; but after two days of service my successor resigned and I was re-elected. Leaving the Platte, we went up the Sweetwater. In our way we were met by fugitives fleeing toward the settlements from Indian raids[47] all along the overland stage route. They had stopped the stages, killed the passengers and drivers, robbed and burned the stations, and had driven off the relays of horses and mules. We met soldiers rushing away in fear, and their officers commanded us to retreat also. We heard their stories and went on. One day we came up with a fine-looking train, whose animals, like ours, were nearly all horses or mules, and which traveled at about the same gait. We camped together that night beside a small lake. There was a proposition to join forces. The captains of both trains resigned, and the companies resolved to become one train and to choose a captain. I was again re-elected, almost unanimously. I made them a brief address in which I outlined my policy as to guarding stock, compactness in traveling, defense of the corral, settlements of quarrels, treatment of friendly Indians, and keeping the Sabbath. It apparently gave good satisfaction, and if any hesitated in assenting to the new *regime*, they were quite won over the next day, when they saw me take a horse, about midafternoon, and riding ahead out of sight, select a fine camp, where was water and grass, and a good place for defence.

This was my usual custom, and I generally went alone. The danger was often great, and I feared to send another, who might not be as good a shot as myself, or as quick to discover danger and avoid it. My company used to congratulate themselves on the excellent camps I selected. These were in striking contrast with those of other trains, which often tied up to the sage bushes, with no water or grass for the stock, their captains, none of them, daring to take the risks I ran daily. One evening, not twenty rods from our camp, I found a *fresh dug grave!* A rough board at its head informed us that there the Indians had attacked their train, killed several, and that *two women and their children had been captured and carried off!* This sad writing was dated *the day before!* Our men rested uneasily that night. Few of us slept. We were thinking of the sad fate of *those wives and children!* The Fourth of July we were at Fort Bridger,[48] near the source of the Sweetwater. Our boys celebrated the day by throwing snowballs at each other from a bank of snow on the slope. I called on Capt. Bridger, the first officer of the Fort, and consulted him about our route to Fort Hall. At first he said, "Don't go; the Indians are bad." Seeing I was bent on going, he asked, "How many *men* have you?" I replied, "Sixty or seventy." Eyeing me sharply, he asked with emphasis, "How many MEN have you?" I saw his meaning and replied, "I think some twenty-five or thirty will fight to the death." "Well," said he, "if you are correct you can go through." Taking down his maps and charts he traced out our course to the "Lauder's Cut-off" trail, and thence to Fort Hall, adding, as he pointed to this place and that on the route, "Take care *there!* I had a battle at that place and lost so many, or killed so many; and there I was waylaid and attacked by so many hostiles." The old Indian warrior was delighted to see men of pluck.

THE SOUTH PASS

Following up the Sweetwater to its sources we entered the celebrated South Pass, the gateway through the Rocky Mountains. We had been looking forward to this pass, and our journey through it, as an event in travel never to be forgotten. Well, we entered it, and were nearly through it before any of us were aware of it! True it was, the streams we crossed no more flowed eastward, but west; but the significance of that fact had not been appreciated, and we little knew that we were passing into a new order of things. The Sweetwater we had just left we were to see no more! Its waters would flow into the Platte, the Platte into the Missouri, the Missouri into the Mississippi, the

Mississippi into the Gulf of Mexico, and that into the Atlantic Ocean! On the other hand, these westward-flowing brooks would flow into Green River, Green River into the Colorado, the Colorado into the Gulf of California, and that into the Pacific! How near their beginnings; how wide apart their destination! The South Pass, instead of being a narrow gateway between lofty cliffs, crowding upon us from either side, was a plain wide enough for vast armies to pass through—a highway for nations, I judge it to be, from ten to twenty miles wide; and but for some one to tell them, not one in ten of our company would have dreamed of the passage till it was over! Even so do most of our race pass through the great moral crises of life, which determine their everlasting future, quite unaware of it at the time!

Descending gradually westward, we came down upon the east branch of Green River. It was about the 12th of July, and this river overflowed all its banks. It was, where we struck it, from twenty-five to fifty rods wide. It was too deep to be forded; the current was swift, and the waters very cold. All around us were snowclad peaks, and we passed over drifts in valleys perhaps twenty feet deep. How should we cross this river? Our plan was quickly formed and executed too. I selected a committee of experts, examined all our wagon-beds, selected two of the tightest and best made, took them off the axles, caulked them as tight as possible, and otherwise made them fit for boating, and put them into the water. The next morning they were soaked tight. We crossed the river with the earliest light, and the landing place was selected. A wagon was taken in pieces and put in one boat, and its baggage put in the other, and rowed over. Men were there to put it up by the time another could cross; and so it came to pass that nearly forty wagons were taken over that day. The horses were forced into the cold river and obliged to swim over. The next day we were on our way. At the second branch we found a ferry boat. I bought it, took my train over, and sold it for five dollars less to the train behind.

AN EFFORT TO BREAK UP OUR SABBATH-KEEPING CUSTOM

There was a man from Iowa, a Dr. Jones, who had fallen into our company on the way, who disliked Sabbath keeping and all religion. He was a restless, nervous, Democratic politician of the Vallandigham stripe,[49] opposed to Lincoln, to abolition and the war, and was intensely dissatisfied with the Republicans of Iowa. The reason for leaving his own train and joining ours was, I believe, the better time we were making, the better camps, and better discipline and order maintained. Soon after joining us he began to vent his spleen against the Abolitionists and the "Puritan captain;" but he made no sensible progress till we reached the third fork of Green River. Coming to it Saturday night, we camped there for the Sabbath. Mosquitoes swarmed in all the air, and we all suffered more or less from them. This was a devil-send to him, and he improved it. From Sabbath morn till Sabbath noon he went from tent to tent, bearing a petition to the Captain to lift our tents and move out of this horrible place. By noon he had got a large majority of the names affixed to his petition, and came bringing it to me. I called a meeting and all came together. Dr. Jones read his petition and made a speech, and closed by saying we had to go only six miles to get rid of the pests, and triumphantly introduced a man who had been over into a nook in the mountains six miles off, on our route, and *he saw no mosquitoes there!*

Of course I knew the main object was to get us to break the Sabbath *that day, and then make it a precedent* for Sabbath traveling ever after. I answered him saying I was ever ready to travel on the Sabbath when necessity required it. The mosquitoes were very bad, I knew, but there was no prospect of bettering our condition in that respect by going over yonder. I then turned to his witness and asked, "Are you not the man who about eight o'clock went up yonder hill with a rifle?" "Yes." "Did you not go along the skirts of yonder hills?" "Yes." "Well, sir, I was where I could see you till your return down yonder divide. *You never went over to the nook in the mountains the Doctor speaks of.* You did not go two miles from camp." "Well," said he, "*I could look over there,* and I did not see any!" "Could not see any! That valley is *six miles off;* and did you suppose there were none because you *could not see them four miles off?*" An outburst of laughter followed. Dr. Jones called for a vote. As I was about to put it, some one said, "If we vote to roll out, I suppose you will go along with us, Captain?" "Oh, no," said I. "I don't go when the reason for this action is so transparent." There was a sensation, a rapid exchange of words, such as, "Then I wont go," and, "I wont," and, "That alters the case," when one said, "I move this matter be indefinitely postponed," and that vote was carried almost unanimously, and that was the last attempt to induce our train, like the others, to travel on the Lord's Day.

SIX RETURNING MINERS KILLED

One evening we were met by eight miners returning homeward to the States. Each had two mules; one he rode, the other carried his clothes, provisions, blankets, and perhaps his gold. We invited them to share the hospitalities of our camp. They staid with us over night and gave us much valuable information, as to our route and the mines.

They were fine fellows. They left us early the next morning. As my train was about to start, I took my station as usual some distance ahead, holding the foremost back till the last wagon was in line, for I never allowed my train to stretch out in unreasonable length. Hence no straglers were captured from our train. While waiting and looking over the adjacent hills, I discovered the upper half of an Indian's head looking down upon us. Looking steadily at it, it slowly sunk down like that of a partridge till it was out of sight. I knew what was up. So bidding the train move on, I stood still, gun in hand, and as each wagon passed me I called out one of its armed men and when the last went by, I had about forty at my side. The Indians finding they were discovered soon appeared on their ponies and rode back and forth on the hillside at the top of their speed. They made threatening gestures but were careful to keep out of reach of our rifle balls. They ransacked our camp ground for plunder, and the last we saw of them they were taking our back track, and making haste to overtake the eight miners who had left us half an hour before. We knew they would be overtaken, and probably all be slain!

And so it proved in the case of all but two, and they lost everything but life. Some half a dozen miles distant they were overtaken. Seeing some thirty or forty Indians in hot pursuit, the miners dismounted and standing behind their animals fought like heroes for two or three hours, till six of the eight were killed, and I believe all their animals. One of them, a Mr. Parmalee from Illinois, when dying said to his comrade, "Tom, I am dying. Load my rifle for me, and level it across my dead mule. Then run and save yourself. May be the Indians will rush up for booty, and I can kill one more of these robbers before I die!" Tom did so, and as he was running through the sage brush, he heard the crack of the well known rifle and looking back he saw consternation among the Indians, and concluded Parmelee had been as good as his word.

While this unequal battle was going on, there came upon the scene a train of from thirty to fifty men. They rushed to the top of a hill near by, corraled, and looked on and never lifted a finger to help the beleaguered miners! "A sally of half a dozen of them," said Johnson, one of the escaped men to me, "would have saved most of us." What a crime it is sometimes to yield to coward fear! "And the fearful," etc., "shall have their part in the lake of fire, etc." I will add, that no sooner was this disgraceful cowardice known abroad than the burst of indignation was such all along the line, that the said train broke up and its members made haste to hide themselves in other trains.

A STAMPEDE

Just before reaching Fort Hall,[50] we overtook a train and camped near by it. It was Saturday evening and I invited them to stay with us over Sabbath and attend the preaching service, which I held in our corral every Sabbath. They partly agreed to do so. But when the morning came, they moved on as usual. They had not proceeded far, before an unaccountable panic seized upon nearly every animal in the train. It was the noted *"stampede,"* so often spoken of by travelers in connection with migrations across the Western plains. To describe one, is to describe all.

That Sabbath morning was one of unusual quiet. Scarce a leaf was disturbed by the breeze. The path skirted along the border of a marsh, in the center of which was a shallow lake. The teams were mainly made up of several yoke of oxen and cows. They were nearly all lame and footsore and lean too, from incessant travel over a thousand miles of desert. Tired out and stupid, they little cared for the crack of the resounding bull-whip, or the sharp goad carried by some of the drivers; mechanically they moved on with slow and measured step, as if all sensibility and life had departed from them!

In an instant all this was changed! An uncontrollable frenzy had seized every animal in the train. His dull eye now glared like a fire ball and protruded from its socket! With a moan which ran over all the notes, and lugubrious and startling beyond description, the poor creatures leaped into the air, and rushed headlong and reckless to right or left against trees or rocks. In some cases the leaders vaulted into covered wagons filled with women and children, and others became hopelessly wedged together. And the din of crushing wagons, the looing of the frantic beasts, the shrieks of women and children, the crack of the whip, and the oaths of the excited drivers combined to create a scene wild beyond description.

In this case, in addition to the wounded, one woman and a child were killed outright, and we passed their fresh dug graves on Monday morning. The cause of the stampede, who can tell! It reminds the looker-on of a scene described in the New Testament, which occurred in Gadara, where "the devils entering the herd of swine, threw them headlong down the steep and they perished in the waters." But I take it, that at first the smell of blood, or something like it, excites one animal to utter his startling moan. This excites all the rest, and they moan also, and the bedlam of these wild bellowings does all the rest, for it is enough to waken the dead and kill the living.

FORT HALL AND CROSSING THE PORTENEUF

At length we reached Fort Hall, which is no fort, and never was, in any American sense. It used to be a French or English trading post simply. Here we first came upon the Snake River, the great southern fork of the Columbia. A dozen miles west of it the trail crossed a deep but sluggish stream called the Porteneuf. There was no way of crossing except by a small ferry boat. Between this ferry and Fort Hall lay scattered along the trail perhaps a dozen trains, waiting their turn to be ferried across. None of them lifted a finger to help the wornout ferrymen who had been working night and day for weeks, but lounged about, played ball or cards, drank whiskey, etc. I rode forward to the ferryman to learn when we could cross over. He was cross as a bear and hardly gave me a civil answer. "Somewhere from a week to ten days," was all I could get out of him. Seeing how it was, I resolved on a little strategy. Riding back I ordered the train to hitch up and follow me. Passing one camp after another each called out, "No use in going ahead, you can't cross till we do. We are booked before you!"

But we went on till we reached the river and camped hard by the ferry. The horses put to pasture, I took half a dozen of my most robust and willing men and we went down to the ferry. We watched the ways of managing the boat, the putting on of freight, wagons and horses, and when we thought we "knew the ropes," I stepped aboard and said, "Captain! take a rest, you and your men; let us try our hand a turn. Give your orders, Captain, and we will do the work." They lay down, poor wearied men, and we went at the work with a will. How the boat spun through the water. How quickly the wagons were trundled on board, and the quick trips made them stare! The captain's rigid face began to relax. He inquired what was the name of my train and when told, asked, "And is that the *abolition* train so much spoken against?" I said "Very likely. We are all free men ourselves and we like to see others free, too. "I see! I see!" said he with a smile. Taking me aside he whispered, "Get your train down here and this afternoon we will put you over." I did so, and before dark, my whole train was over and ready to start out the next morning. "That is the finest company of men and horses," said the captain, "which has crossed the river this season," and when I asked him to count our wagons he refused and left it all to me. Thus by this maneuver we saved a week's delay at least. There is nothing lost, in the long run, by being generous and helpful to men in need, even if they are strangers and we never expect to meet them again.

DOWN THE SNAKE RIVER

The Snake River is tortuous as a snake's path in its course, and hence its name. It runs through a vast sage brush plain so destitute of forage and trees that scarce a Jack rabbit can find pasture and where a sage hen is rarely seen. In journeying down it on the south and west side we could only find feed for our hungry animals once in fifteen or twenty miles, when we came to small creeks on their way to the river. No buffalo or wild horses are found here. Now and then a deer or antelope is seen and half-starved wolves in hot pursuit. At one of these creeks our train and another spent a couple days. I went some distance down the brook, fishing for trout. A one-armed man not of my company went along, too, and went farther than I did. That night he did not come back! The next day his brother and some others went after him. They found his tracks and those of Indians, too, and saw where they had captured him and led him to the Snake River, where they crossed over, and they had to give him up! Poor one armed traveler over the plains! He was never heard of afterward. "The Indian knows his resting place!"

A SWARM OF WINGED ANTS

Not far from this stream, Goose Creek, we encountered a great cloud of winged ants. Several of us were on horseback just ahead of the train, when we saw beyond us, and stretching across our path, what seemed a layer of mist or a foggy wreath. It was perhaps forty rods long, thirty feet in height, and perhaps ten rods through. What could it be? Was it dust or fog or smoke? While we were philosophizing we came against it, or it struck us, and then we knew. *It was a cloud of flying ants.* As they swept against us the whole train stopped. The horses snorted, thrust their noses down between their knees to brush them from their nostrils. Hundreds dashed against my face at a time. We could not open an eye nor see an inch before us. The air was hot and sickening. We plied our whips and spurs to our crazy horses, and holding our breath dashed headlong forward some ten or twelve rods, when we were through them. Had that swarm been a quarter of a mile thick, I suspect nearly every man and horse would have died. To say nothing about their picking our bones, we could not have endured *that hot and intensely ant-scented air.* The heat, I supposed, was from their breath and the warmth of their bodies. Whether such swarms of flying ants are common in this part of the plain I know not. I think I once read an account of something like this, just where, I cannot at this moment call to mind. But it made me think of the swarms of flies which filled all the air of Egypt, and appreciate the plague as never before.[51]

A CASE OF DISCIPLINE

"The course of true love does not always run smooth." This was illustrated in my train one morning near this time. It shows also *the stern decision* the chief officer of a train is sometimes obliged to exercise. As we were about to break camp one morning two men came to me with the complaint that their partner had refused to hitch his horses to the wagon, was packing his *own* baggage upon them, and about to leave his partners behind. I went at once and personally arrested him as he was about to proceed. He was mad and drew a revolver, but I had mine and demanded an explanation. From the testimony it came out that the three men were from Beaver Dam, Wis. That there they had agreed to go to the mines together. One was to furnish the wagon, another the supplies, and the third the team. Up to this time each had fulfilled his part, but here our man of the horses broke his engagement, and swore he would leave the wagon and proceed with his horses. I reasoned with him; showed him that as a man he should stand by his engagement. To break it here meant the death of his two partners, unless others were more merciful then he. And finally I told him I was bound to see to it that the contracts made at home, so vital now, should be carried out here! He said I had no legal authority over him, and that he should do as he had a mind to. I said, "We shall see! Unpack your horses at once and hitch them to the wagon!" He raised his revolver and dared any one to lay a hand on his horses. I ordered every man to draw his weapon and sixty revolvers came forth quick. "Now stand away from him!" The clicking of revolvers being cocked, made one's hair stand on end. "Who will lay a hand on my horses?" said he. "I will," I replied, "if no one else will. Stop your threatening and unpack your horses. I give you just five minutes to decide whether you will do it. Every man level his pistol upon him, and if he raises his weapon fire on him!" Instantly he was covered by some sixty pistols. "Can I speak to Mr. So and So?" he asked. "Yes, but do your talking quick; this train is not going to be stopped very long by such conduct as this." The man went to him. In a whisper he asked: "Do you suppose they will shoot me if I resist?" The reply was: "Yes, they will put *sixty balls through you!* They will do it sure." These were several too many, and he threw down his weapon in disgust upon the ground and unpacked his horses, and we helped him put them into the wagon. I left him with the remark, "See to it that this foolishness is not repeated again in this train!" Some days after while walking with him alone, he used some such language as this: "Captain, in general, I think I am an average man, but every now and then the devil gets into me and I am the biggest fool out. That is just what I was the other day. Now I want to ask you, as a favor, to take my money when I am in the mines, as fast as I get $50 and send it to my wife before I spend it in one of these fits of folly." Well, I partly agreed to do so, and from that time and for two years, we were warm friends. And when I returned some two years after I brought to Wisconsin $200, which I sent to his wife in Beaver Dam.

An ounce of prompt and resolute decision is often worth a ton of vacillation and palaver.

MASSACRE OF THE IOWA CITY TRAIN

As we proceeded down the river, a terrible massacre of a train from Iowa City was perpetrated by these worse than Bedouin Arabs. When attacked they were five or six miles ahead of us. The train consisted of twelve to twenty wagons, and was commanded by a Capt. Adams. He was, perhaps, the first one killed, the Indians coming upon either side and killing him almost instantly. His wagon arrested, the rest were obliged to stop and an attack was made on every wagon by some 200 hostiles. Many fled in to the sage brush and escaped. Some fifteen were killed or wounded. The Indians took all the horses, from sixty to seventy, and robbed the wagons of all their valuables. Captain Kennedy's train coming up, drove the Indians away, and picked up the fugitives. The only horse saved was rescued from an Indian by one of my train named Hank Humphrey, a powerful man, who happened to be ahead and witnessed the attack. An Indian mounting a large iron-gray horse belonging to the train had some difficulty in managing him, when Hank seized the horse and dismounted the Indian, who ran away.

Hank vaulted upon his back and at full speed hastened to inform our train, which he did in perhaps forty minutes. He also informed Captain Kennedy's train, as he flew past it, of what was going on.

In ten minutes my train was moving forward with all possible speed, and a company of sharpshooters struck off to the left to cut off their retreat to the mountains. But the Kennedy train really resuced them, and when we struck the Indians' trail they had passed and were beyond our reach.

Coming back to the road just where the attack was made, our animals were so tired we could not proceed and had to stop right there, though there was little forage. We expected an attack that night. I put the camp in order, and, with Ives our famous hunter, stationed ourselves in a nest of rocks which commanded the ravine down which they were expected to come. We thought it quite likely we should be killed, but hoped so to demoralize them by vigorous defence of our castle as to save our train. But the long night passed, and no attack.

The next morning was the Sabbath, and for once we hitched up and drove forward five miles to where there was grass and water, and where lay our dead and wounded fellow-travelers. We at once undertook our share of the work burying the dead, caring for the wounded, providing places for the fugitives in the trains, and furnishing them with provisions and clothing.

About noon several of the horses of the robbed train were artfully led out upon a hillside in full view and appeared to be loose and feeding at leisure. Captain Kennedy came and proposed we should go out and drive them in. I objected, saying it was a ruse of the Indians to get us out there to shoot us from their ambuscades. That each horse, no doubt, had a lasso attached to his foot, and an Indian was crawling after him and when we came nigh would shoot us, then mount and run away. But Captain Kennedy would go, and told others Bristol was a coward. In an hour or two he sent to me saying he had fallen into an ambush, was badly wounded, and wished me to come to his rescue. I did so, but they fled at our approach. Captain Kennedy was brought off, but two of his men were left dead in the sage brush. I tried to find them but could not.

Returning I found we had twenty-one on hand killed or wounded. Two of them were women. How hard it was for me to persuade the wives of the men left in the field not to insist on our going back to recover their bodies, as in that case we should probably lose more men. Captain Kennedy's wound was at first considered mortal, as it struck him in the abdomen and came out behind, near the backbone, and was supposed to have passed through the intestines. It afterward proved to have gone around in the muscles, and after a week or so he was able to be carried along.

For various reasons his train had lost all confidence in their officers, and, on the other hand, had unwarranted confidence in our train. They proposed to disband and join us. I objected, as it would make a body too unwieldy. At their earnest request we agreed to keep near them in our travel and camp by them for a time. This came from my going miles ahead of my train each afternoon to find it.

Now and then a grumbler would criticise my camps and I had plenty of friends to inform me of it. But I took no notice of it till the next afternoon, when I would ride up to the complainer's wagon, and calling him out would say: "Here, take this horse and ride forward and select our camp to-night. I am tired and you must go. Be careful, select a good camp, you know our people are critical. Remember the essentials—good water, grass, wood, and a defensible camp. Now go ahead and don't let the grass grow under your horse's feet until you have found it." "No, captain, I cannot select one. Send some one else." "No, you must go. A man who can criticise a poor camp should be able to select a better one. Go ahead, you have no time to lose." Now it is not every fool who can select a good camp, especially where few or none are to be found. In nine cases out of ten our novice and fault finder made an ignominious blunder, and when I formed the corral and gave out the orders for the night, I usually added in such cases, "The train is indebted to Mr. So and So for the selection of this camp," and if a bad one he did not soon hear the last of it. I found this a potent method for suppressing unreasonable criticisms, and one application was sufficient. This was much better than an altercation, and my company loudly applauded my course.

THE MIDNIGHT ATTACK AT ROCK CREEK

Still following down the left bank of the Snake River we came to Rock Creek. Going ahead of my train in search of a camp I observed in the trail fresh tracks of Indians, also making for Rock Creek. They were but a few hours ahead of us. I went cautiously forward till I came to it. It ran in a deep canyon. Finding a path down into it, I camped there. My suspicion of trouble at hand led me to look over the ground very carefully and determine what to do in case of an attack. When the time came to set the guards, I went to Ives, our famous hunter, and said: "Ives, I have a place for you to-night, I expect an attack before morning." "All right," he answered, and chose as his comrade for the night watch one John Henley, a young lawyer from Iowa City. I located them and returned to camp.

About 12 o'clock as I lay half asleep, my ear on the ground, I was aroused by a faint cry for help coming up from the canyon. Springing to my feet I seized my gun and rushed out to the guards who patroled the corral, and demanded whence that cry? The guard had heard none. Being at the end of his beat, another guard came up; he, too, had heard no cry of distress. I was sure somebody was in trouble. While we talked another faint cry came up the trail. We hastened down. It was dark as Egypt, and one of the guards stumbled over a prostrate body, and we turned and took up the body of Henley, the young lawyer, and bore it to camp. Limp it was and hung down heavily. The camp reached, the doctor was called and restoratives were applied. Henley came to consciousness and told us he had been wounded by an Indian arrow, and had come to tell us the Indians were after the stock. The great arrow was then apparently embedded in his breast.

It had penetrated six or eight thicknesses of his Oregon blanket, his coat sleeve and the fleshy part of his forearm, had then gone through his coat, vest and underclothes, and was apparently deep in his chest. All these garments were pinned to his person by this arrow. The blood was slowly oozing out. Leaving him with the doctor, and expecting he would soon die, I aroused the whole camp, set it in order for a fight and called out my sage bush men and sharpshooters. Oh! how tardily they came, one by one. Repeated calls at the top of my voice scarcely hastened them. Every second was a minute to me! I wanted to fly to the side of Ives. I could not wait, and left with half our number, leaving orders for the rest to follow. We crept stealthily along the bluff till near the place of attack. Here along the cliff overlooking Ives' position, I located the men, one here, one there, with orders to shoot any one without a hat. Wild Indians never wear hats. I myself crept down the rocks near to where I had stationed Ives. I knew if he discovered me he would shoot me for an Indian, but I was so anxious for him I wanted to be near him in case of an attack. I had not long to wait; a bright flash of his gun burst upon the dark valley, the loud report rang and reverberated along the cliffs like a park of artillery. Some twenty feet before him an Indian with half-drawn bow stood a second and then fell as the darkness closed in, and all was silence again. A few minutes and the dying warrior commenced striking out wildly with arms and legs; I could hear distinctly his motions and efforts to rise. By and by he began to roll over and then over again. After a time he reached the river bank, fell over, a loud splash, and then all was still again.

All night we lay and watched the pass, and one there was I know who not only watched but *prayed* also. It is a very pretty thing to talk the soft words of non-resistance when no enemy is nigh, but in such an hour as this, it is not only sheer nonsense, but high treason to humanity and God.

As the first rays of morning began to modify the darkness, I descried an Indian on horseback, swaying back and forth, trying to make out just where we were. My shotgun, though heavily loaded, would hardly reach him, and I crawled back to where Hank Humphrey lay, and took him, with his rifle, to a point near the river, where we hoped to see the Indian. But he was gone. While we lay there together in the sage brush, I saw what seemed the outline of an Indian's body in a bunch of willows. The strong wind rushing through the narrow pass swayed the willows to and fro, and as they leaned this way and that, so leaned his body. Some time I watched it, when a sudden gust revealed him. Instantly my gun was up, but Hank knocked it down, saying, "Stop, Captain, it's an ox." A leap over the bank, and the Indian was out of sight.

Bitterly Hank reproached himself for this indiscretion, which had saved a murderer's life. I now called to Ives, and he came out from behind a rock, and when I told him where we had been since he sent wounded Henley up to the camp, he replied that he knew the Captain was not far off; just where, he could not tell. And when I told him how near I crawled down to him, he trembled to think of the danger ran. Believing that Henley was dead by this time, I believed I had a commission to destroy his murderer. I asked my lieutenant to go a little above and with some men cut off the retreat of the Indians, while I would cross over where we were, and follow up their trail. He objected, saying there might be hundreds of hostiles there. I said, Then I will go alone, and calling our company dog I jumped into the river, and following it up a dozen rods under the overhanging willows, I found where the Indians had crawled up the bank, and went up also, and pulled up the dog. To my surprise, I found myself followed by two young men — McComb and Alexander Hargrave. They would not see me go alone.

When out of the river, we found the trail so difficult we had to break a path for the dog. Reaching the wall on that side, I saw the marks of a wet foot on a rock, which showed he had gone up the cliff there. I turned quickly to the right, looking on the ground as if still following the track. When we had turned a corner, and were out of sight, I said:

"That Indian went up the rocks where we first came to the wall. Hargrave, linger here several minutes, till McComb and I can go up this ravine and reach the top of the cliff. Then do you go back and follow the Indian up the rocks, rout him out, and we will have him."

But it took us longer to reach the summit than Hargrave expected, and he went back. Our Indian, seeing him come back alone, left his hiding place. Just then I appeared on the plateau. He was some forty rods off, and could easily have kept out of reach. He was armed with a bow and arrows, and when he saw me he shook his fists in my face, and ran to meet me. I, too, ran to meet him. We were in full sight of a hundred men of my own train and Kennedy's, who saw us running together from the opposite bluff, and set up a universal shout. My train had great confidence in my coolness and marksmanship, and, I think, had no fear of the result, but wondered that while he ran fast I ran toward him rather slowly. The reason was, I wished to preserve my breath and steadiness of nerve.

Coming within eight or ten rods, he turned to run from me. I raised my gun, and be began dodging to right and left; but that did not prevent his receiving sixteen heavy shot in his back, just above the heart. His weapons fell out of his hands; he staggered, but laid hold of the sage brush with both his hands to hold himself up. McComb coming up, trembled so with excitement that he had to rest his rifle on my shoulder; but the ball flew aside from the mark. And now the firing began from the other side the river, and so thick the balls flew about me and McComb that I had to swing my hat and order them to stop.

In ten minutes fifty men had crossed the river, come over the bluff, and surrounded the wounded warrior. They asked the privilege of scalping him. This I refused. But unknown to me, they did it, and presented it to Henley, who survived, his chest not having been mortally pierced by the arrow. This Indian was a monster in size. His neck and shoulders were like those of a bullock. In his dying moments he struck a man and knocked him nearly a rod. The man said to me, "His stroke was like the kick of a horse." We afterward learned from friendly Indians that he was a big chief among the Bannocks, that they regarded him as the strongest man in the world. That at Fort Hall he whipped four men who set upon him at once. They also gave us his name. I have forgotten it, but it signified "Big Thief." As we left camp that morning, Indians rose up out of the sage brush near our camp and ran to where the two Indians were killed, showing that they had been spectators of all that had passed. Nor had we proceeded far before the smoke of signal fires began to ascend from hilltops in different directions around us, some of them ten miles distant! And then we knew well the whole Bannock tribe was upon us. Most of the people in our train and Kennedy's were badly scared. We saw Indians on horses dashing over the hills at full speed to carry the news to the scattered warriors. The view I took of the situation differed widely from the rest. I said, "We are safer now than ever. They are mad, but they are *scared, too.* Their invincible chief attacked us by night but was outwitted and killed; he and his companion. They will hover around but run when we steal through the brush to get at them." And so it proved. They followed us perhaps 200 miles but did not dare attack us. At length we drew near Catharine Creek, the western limit of the Bannock range. They determined there to make a stand and sent forward a chief and three braves to lie in ambush, spy out our camp defences, and attack us with their whole force by night. Going forward to select a camp as usual, there went with me one Geiger. Passing through the willows which lined the creek, I observed fresh footsteps of Indians, and also a strong *smell* of Indians. With quickened step I hurried through and made for an open space some twenty rods square and sat down in the middle of it. Geiger coming up asked, "What's your hurry, Captain?" I said there are Indians there; I smelt them and saw their fresh tracks also. In an hour or so the train filed down the long hill. Most of the men, eager for game, came rushing on ahead, gun in hand, and as they came near the willows spread out like a fan. In doing so they unwittingly surrounded the Indians, and seeing them hid in the bushes quickly took them prisoners and brought them to me. While I was examining them and considering what to do with them, we were startled by the sound of a bugle approaching us from the opposite direction. Soon the advance guard of a regiment of United States soldiers and cavalry came filing around the hills! Hearing of the troubles on the plains, the United States Government had sent out from Oregon these troops to help the beleaguered emigrants. When the commanding officer's tent was pitched, he sent a squad of soldiers to take the Indians to him. On the way they skipped right and left, and all four escaped. They soon rejoined their forces concealed behind the hills and told them that the game was up, there were too many of us now in the valley to be attacked. Their chagrin was great and they came out upon the hillsides in full view, and there they ran their ponies for full half an hour and thus worked off their wrath and gave vent to their vengeance. Then they slowly took the backward track and we saw them no more.

AN ESCORT ASKED AND DENIED

I think a full thousand persons were camped upon Catharine Creek. We staid there a week and recruited our hungry horses. As the time drew near when we were to continue our journey, a petition was gotten up for an escort of soldiers to accompany us to Oregon. Nearly every one signed it. It was presented by an able committee and well argued by a lawyer. Col. Maury, looking over the long list, said: "I don't see Capt. Bristol's name here?" The lawyer replied that he would not sign it. "Why not?" said Col. Maury. One of the committee said Capt. Bristol was a man without personal fear, and would run risks no sensible man could approve. The colonel called an orderly and bade him bring me to him. When I came, he said: "I see your name is not on this petition for an escort. Will you let us hear your reasons for not thinking an escort should be granted?" I replied my principal reason was that I thought the *trains behind* us would be in greater danger than we. That his whole force would be needed between this place and Fort Hall. That, if we would act the part of men, keep a good lookout, keep close together and select defensible camps, we would go through all right. Besides, if an escort were given us, our men would become careless and lean wholly on the soldiers for defence. But if we went without them, we would all be watchful, prepared, and therefore safe. Turning to one Capt. Crawford—the senior captain of the regiment—the colonel asked: "What do you think of that, Capt. Crawford?" "*That is sensible*," he replied, and half a dozen other officers assented also. The colonel then said to the committee: "The view presented by Capt. Bristol is not only sensible, but it is patriotic. I agree with him entirely, and if you will heed his advice to rely on yourselves and keep close together, you will go through safely. I cannot give you an escort."

The meeting broke up. The committee went out swearing mad and poured out their wrath without measure upon "Bristol's dare-devilism which had deprived us of an escort, and, no doubt, would prove the ruin of us all." And for once I was thoroughly unpopular, even in my own train. I offered to resign and have the train choose another captain. But no one seconded my suggestion and no one seemed to covet the privilege of running the risks I took every day in going forward and selecting our camps. When we reached Oregon and before, I believe, all were glad we were not bothered with the escort and coerced in our camps and disciplined by them. The truth was, I had no very exalted opinion of the fighting qualities of half the soldiers. Their method of fighting was objectionable. Better ten men who can crawl half a mile in the brush to shoot them singly, than a round hundred fighting as civilized soldiers usually do. The greatest instance of cowardice on the plains, I can remember, was that of a large soldier, wearing the United States' uniform, who joined us on our way. In a skirmish, a little Indian, not weighing much over a hundred pounds, chased this big, tall soldier nearly a quarter of a mile, each running at the top of his speed. At last the big soldier *jumped into Snake River!* But the water was only about four feet deep where he struck it, and rising, he took refuge under a shelving rock. No doubt that little Indian laughs about it to this day, if he is alive.

MASSACRE OF THE VAN ZANT TRAIN

Pursuing our journey, we camped one night on Castle Creek. About a mile from this we came upon the ruins of the "Van Zant" train, which a year before was here ambushed and captured by the Indians. It was a sad sight — the charred remains of wagons, the bones of cattle and horses, and the skulls of murdered men and women! Some of the skulls were perforated with rifle bullets. These were scattered about, the work of these devils of the desert. I afterward fell in with one of the two who alone escaped that massacre. And the tale of horror he told was frightful. And he wept like a child, as he narrated to me how his lady love was slain there. How she stood by him night and day through all the siege and defence. How she loaded guns for him, encouraged him and brought food to him, till at last she fell at his side, perforated with balls and faint with hunger and thirst and loss of blood. I wish I could repeat her dying words to him — so brave, so sensible, so affectionate, even in death — but they are gone from me.

The substance of his story was this:

The Van Zant train was, I think, made up in Illinois and Wisconsin. It consisted mainly of families, who were *en route* for Oregon, and numbered some thirty-five persons.

At Castle Creek they were visited by a band of Indians, who as usual asked for bread and meat, sugar, and what else they fancied. These were promptly given in the vain hope of propitiating their favor. The next day the train had got but a mile from their camp, when the same Indians they had fed the night before surrounded them and began to fire upon them! The men lay behind their dead animals and wagons, and tried to defend themselves. And this they did all that day, the women loading guns and taking care of the wounded and the frenzied cattle. All night they were held in siege, and not a drop of water was to be had.

The next day the battle was kept up, nearly all the cattle were killed, and all but half a dozen women and men.

The stench of the putrefying corpses as well as the awful thirst made their stay there impossible and on the morning of the third day they rushed out, not caring whether they lived or died. One or two were killed, but the savages were so intent on plunder, they could not stop to kill the rest, and four succeeded in walking away from them. One died the next day, and they ate a part of his body. Another gave out and besought the two stronger to leave him and go forward for help. He was never seen afterward, was doubtless eaten up by wolves. The two left followed along the trail, living on reptiles, raw fish and bark till they came to the settlements. Such was the fate of the "Van Zant train," and it is but a specimen of the heartless cruelty of these fiends of the forest.

And we threw down the skulls and bones resolved, that if they got our skulls, *they would have to pay for them!* And if any of us had started out on this trip, with the soft sentiment that the white man is always to blame for these Indian troubles, their minds were disabused of that false idea by this time. Drawing near the eastern boundary of Oregon, we were overtaken by a band of prospecting miners, who had first discovered the gold mines of Idaho, but were driven off by Indians. One of their number, a Mr. Grimes from Oregon, was shot down by them while engaged in digging for gold. The rest fled, leaving his body unburied, and were now *en route* for Auburn, for help and supplies. Going up Burnt River, we met a band of three hundred horses, driven at headlong speed by some Indians. We were in a defile, and I demanded what they were doing with them. One of them replied, "Salt Lake!" "Salt Lake!" This was plausible, and we let them pass. The next day we found they had all been raided from the miners at Auburn.

THE SETTLEMENTS REACHED—FAREWELL SPEECH

Early in November we reached Grass Valley, ten miles from the town of Auburn, and were now quite within the bounds of civilization. There was no more occasion for a nightly guard, a captain, or an organization. I led my train out upon a beautiful camping ground, and forming them as usual in a circle of wagons, I gave notice, that at seven o'clock that evening I wished all the members of the train to come together, as I proposed then to resign the office I had so long held, and to make them a farewell speech.

Prompt to the moment the camp bell was rung, and all train was at hand, and many others with them. In my speech I congratulated my companions on our arrival at the end of a journey of over 2,000 miles, the greater part of it through a country destitute of forage and other supplies, and infested with hostile tribes intent on robbery and murder. That now after some seven months of weary travel by day and of watching by night, we had reached a land of peace, of plenty and of rest. That in all the long journey we had not lost a man or scarcely a beast. But we were all here to-night, not only alive, but all in good health. Fit it was we should congratulate each other on our singular success and express our gratitude to that Great Protector who had watched over us by night and by day. I thanked them for their loyalty to me as their chief officer and the confidence shown in having thrice elected me to the office I held. I felt this the more sensibly since so far as I knew ours was the only train which had crossed the plains this year, standing by their captain all the way through. While most of the trains had been rent by serious diversions ours never had one to speak of. That it was a great pleasure to me, and no doubt ever would be, to remember that in our long journey we had regularly reverenced the Sabbath day, and tried to keep it holy. That since we started, in but one instance had we harnessed our teams on that day, and then only to travel five miles to assist and protect some emigrants who had been attacked and robbed by Indians the night before.

I thanked them for their uniform attendance on such sermons as I had been able to give them on the Lord's day. I referred to the pleasing fact that instead of falling behind other trains, on account of resting on the Sabbath day, we had out-traveled them all, and left them behind us. That the weekly rest had enabled us to keep our horses in good condition, had been a source of health and comfort to us all, and that this illustrates what will prove true of all the commandments of God, if we observe them, that they are all laid upon us in love, and that "in keeping them there is great reward." I remarked that I had received compliments from time to time from nearly all of them for the excellent camps I had selected and for wise management of affairs in emergencies. That I thanked them for such friendly words, but I wished here very emphatically to say, that whatever of success had attended my administration, it was due to Him who said, "If any man lack wisdom, let him ask of God, who giveth to all men liberally, and upbraideth not." That every day in the long journey I had asked the Lord to give me wisdom to select our camps and in all our affairs to be my guide and helper. That when I asked I believed he *would* do so, and now that we are through and looking back, I believed he *had* done so.

Wishing them all success in their varied pursuits, a happy return to their families in due time, and a happier meeting by and by in that better country, when the toils of life are over, I tendered my resignation. Rounds of applause followed. A lawyer stepped forward, called the train to order, and a committee was appointed on resolutions. Congratulatory speeches were made, and then the committee reported a series of resolutions too complimentary to their captain to be inserted here. As we were yet to move on ten miles further to Auburn it was voted unanimously that their captain should proceed at the head of their train and corral them there, which I did the following day. From this last encampment we gradually separated and went our several ways, the most of us to meet no more till from our sight these heavens and earth have passed away.

Long years have passed since then—twenty and five of them— but the attachment then formed to those companions in tribulation is as fresh and strong as it was then. It was a great pleasure to meet several of them during a subsequent residence of nearly two years in Idaho and to share with them the hospitalities of a miner's home. They were all as brothers to me, nor do I think I was less to them. There is a strange fascination that binds us to the companions of our struggles and sorrows. I remember how the old revolutionary soldiers used to gather under my grandfather's roof and recount with much zest and often with tears of joy the marches they made together, the battles they fought, the sufferings endured and the hairbreadth escapes they ran. They told of hunger endured, wounds received, rags they wore, of cracked and bleeding feet marking with gory stains the frozen sod, as they marched and counter-marched, during the seven years of war.

O! how these old soldiers loved one another! Even so in like manner our lesser perils had knit our hearts together, and neither time nor space shall quench the fires which then were kindled. Who can tell but that in the endless future the sorrows and struggles of the earthly life shall contribute immensely to its bliss?

OFF FOR IDAHO

A rrived at Auburn I began at once to prospect the hills and valleys for mining claims. But while I could find "the color" or small particles of gold almost anywhere over a large section of country, there were a few places where it was concentrated in paying quantities.

The news from Idaho being favorable, Messrs. Bainan and Walcott, McComb and myself formed a company, sold our cabin and all we could spare and invested in a couple of yoke of oxen, a wagon and supplies, and started off for the new mining placer. It was midwinter and bitterly cold, and much we suffered before we reached the end of our journey, 300 miles distant. Once on our way we walked or ran all night to keep from being frozen to death, for we camped where not a stick of dry wood could be found nor other wood save green willows or alder. On another our favorite ox came to us about midnight, alkalied and leaning his head against me, seemed to say, "I am deathly sick, master, and have come to you for help." In spite of all we could do he died, and we had to proceed with a "spike team," as the miners called it. Reaching the mountain we managed to climb over with our three oxen and the forward wheels of our wagon, to which were lashed our blankets and a little food. The rest of our provisions we had freighted over at $12 per hundred pounds. The last three days our poor oxen ate nothing, and when we butchered them Deacon Bainan said there was not tallow enough in them all to grease *one pair of boots*. And I think he was correct.

We located at Placerville, and at once commenced sawing our lumber by hand. We had brought along a saw from Auburn for that purpose. Lumber was bringing, I think, $30 per hundred feet, and we could earn about $5 a day to the hand above the expense of living. Flour was $50 per one hundred pounds. Bacon the same, and other things in proportion. My partners being well settled for the winter in a fair business, I proposed to strike out for myself and did so. Went over to Mores creek (now Idaho City) and formed a partnership with one William Henry from Illinois.

RICH MINES UNDER HOUSES

My partner's cabin was built on a bench thirty rods above the creek. The snow was four feet deep. There were twenty other cabins near us, and the difficulty of bringing water from the creek led us to hire a man to dig a well. At a depth of eighteen feet the well-digger struck the bed rock. He found no water, but seeing pieces of gold in his bucket he went to the river with a pan full of dirt and washed out $2.50 in gold. He went to the saloon and showed his find. Each gambler dropped his cards, paper and pencil in hand, ran up the beach and posted on a pine tree, some such notice as this: "I ——— claim 60 feet west of this notice for mining purposes, etc." Thus in half an hour the whole beach for half a mile along the side of the Creek was taken up by gamblers, the rest of us being away in the hills prospecting. All these claims were fabulously rich. That on which our cabin was built was worth $250,000 the day it was taken up, for it yielded about $500,000. Three brothers named White held this claim and the one adjoining. They employed a force of seventeen men by day and as many by night. Their clean-up usually amounted to about $2,000 a day. This was, at least, $1,500 beyond expenses. They took turns at superintending the mine, and while one was doing this the other two were sleeping, gambling or otherwise dissipating.

They mined under our house till we had to leave it and it tumbled into the excavation. They took an immense sum, but the last I heard of them they were all poor. It is a saying among gamblers that "riches got by gambling never abide long by the winner."

SETTLEMENT OF BOISE VALLEY

The heavy snowfall, some five feet deep, impeded all prospecting, and for a few days I had nothing to do. So I betook myself to figuring out the problem of the next year's supply of vegetables and grain for the Idaho miners. I had heard that the valley of the Boise River, some fifty miles distant, was warm and fertile and spent a day in figuring the expense and profits of an expedition there, taking along our starving horses, and cultivating 500 acres of land, marketing, etc. William Henry looked over my shoulder occasionally and, wishing to have some fun, went all over town and invited everybody to come to our house that evening.

Of course I was ignorant of all this. But as evening was coming on, men began to drop in until the cabin was full, and I wondered what was up. Soon a dignified man rapped three times on the table and called the meeting to order. All was still and he began his speech, somewhat as follows: "Fellow citizens! Our usually quiet community, I am grieved to say, has of late become excited and alarmed, by certain strange and suspicious actions, by one of our citizens from whom we had hoped better things! Not to be further tedious, I will now call upon Capt. or Rev. Bristol, to rise and explain to this honorable assembly, the meaning of certain suspicious papers known to be in his possession, and to show the intent of formidable arrays of figures and hieroglyphics found therein!" After a hearty laugh, in which all joined, I took the floor and explained the situation. Our starving mules and horses, the high prices of potatoes and grain, the probable want of hay and vegetables in all the mining camps next summer, and the high prices we should have to pay for them.

Then I turned to Boise Valley, its adaptability to agriculture and gardening, the way to get there, how many men it would take to break a road through the snow, and the horses we could take by so doing, the saving of human life and money, too, in Idaho by this move. When I was through objections were heard and replied to, and by 12 o'clock the whole crowd had been converted to my views, and were eager to start off the next day. But I persuaded them to delay a couple of days and get a good ready.

In two days were were on the move, some fifty men and 300 half starved horses, mules and asses. The snow was five feet on a level, and thus we proceeded. Thirty men went forward as pathfinders and path-breakers through the snow. They followed each other in single file, those forward floundering along a few rods, and then when tired out falling out till the other path-breakers had passed, and then falling in again. Then came the animals, the strongest in advance, and drives intermingled to keep them all in motion. In this way a fine path was made for the feebler animals.

We made perhaps ten miles the first day, and twenty the second. The snow became less and less in depth as we descended toward the valley. On the third day toward evening, we looked down upon the great valley. Far as the eye could reach no snow was there! and grass in abundance was everywhere! Even on the foot hills, tufts of rich bunch grass cropping out of the snow tempted our starving animals to rush out of the trail for a mouthful. But when we came in full view of the vast pasture lands, free from snow, not only the men swung their hats and cheered, but our animals, whinnying and braying, expressed their joy, and then ran pell-mell down into the valley! Many of the men took out their knives, cut a sackful of hay and carrying it back to some favorite animal, which had given out by the way, fed it to him, and led him also into the valley.

We began at once to stake off claims of one hundred and sixty acres each, for farming purposes, and soon the whole valley was largely taken up by these claims for fifteen miles.

THE INDIANS STAMPEDE OUR HORSES

No Indians were in the valley when we entered it. We had been in it perhaps three weeks, when learning that we were there they made a raid upon us one stormy night.

The wind was howling fiercely, and the rain fell in torrents. Near midnight, the wild neighings of horses and braying of mules was heard above the thunder of the storm, as they rushed past us up the valley at the top of their speed, as if a troop of devils were after them. My own riding horse, tied fast to a tree under which I had spread my tent and was trying to sleep, fairly bawled out his terror, and leaped and plunged as if a tiger was upon him. I rushed out gun in hand, and succeeded in keeping him from breaking his rope. No doubt an Indian was at hand, and scaring him as only an Indian can. But it was so dark I could not see an object five feet distant. All I could do was to hold my horse, and listen to the unearthly wail of the terrified animals, as they died away in the distance. The next morning we found they had taken from us one hundred and twenty-five horses and mules, not one of which was ever recovered.

A few of our company followed them to the crossing of the Boise River, some ten miles above, and gave up the pursuit. They passed a dozen of dead or dying horses, which were not able to keep up with the rest, and were shot with an arrow and left to die a lingering death. Of course we put them out of their misery. But what cared these Indians for the sufferings of a horse? Or even of a man? Their tender mercies are cruel. It was not long before the stolen animals were replaced by others. The sound of the ax and of falling trees was heard all along the Boise, in the patches of timber which lined its banks. Houses began to show themselves on every quarter section.

Taking up a ranch in the valley, I became associated with Messrs. Richie and Davis, in the cultivation of a farm. We built a log house and a strong stockade, where nightly we gathered our horses and cows, to save them from Indian raids. The gate opened within twenty feet of our door and the bars were pinned to their posts. We had port-holes through which we could shoot in case of a siege. A chinking left out at the head of my bed enabled me to look out at the corral gate and to shoot through it if necessary. One night about twelve o'clock some horses came running up to our yard. A falling bar startled me and I was soon out at the gate, gun in hand. I saw an Indian crouch behind a sage bush. Knowing that he was armed, I pretended not to notice him, but went around among the horses, to get a better sight at him. But the wily thief crawled away. For half an hour in looking for him, I was exposed to instant death from an arrow. Not finding him I put up the bar again, went in to the cabin and lay down. Meantime the thieves stole up, and taking down the bars noiselessly, at a flap of their blankets, all our horses rushed out pell-mell together and started off at full speed with those of our neighbors! Quickly I was out among them.

But such was the dust raised that I could see no one, and dared not fire lest I should wound or kill our own horses rather than the Indians. So they were soon out of sight and hearing.

This time we lost all our stock, and so did many of our neighbors. Other raids they made with equal success. After one of them some of the settlers followed them, and after a battle drew them into a rocky fastness, where they besieged them for several days, but one night most of them crawled out and escaped; several of them, however, had been killed.

Should any one ask, what use the Indians had for so many horses? I answer, *They ate them!* At one place we found the heads and bones of perhaps thirty, which they had recently eaten.

INDIANS OUTWITTED

Two of the miners visiting us went down the valley to Snake River and camped near a crossing. They saw two Indians watching them on the other side. They hailed them and asked in Chinook where they were going. The Indians replied by asking back the same question? The miners replied, "Going to steal horses." the Indians said that was what they were going to do. Were there not some up the Boise? Yes, and fat ones, too, was the reply. Both parties cooked their bacon and coffee, wrapped themselves in their blankets, leaving their hats and blankets as if a man was still in them, crawled behind some bushes and waited developments. In the light of the moon, they saw the Indians slowly crossing the river, and then stealing softly up toward the smoldering camp-fire, discharged their arrows into what seemed the men in their blankets. At that instant the miners also fired! and there were two less of a race whose principal business is to rob and to kill.

In spite of Indian raids, want of farming implements and seed, we raised an immense amount of produce that year in Boise Valley.

I and my partners planted twenty acres of potatoes. For seed potatoes, we had to send to Oregon, and import from thence 2,500 pounds. For perhaps four hundred miles they were brought on the backs of mules and horses, and when they arrived they cost us thirty-three cents a pound, or *about twenty dollars a bushel*, and the seed for the twenty acres, eight hundred and twenty-five dollars! We also planted corn, melons, etc., nearly all of which were reasonably profitable. Our potato crop we sold at from ten to twelve thousand dollars. Our hay we sold at seventy-five dollars a ton. Hay brought that year two hundred dollars a ton, in Idaho City, sixty miles distant, and for months we were offering one hundred dollars a ton for carrying our hay to that market.

STEAMBOAT SPRINGS

Six miles from us was what was called "Steamboat Springs." This was a spring of boiling water which was poured out of a crevice or hole in a rock, with such hissing noise and force, that it strikingly reminded us of a steam engine blowing off steam.

Some ranch men, wiser than we were, saw how they could utilize it. They took up a claim below it, and led forth its smoking waters into several ditches, and through extensive vegetable gardens. The land was not only irrigated but *warmed*. The late frosts were kept off, and they put vegetables into the market three weeks earlier than we could. So also in the fall they supplied the market four weeks longer than we could.

BUILDING OF FORT BOISE

During the summer a regiment of cavalry was sent by the Government from Oregon to Idaho to build a fort, and to protect the miners and farmers there. The commander of this force had heard of me from Col. Maury, and on his arrival in Boise Valley, sent for me to visit his camp.

He informed me of his business, to build a fort large enough to accommodate a force of one thousand men, and for this purpose $500,000 had been made subject to his order. It must be located within fifty miles of the mouth of the Boise; it must be in a healthy locality, have good water and plenty of wood and forage. Also, that there must be timber near, and of good quality, as he would have to erect two sawmills, to furnish the amount of lumber required for a fort. Did I know of such a location for a fort? I replied that I knew of two, either of which would fill the bill. After two weeks spent in looking at localities recommended by others he fixed upon the one

I had recommended as most suitable, and there he commenced at once to build.[52]

BOISE CITY

The fort being located and hundreds of workmen gathered there, the necessity for a town or city became at once apparent. Half a dozen officers from the fort and several prominent citizens met at my house and formed a town site company. There were seventeen of us in all. We divided the stock into eighteen shares. Of these two shares were voted to me and the other sixteen shareholders had one each. I was the president of the company. We had our plat surveyed, lithographed, and a copy sent to each member of the territorial Legislature, then in session at Lewiston. We invited the legislators to visit us and agreed to pay their expenses. They came and were most hospitably entertained; they were shown the fine grounds we had set apart for the legislative and State buildings, and when they went back they voted to make our city on paper the capital of the territory. And to-day Boise City is the most important town in the Territory. The governmental buildings are all on "Capital Square," the churches on "Church Square," and the educational buildings on "Schoolhouse Block," and every street in the city bears the name we gave it, before scarce a house was there.

Let no one think I became a millionaire because I owned one-ninth of Boise City. I did not make a hundred dollars out of it. Our expenses were large, and besides this I gave away to worthy persons all my best lots.

OWYHEE MINES

Among the rich mining sections of Idaho were those situated on one of the branches of the Owyhee River, which empties into the Snake on its southwesterly side. They were discovered by one Jordan early in the summer of 1864. He was a brave man, and possessed of many fine qualities. I had no special acquaintance with him, but no sooner had he made his discovery, than he came to me and offered me an equal partnership with him in his claims, if I would go with him and help develop them. I thanked him but declined, on the ground that I intended to leave for the States in the coming fall or winter. But he stood by me a whole day and argued the case, and when he found I could not be persuaded, he went away downcast and greatly disappointed. Poor fellow, he returned to his claims and soon after was killed by Indians as he was looking after his horses. Jordan River was so named after him, and not after the Jordan of Scripture, as many suppose.

CHAPTER
18

RETURNING HOMEWARD—
TRIP TO WALLA WALLA

I n December, 1864,[53] Capt. Hughes, quartermaster of the fort, was
summoned to report at San Francisco. He was a fine officer and
a special friend of mine, and he invited me to share a seat with him
in his carriage as far as Walla Walla. Settling up my affairs, I found
I had accumulated seven or eight thousand dollars during my stay in
Idaho. A part of this I collected, and a part was intrusted to a friend
for future collection and to be sent as fast as received by express to
Wisconsin. Alas, of this latter I received next to nothing. For though
collected, my friend loaned it for a few days to a merchant in Idaho
City, but before it was repaid the man was burnt out and I lost it all.
Before leaving the citizens demanded a farewell speech, which I gave
them, and left with Capt. Hughes and his escort. A couple of weeks
or so brought us to Walla Walla.

DOWN THE COLUMBIA

Boarding a steamer at Wallula, the river port of Walla Walla, we started
down the Columbia for Portland. The trip is full of startling sensations
from Wallula to the foot of the Cascades or lower falls of the river.
Once taken it is never forgotten. First of all it is a great river and
discharges a vast volume of water into the ocean. Then it is remarkable
for its summer flood—like "Jordan overflowing all its banks in time
of harvest"—several months after the spring rains have ceased to
fall. This arises from the melting of the snows at that season on vast
mountain ranges whence this great river derives its waters. Remarkable, too, it is for the vast shoals of salmon which, at a set time in
the year, come up from unknown pasture grounds far away in the
depths of the ocean, and, entering its mouth at Astoria, ascend its
cataracts and rapids, nor stop in their mad race till they have reached
its sources—1,000 to 2,500 miles distant.

Not one in fifty of its tributaries fails to receive great numbers of these valuable fish. I have seen them so thick I could kill them with a shovel. They are the principal article of food for the Indians over the vast territory it drains. While from the lower rapids to Astoria a hundred canneries catch and cure and send to distant markets more salmon than, perhaps, all other rivers of the world united.

But *the feature* of this river which especially startles the traveler as the steamboat leaves Wallula, is the headlong speed of the boat as it rushes down the rapids. I think the flow of the river is equal to six or eight knots an hour. The surface is, much of it, white with foam and broken up into unnumbered hillocks of leaping waters. Had I been called upon to give it a name, I should surely have called "Mad River." But what made our headlong plunge down thereon seem madness intensified, was the sight of immense boulders strewn in uncounted numbers over the river bed, and directly under our boat, and sometimes so near the surface that it seemed a miracle that we did not strike them, and our boat be dashed in pieces. We wondered if the water had not moved some of them on a little, and nearer the surface, since the last trip was made? Too near to be passed over in safety? Why not? Had not all these boulders been floated or rolled down to their present position, some of them from a hundred miles above? And if it was continually moving them on, what assurance could the last survey give of present safety? But worse than such conjectures was the actual sight of a reef of jagged rocks projecting quite out into the current and directly before us. We were running straight upon it. It was a grand sight — the mighty Columbia, rearing twenty feet high and leaping like a mad horse upon that barrier, and then to witness the recoil as, dashed into fragments it fell back discomfited, and thenceforth pursuing its way, for a time at least, with much less of self-confidence and arrogant pride.

But how about our boat, laden with valuable freight, and a hundred human beings? We are scarce twenty rods distant from the reef. One minute and we shall be on it! Is not the helmsman asleep? Or more likely he is insane, and bent on dashing us all to pieces! And now we are just upon it, ready to shriek with terror or leap overboard, when our boat is uplifted by a mighty wave of recoiling waters, and aided by a skillful turn of the helm, is thrown into a side channel, and the danger is past!

Through several of these hairbreadth escapes the voyager passes, ere he reaches the quiet flow of the Lower Columbia. Yet so skillful are the navigators of these rapids that rarely an accident happens or a life is lost. So dangerous are some parts that a railroad is built around them, and navigation suspended. In one part, for several miles, the water flows gently, and down upon the bottom, several fathoms below the keel of our ship, are seen *large pine stumps*, standing erect as when alive and growing. Fremont, I think it was (possibly Lewis and Clarke), accounted for this, by a landslide, long ago, down into the bed of the river. The objection to this is, had that been the case, the stumps would be at all angles, instead of all standing erect, pointing to the zenith, as when they were growing. The true solution probably is that they are in place, or as they grew in a deep valley, and that a big landslide *below* dammed up the river and raised its waters over the valley, killed the trees, and hence these stumps, and hence this depth of quiet water.

The lower part of the Columbia contrasts widely with the part just described. Emerging from the Cascade ranges, it assumes at once a new character. It now has a depth and gentleness of flow, and an amplitude of navigable channel, which is the admiration of all. For 100 miles, more or less, it moves on slowly and majestically toward the sea, and when it reaches Astoria it has a breadth of miles and a grandeur equal to the Mississippi or the Hudson.

PORTLAND

The steamer from the Cascades carried us to Portland, where I spent a couple of weeks. I was pleased with the place that I half made up my mind to buy a home and locate there. In pursuance of this, I crossed over to East Portland, on the other side the Willamette, to look at some places for sale there. One was shown me of 160 acres, with a fair sized two-story house and outbuildings, for some less than $3,000. I concluded I would buy it, but going back with the land agent to look up the title, I was buttonholed by another man, who offered me another piece of property quite as cheap. Then another took me in hand, and so much property was crowded upon me, and at such low prices, that I was scared, and inly resolved I would not buy where everybody was trying to sell out and leave. So declining them all, I bought a ticket for San Francisco and left.

This was twenty-four years ago. Sixteen years thereafter, on a visit to Portland, I went over the river, and lo! that 160 acre lot, offered me for less than $3,000, was now in the center of the city of East Portland, and not one acre could be purchased for $1,000.

SAN FRANCISCO

Reaching San Francisco, I found the city immensely changed from what it was thirteen years before, at my last visit, but in nothing more than in the expense of living. In 1851, hotel bills were all the way from $3 a day to $10. A single meal, however plain and unpretentious, was $1. Now, in 1864, the usual charge for a square meal (as the miners call it) was from twenty-five cents to half a dollar. I took a room at the Railroad House, and a very desirable one, too; two beds were in it, it was large and furnished with books, writing material, etc., and all my companion and I paid was fifty cents each a day. Two large restaurants were attached to the hotel. One for families and ladies, the other for men and transient boarders; and in either of them a liberal patronage of the bill of fare seldom made the expense over thirty-seven cents for a meal. And I daily saw 500 men go into the "Lick Restaurant" and get a fair dinner there *for ten cents each.* Indeed, San Francisco had, during those thirteen years, taken a long step forward, and from being the most expensive city on each to live in, had now become one of the very cheapest.

I was surprised to find that California still adhered strictly to the gold and silver basis, notwithstanding the National law making greenbacks legal tender for payment of debts. California was truly a loyal State, but her courts, her legislature, and all her citizens, tacitly ignored the Greenback Act of Congress, and only gold and silver were currency within her bounds. The National paper was indeed here, but it was not treated as money, but was bought and sold by brokers, the same as mining stocks, or bonds of States and cities. Suits had been started several times in the courts, to compel creditors to take greenbacks at their face for debts, but the judges put the cases off from time to time, or persuaded the parties to withdraw them.

The ground generally taken by the leading men of the State was, that while the National Legal Tender Act was a necessity in carrying on the war, the case of California, as a gold-producing State, was exceptional. She ought to retain her gold against future emergencies. Happily she did so, and it enabled her, when the war was over, to open her vaults and allow her coin to flow over the mountains, and enable the Government the sooner to resume specie payments, and bring her credit up to par and above it among the nations of the earth. While in the city I bought $1,000 in currency for $650 in gold. After a month's stay I left for New York. Nothing of special interest occurred on the passage.

CHAPTER

19

AT HOME AGAIN

Arrived at New York, I found the great city full of business, and in full tide of prosperity, with scarce a sign of the great war now in progress, and hastening to its close.[54] The expense of living was frightful, and contrasted strongly with San Francisco. I think my room in the hotel cost me $3 a day. But everything was on a greenback basis.

From the city I hastened to visit kindred and friends in Connecticut, Rhode Island, Massachusetts, New York State, and Ohio, bringing up at my home in Dartford, Wis., about the first of April, 1864. I found on my arrival another minister occupying my old pulpit, and acting pastor of the church. He proposed at once to resign, but I opposed with all my might, saying that I much preferred to engage in evangelistic work, assisting the churches in their special meetings, unembarrassed by pastoral care and work. That as my home was there, I would pay for his support more than any one else in the parish. But nothing could change his purpose, saying that neither himself or any other man could satisfy the people, while the old pastor, endeared to them by so many thrilling memories, was at hand and able to serve them. So, much to my regret he left, and I soon found myself in the old traces again.

After I had served them a year or so, there came a call from two churches, Brandon and Springvale, to preach alternately to each of them, giving Brandon the morning sermon on the Sabbath and to Springvale that of the afternoon. Both of these churches were endeared to me by revival meetings I had held in them years before. They were only five miles apart. Reluctantly I left Dartford for the new field and labored there till near the end of 1867. Little of note occurred during my stay there.

In each church we held revival meetings and quite a number were, we trust, added to the Lord in both places. But a great and sore trial was now coming upon me. The nerve power so indispensable to sustained effort in preaching—especially in protracted efforts—

now began to fail me. Calls came to me from all sides to aid my brethren in these harvest seasons of the churches. But the vigor of former years had departed. A sermon, energetic during the first fifteen minutes, became weak and labored as it approached its conclusion. A week or two of continuous effort prostrated me completely. I felt intensely sad at this, and it was a question of anxious thought, Whence is this? Have I not in some way grieved from my heart the Divine Spirit, so that as in the case of Israel of old, he goes no more forth with me, to fight the battles of the Lord? Over and over again I reviewed the past stopping at each questionable place and asking, Did I here do just what was right? And did I not at this point let go of that Divine hand which so gently and so tenderly led me, during those years of success and power? But to these earnest interrogations there came no satisfactory response.

God was trying me, while yet he was leading me through a dark place. But light was beyond, and all the while I was approaching it. In some such way it came.

THE SERMON IN THE APPLE TREE

Walking one day in my orchard, I came to an apple tree which I greatly prized. It had borne great crops for years of excellent fruit. But now, alas, its fruit was small and withered, the leaves were turning yellow and that year, though comparatively young, it had made little growth! It was evident its period of fruit bearing was past and God had shifted over upon other and younger trees, the burdens it had been wont to carry. As I stood looking at it, I read there written among the branches—God's inexorable law—that not always on earth shall even the best employed powers retain their vigor or fruitfulness, but like this tree, must ultimately wither and give place to others. That this has been true of other men—the latchet of whose shoes I am not worth to unloose, and why not in my case as well? And decadence in abilities and success is no more proof of God's displeasure than of his wrath against this tree. And I went out of that orchard a wiser and happier man!—thanking God for the past, reconciled to the present, and looking hopefully toward the future. Since then I have daily thanked the Lord for abilities still retained, and have sought to use them, well and wisely.

THE SKEPTIC'S CONVERSION

In one of these meetings of days—held during my pastorate in Springvale—there occurred a somewhat remarkable conversion. It was that of Mr. Eugene Ely, now a resident of Iowa, a licentiate preacher, an accomplished instructor of youth and in other walks a most devout and useful man. Should his eye fall upon this narration, I trust he will pardon this exposure to the public of a conference eminently private and confidential, for the sake of the benefit it is hoped others may derive from it. Mr. Ely had years before married a most excellent lady in my church, the daughter of its former pastor, a Miss Julia Lamb.

Mr. Ely was a well-educated man, had taught school, and had been an officer in the Union army. But alas, he was a disbeliever in the Bible, and quite pronounced and outspoken in his sentiments of disbelief. But his wife, her sister and brother were decided Christians and were praying for him continually. They desired he should have a talk with me on the subject. He would be pleased to do so, as he regarded Mr. Bristol as a candid man, but it would do no good for he had objections to the Bible and all revealed religion no man on earth could remove! It was while holding a series of meetings in Springvale that an opportunity occurred. I was boarding with Mr. Edward Lamb and his sister, when Mr. Ely and wife came to pay them a visit, and perhaps also to attend some of the meetings.

This brought us in contact and afforded the opportunity for the coveted conversation, and we took a whole day for it, a day never to be forgotten by him or by me. It was a snowy day and little could be done without. So at the breakfast table Mr. Lamb said: "Eugene, I will do the chores and do you and Mr. Bristol go into the parlor and have a good talk to-day." All the family indorsed heartily the suggestion. So we went in and the door was shut. Turning at once to the matter uppermost in each of our minds, I opened by showing briefly what were the great and benevolent principles the Bible teaches and seeks by highest rewards to implant in the hearts of men, and what an Eden restored it would soon create in our world, would all mankind adopt and practice them. Was such a religion begotten and brought forth by a generation of liars or of fools? Could a bad tree bring forth such good fruit? Mr. Ely admitted there was force in these considerations.

But the objections were strong enough to set it all aside. Should he mention some of them? Yes, surely. I would be glad to hear them. He presented one. I admitted its plausibility, and taking his line of thought I added a further consideration which gave it additional force. He thanked me for it and asked, How can you answer them? I then gave the considerations which to my mind completely neutralized the force of those objections to the Bible. He listened candidly, and at length said, "We will lay that objection to the Bible aside. I don't think it has much force. He brought forth another, and this was treated like its predecessor and like it laid aside. And so the discussion went on all the forenoon, the utmost candor prevailing all through. We were seeking the truth, and the God of truth was there helping us to disentangle it from error. We were called to dinner, after which Mr. Ely went to his room a moment and his anxious wife asked about the discussion and he replied, "The pleasantest I ever had in my life." "Did he answer your objections?" "Yes and with the utmost fairness. He is the most candid of men. But I have not presented my strongest. I have reserved them to this afternoon. Those objections I know he cannot answer, or any one else."

We returned to the parlor, and took up the thread of argument where we dropped it for dinner. Other objections were brought forward, and resulted as in the forenoon — till near night Mr. Ely brought forth not only his strong, but one which he considered *the unanswerable* argument against the Bible. The answer I gave startled him! Springing to his feet he said, "Please state that again!" I did so in other language. He saw it was fatal. It undermined his great objection completely. And there he stood disarmed and naked before God and all the sweeping claims of religion and the Bible. I had felt all that day, and I presume so had he, that the room was full of light! That exposing error and presenting truth, we were aided by a prompter unseen.

The sun was setting, and Mr. Ely, taking his hat went out into an adjacent wood, I presume to pray. Returning at tea, he said I must go home. Why? He had some rails to haul, etc. I asked if there was not something in the line of duty far more important than hauling rails? He thought a moment and said, I will go to meeting to-night. We went. I tried to preach. But my nerve-power was gone, used up by the day's discussion. Preaching this night was rowing against wind, and wave and tide. After speaking feebly some fifteen minutes, I closed the book and said, Brethren, I am too weary to preach to-night. I must turn over upon your shoulders the burden and responsibilities of this meeting. Deacon Savage prayed and then there was an oppressive silence, and I rose and said, "Perhaps there is in this house some one not a Christian, whose hour of supreme interest has come; the hour whose decision and action will determine an endless future!

"Such a crisis occurs some time in the history of us all! Oh, the value of that hour, when the Spirit hovering over a convicted sinner, whispers: 'Now is the accepted time, to-day is the day of salvation!' Had poor, begging, blind Bartimeus, sitting pensive by the wayside when Jesus passed by neglected, even for ten minutes, to cry 'Jesus, thou son of David, have mercy on me,' how different had been his history and everlasting destiny!"

Mr. Ely sprang to his feet and said, "I am a great sinner! It don't seem possible God can forgive me. But if any of you can pray for me I ask you to do so, and I will try to pray for myself." So saying, and not waiting for others, he fell upon his knees and offered up the first public prayer of his life. Others were also moved to pray, and there was no lack of interest to the close of the meeting. When we returned home, in our family prayer each one, including Mr. Ely, led the others at the Lord's altar.

From that notable day unto this, covering a period of more than twenty years, there has been a family altar in Mr. Ely's house, and the sight is not unusual in the church which he attends, of himself and wife and four promising children, all sitting around the Lord's table and showing forth his death, till he shall come! The number of conversions in this revival was small. Speaking of this rather mournfully, subsequently in a prayer-meeting, Miss Elizabeth Lamb rose and asked me what I thought the conversion of Mr. Ely was worth? The question took me aback. I felt justly reproved, and never after murmured over the small success of that effort. Years after Mr. Ely wrote me offering me one or two hundred dollars, if I would write out a synopsis of that conversation. In vain I tried to reproduce it. It came upon us as a vision, and as a vision it passed away. Dr. Lyman Beecher,[55] while President of Lane Seminary, once told his students of holding revival meetings among the pioneer settlements, and that the power of his sermons astonished not only the people, but himself. When he returned to the seminary he tried to reproduce them, but could not. He added, that like many of the experiences of life, they would be profaned by a rehearsal.

RIPON COLLEGE

Not long after my return from California I received a call from Rev. Dr. Merriman, President of Ripon College.[56] He was one of the ablest preachers in the State, an acute reasoner, a man of scholarly attainments and otherwise eminently fitted to preside over and develop the youthful college. But at that day it had next to no endowment fund, and worse than that, there was hanging over it a $20,000 debt. President Merriman at once determined to remove that debt and put the College on such a basis that its annual income and expenses should balance each other. The financial condition of the country made it impossible to get money in the East. The West, and especially Wisconsin, must first indorse the youthful college and show faith in its

future by canceling that debt. This was plausible, if not wholly reasonable. So President Merriman undertook to raise the $20,000 in
Wisconsin. A whole year was spent at it, the ground canvassed over
and over, and at its end only a little over $18,000 had been subscribed
and all this on condition of the whole being subscribed by responsible
parties. Worn down with the long labor, discouraged by the meager
results and not knowing where to go for the remaining $2,000, the
good man rode up to my house to stay a few days, he said, and rest
and then go back to the college, resign his office and abandon the
institution to its fate. Of course, he was welcomed with a brother's
love and sympathy.

While he was resting, being one of the trustees I looked over
the list of subscriptions and saw it was reliable so far as I knew the
men. I asked if the college had not some property we could sell and
raise a part of the money. Yes, there were some lots down by the
railroad depot. We concluded we could get a Mr. Catlin to take them
for $300 or $400. Then there was this horse he had been riding, and
now in my stable. Then there was a second-hand carriage. Thus we
figured down the debt till it was reduced to some $1,300 or $1,400.
Here "was the rub." How could we raise that? We were sitting near
a small bureau and I opened one of its drawers and taking thence a
small box I took out a couple of $500 bills and spread them on his
knee. Then two $100 bills and then in lesser bills the lacking amount
was made up. A more astonished man one rarely sees! "*Do you mean
that?*" said he. "Certainly, put it in your purse and lie down upon it
and go to sleep. Rest with me a week and recruit your strength and
then I will let you go back to the college." "Not a bit of it," he replied,
"I am well now; I must go right back and tell the professors the joyful
news. I can't keep it pent up all that time; let me have my horse."
And I could not persuade him even to stay with me to tea. Cantering
away he was quickly in Ripon, and I was told that entering the town
he saw across the street a friend of the college and also one of the
subscribers, and he called out, "Prepare to pay your subscription; the
$20,000 is raised! *I have seen the money.*" And then was great joy in
that city. * * * In thus helping to relieve the college, while it was a
great pleasure to me, as also the memory of it ever since, I claim no
special credit for it. For I truly feel that he, who has the power to
give, is under greater obligation to be grateful, than he who receives.
"It is more blessed to give than to receive."

CHAPTER
20

THE THIRD JOURNEY TO CALIFORNIA

The year 1867 opened upon me weaker in nerve power than ever before. I was obliged to curtail my labors and confine them to Springvale. The long cold winters of Wisconsin confining me so much indoors, and interfering so much with regular outdoor exercise, was steadily aggravating my nervous troubles, and I resolved to try again the healing virtue of a California climate. Early in the autumn I sold out, and left with my family for the Golden State. Our route was via New York, Panama, and the Pacific. Even so late as 1867, twenty years ago, no railroad had crossed the western plains, and the quickest route to San Francisco from Wisconsin was that which took us one thousand miles east to New York, thence twenty-five hundred to Panama, then three or four thousand more to the Golden gate; and all to reach a county scarce two thousand miles west! The voyage was without incident, and quite lacking in interest to one who, like myself, had passed over the route three times before.[57] Arrived at San Francisco, we went southwesterly about one hundred miles, to San Benito county, and took up our residence in San Juan. The families to whom I bore letters of recommendation received us with characteristic California hospitality.

The sea voyage had done me no good. I was far from well, and concluded it was my duty to cast off care, and recreate, as best I could, for some months at least. To this end I wandered over the hills, carrying a gun on my shoulder, and capturing game wherever I could find it. Nothing more completely diverts a man's thoughts from old channels, and scatters them broadcast upon new and changing objects. The physical exercise is so varied, going up hill and down, one hour clambering over fences and rocks, and climbing the hills, and the next crawling on all fours through the tangled thicket, or running down hills. Then the excitement of the chase affords a salutary exhilaration of the spirits. For two months or so I tried this best of remedies for nerves, worn and wearied by overwork and care.

HUNTING NEAR SAN JUAN

There was a great deal of game near San Juan, and not infrequently I returned from a day's excursion heavily laden with the prey I had taken. Perhaps it may interest some of the boys who read this book, and girls, too, to have a more particular account of some of these strollings over the mountains, and scenes of the chase and the hunt. For their sakes I will relate some of them, for I have ever loved to amuse them with an innocent story. Amusement holds an important place in human life, and at no stage is there a greater demand for it than in childhood and youth. Older people, if there are any who have got beyond such things, may skip this chapter, and pass to the one which follows it.

San Juan is on the north side of the Gabilan Mountains, and these mountains abounded in wild hogs, wild cats, deer, panther, bear, wolves, raccoons, rabbits, squirrels and quail in infinite numbers. Years ago there were here great herds of elk, wild horses and cattle; but there were none here at the period of my visit. The shepherds who pastured their flocks in the vicinity of these mountains, complained much of the depredations of wild boars, coming out of the thickets by night, ripping up the sheep with their great tusks, and devouring them. Usually they would run back with their prey into the thickets when attacked by the shepherd and his dogs; but not always. Now and then an old wild boar,[58] who feared neither wolf nor bear, would stand his ground, and crunch his mutton fearlessly in the face of the owner. If attacked he would give battle, in which case the shepherd usually sought refuge in a tree, and staid there till the boar was tired of waiting for him to come down, and walked away. And woe to his dogs if one of them received a side-winder from one of those terrible tusks.

Near San Juan was one famous for his size, his ferocity, his depredations, his daring, and his many encounters with armed men and dogs. I heard so much about him that I rather wanted to see him, and soon had an opportunity. I and my nephew, Selwyn Shaw, were invited by Deacon Cowles and son to accompany them on a hunt for wild hogs. The time fixed upon was to be immediately after the first rain, because we could then track them in the soft ground. Accordingly, after the first good shower, my nephew and I mounted our horses and repaired to the place of rendezvous, but Mr. Cowles and son were not there. We soon came upon the fresh tracks of large hogs, and tufts of grass rooted up here and there. There were two of them, and they seemed to be accompanied by a yearling steer. The

game must be near, and much we desired the presence and help of
Mr. Cowles and son; besides, we had no dogs. My nephew went down
toward their house to see if they were coming and to get their dogs.
While he was gone I reconnoitered the grounds and traced them up
the mountain, till they turned into a dense patch of chapparal, nearly
circular, and perhaps ten rods in diameter. Around and around this
I went, till I was sure they had not passed through it, and was certain
they were there. But that steer! Surely he could not have gone in
there!

Again I examined the track and found it was the track of a great
boar, doubtless the one I had heard so much of! If that was so there
was a battle ahead, and either he or we would get hurt. I at once
readjusted my weapons, put a double load of powder in each barrel,
and from twenty to thirty revolver balls, and got my knife in position,
and I waited and waited for the coming of my companions in the
hunt. Finding a point whence I could overlook the valley, I descried
them some two miles off, approaching; but soon they turned from
the direct course and went at right angles to it, toward San Juan. I
concluded some one was sick and they were going for a doctor. On
they went a mile or more, and passed out of sight; so I concluded I
should have to fight out the battle alone, and went back to the lair
of the wild hogs. The truth was the rain of the past night had washed
a gully, narrow but deep, for a mile or two in length, and they had
to go that distance to cross it with their team and wagon. With not
a little caution I peered into the chapparal thicket on hands and knees,
venturing a rod or so within, and then backing out and trying a new
place. Thus I went around it, venturing in toward the center farther
and farther. At length I saw before me, some thirty feet, a black heap!
It was the hogs I was in quest of. I could hear their labored breathing
and an occasional snore! Inch by inch I advanced, my finger on the
trigger, till I could make out a hog's head, resting on the back of
another, and his snout pointing directly at me. I would make sure of
him with one barrel, and defend myself, if attacked, with the other
and my knife. Taking aim I saw a small sapling, an inch in diameter,
standing directly in the line between my eye and the center of the
forehead. Moving aside a little to avoid it, he opened his eyes and
glared at me! A wild grunt and they were all on their feet and rushing
out of the thicket not far from me, and I forced myself outside too,
as quick as they! But there confronted me the famous wild boar of
which I have spoken. And a grand sight it was; especially the tactics
he displayed in showing off his size and prowess as he advanced toward
me. He did not rush upon me at once, but approached steadily and

slowly, now turning this side, now that, his long back rigid with bristles, his tusks protruding three inches outside his upper lip, and his mouth white with foam! His eye glared fiercely upon me, and his hoarse gruntings, and occasional sharp, explosive barkings, were like those of an ourang-outang when aroused and enraged. To show me what he could do with those great tusks, he dropped his head and tore up the ground and scattered the sod. Had I ran I have no doubt he would have followed me and probably have killed me.

Instead of running I steadily advanced, and planting my foot firmly, I gave him the full benefit of one of those terrible double charges I sometimes used. I was thrown back a couple of steps. The boar sprang toward me, but his hind legs gave way and he had to drag his hind parts with his fore feet. I easily avoided him, and poured another shower of balls into his forehead. He quailed a little and I loaded up again. I had discharged that first load at his heart, and just back of the shoulder blade. I did not know then, as I do now, that to an old wild boar this is about the least vulnerable spot about him; for there is a shield there tougher than any sole leather and three-fourths of an inch thick, made so by continual gorings and bruises, in countless battles with his kind. So impenetrable is this shield, and so large, too, that I have no doubt that nineteen out of twenty of my revolver balls flattened against it, and not one of them passed through it. A scattering ball or two flew above the shield and entered the muscles along the backbone, and hence the temporary paralysis of the hind legs. The balls of the second load, discharged at his forehead, were probably also flattened against his thick skull; but they stunned him somewhat and he ceased to advance. Just as I had finished reloading, he turned and began moving down the steep toward a line of chapparal. I followed him slowly, being sure of my game; but getting into the bushes again, he recovered the use of his hind legs and was able to keep out of my way.

While I was following him up I heard the shouts of my comrades, and with their dogs we worried him for perhaps two hours, but could not get a shot at him on account of the thick chapparal bushes. The dogs dared not go near him. Believing he would die, and knowing that his meat was of no account, we left him and went in search of something more palatable. Before night I killed a shoat of 125 pounds, and we packed him on our horse and went home. I may add that once afterward I encountered another wild boar, nearly as large, and that he succumbed only after I had fired into him *eight loads* like those described above, and from a distance not exceeding twenty or thirty feet. This animal also feared neither dog nor man.

HUNTING THE WILD BOAR

A WILD GOOSE HUNT

Soon after this wild hog hunting affair, a gentleman invited me to go
with him after wild geese. My wife's sister, Mrs. Shaw, with whom we
boarded, interested herself not a little in this goose hunt, and not
small was the sport she made over the matter. How nice those geese
would be! She would cook them thus and thus! She could call in friends
to enjoy them with us! Then the feathers! What nice pillows they
would make! Thrown a little upon our mettle, and wishing to get
even with her, we exacted a promise from her before we started, that
she should *pick and dress all* we should shoot, and cook and serve them
up in the most approved style. Yes, she would do that, sure. And so
we started off about seven o'clock one morning. We crossed the San
Benito River and went into the hills a couple of miles, when we
approached a couple of lakelets, each perhaps forty rods wide and
eighty long. My companion said, "Let me lie in ambush at one lake,
and you take the other. In half an hour the geese will come in here
from their pasture grounds in the wheat stubble. Here they get their
drink." As I was going to my assigned lake I broke off a great limb
from a live oak and dragged it after me. As I was seeking a hiding
place I heard my companion shoot, and then a loud squawking of
half a thousand geese. Seeing a little gully by the side of the lake, I
jumped into it and drew the bush over me. Presently the geese began
to come in, flock after flock. At first they aligned on the farther side;
then nearer and nearer, till some of them were within shooting distance. Nearer and yet nearer they came, till trailing my gun upon
them I could take four or five in range.

A flock of great black "honkers" came within six or eight rods
of me. And now they were coming from all directions, and every part
of the little lake was agitated with the alighting flocks. I think there
must have been fifty thousand, and still they were coming. Meantime
I was trailing my gun upon them wherever I could get most in range.
But a shrewd old gander, the boss of the flock, turning his head
sidewise, and peering under the bush, descried danger there! A wild
squawk and the whole fifty thousand instantly took wing. The simultaneous flap of the wings of so many was as the noise of thunder;
but I fired both barrels into the flying mass and there fell not less
than twenty killed or wounded, some on the land and some in the
lake. Instantly there swooped down from high heaven two enormous
eagles, and pounded each upon a wounded goose; but the geese
turning upon their backs, so plied their wings, knocking aside again
and again the talons, that the eagles alighted a few feet distant and

awaited developments. But I was soon there, and claimed my own and drove off the eagles. I could easily have shot them, but I was not after eagles now. Well, I gathered them, all I could run down on the land, and such as floated ashore, till I had gathered twelve! I had killed several more but could not find them on the land, or they were out in the lake and did not float on shore. A flock coming over, I fired and killed two more, which gave me fourteen!

My companion coming over the hill, and seeing my pile, said we would take them and go. He had only one. So we packed them to our cart and drove home. It was about eleven o'clock A.M. when we drove up. Mrs. Shaw was out to meet us, and said triumphantly, "Come, hand over those geese; I am waiting for them." We hesitated, and made her repeat her pledge to pick and dress *all* the geese we should shoot, and cook them too, *and do it all herself*. "Yes, yes, certainly; hand them over." And now the whole household, two families, were out and gathered around the cart, curious to see if we could show a goose. Putting a hand under the curtain we drew forth a goose! "Well done! You have got one poor little goose. It is more than I expected." "Did we not get another?" I asked. "Yes, I believe we did;" and I put down the hand again and drew out another. "Well! you have got two; they will make us a fair meal!" But we drew out another and put it in her hands, then another; and so on and on, till she could hold no more, and dropped "the old geese" in disgust; and so we continued till there lay in the pile fifteen geese! And now it was our turn to laugh, and turn the jokes round the other way. But Mrs. Shaw, with her characteristic good nature, joined us heatily, and went to work to fulfill her promise, and did so, as far as mortal woman could.

CALIFORNIA QUAIL

California is noted for its quail. There are two kinds, mountain quail and lowland quail. Neither variety is like that of the Eastern States. The California quail has a plume dandling upon its head, which trembles and sparkles in rainbow colors, like the spots in a peacock's feather. They abound in vast numbers over all the State. I once saw a flock coming down from the hills to a sheepfold, which I estimated at from three to five thousand. The flock nearly covered a space three rods wide and thirty long. I fired into this flock, but killed only nine.

SOUTHERN CALIFORNIA

Greatly benefited by these hunting excursions, and anxious to find a home and a place where I could resume my employment as a preacher of the Gospel, I left San Juan about the 1st of January, 1868, for a tour into the southern counties, called at this time "Cow Counties," on account of the vast herds of cattle pastured there. I went on horseback, carried my blankets, and otherwise prepared myself to camp out wherever night overtook me. Crossing the Gabilan Mountains, I followed up the Salinas Valley to a crossing opposite the old mission of Soledad, or of Solitude, as it was very properly called. I was obliged to swim my horse across the river. Following up the general course of the Salinas in the direction of San Luis Obispo, I came across a curiosity, which perhaps may be found elsewhere, but was a novelty to me. It was a bed of *gigantic oyster shells*, embedded in a swell of sandy land, evidently once the shore of the ocean. These shells, though in sand, were well preserved. I dug up some that were from four to six inches through the solid shell, and a foot or more long, and perhaps six to eight inches across. One of them was by actual measurement *a foot and a half long*. The oyster it once contained would have filled a two-quart measure, and perhaps a gallon. There were vast numbers of them. In places they formed a stratum two or three feet thick. Singularly, many of them were in position just as they grew, undisturbed by the vast changes which have lifted the lands and deepened the sea, and swept out of life the last remnant of the giant oyster. If any one has the curiosity to see them, or get specimens, they will find them not far from the town of Paso Robles, on the Southern Pacific Railroad, and perhaps twenty-five miles from San Luis Obispo.

The last night before reaching San Luis I spent on the Santa Margarita Ranch. Leaving the Santa Margarita Ranch I passed over to San Luis Obispo, and roamed over that county some two weeks. Thence I proceeded eastward, along the coast, to Santa Barbara. In what was at that time the eastern part, but now the new county of Ventura, is the great Briggs Ranch. It had just been surveyed off into lots, and here I bought a homestead, and here I and my family were soon located and settled down to our proper work. Rest and recreation had restored my stricken nerves to healthful action, and I went up and down the Santa Clara Valley preaching the Gospel, from San Buena Ventura to Santa Paula, a circuit twenty miles long and four wide. In this service I wrought more or less for twelve years; but the old trouble gradually came on, necessitating a curtailment of my preaching appointments, till I was obliged to turn the work over to other and abler hands.

Along with this work I carried on somewhat extensive farming; but for this my preaching days would have been few and feeble. In this latter employment, taking the twenty years together, I have been moderately and satisfactorily successful. That is I have been able to pay all their dues, have supported my family in comfort, have been able to give somewhat to each passing call of benevolence, and lay aside a reasonable reserve against the time when advancing age shall retire myself and my partner from active labor and care. And beyond this, perhaps there is a little sum sufficient to keep up our habit of giving to the end, and in a small way to help our children and others in possible emergencies.

Looking back over the years of our residence in Southern California, I am amazed at the progress made by our State. A few years ago she was nothing agriculturally; to-day she leads nearly all the States in her wool product, the abundance of her wheat and barley, in oranges, lemons, grapes, raisins, prunes, apricots, peaches and pears; as also in her quicksilver and gold. Of course it has other attractions which, with the above, make a home on its soil the hope and desire of nations. The fear of earthquakes, which in an early day kept many from crossing to our coast, has migrated eastward, and bounding over the Sierras and Rocky Mountains, the Mississippi and the Alleghanies, now makes Charleston the seat of its terror and its power.[59] No cyclones here pursue their headlong way, scattering far and wide fences and human dwellings; and even the thunder storm, so common in the East, is here practically unknown, while in number of beautiful and cloudless days, calling forth women and children out of confined rooms into the sunny gardens and fields, it has no parallel, and no competitor on earth. Had Washington, in his reputed "dream of America for a thousand years," foreseen the California that is, and, we trust, is to be, he might well have said of it what Moses said of the inheritance of Joseph (Deut. xxxiii: 13)—"Blessed of the Lord be his land, for the precious things of Heaven, for the dew and the deep which coucheth beneath, and for the precious things put forth by the sun, and for the precious things put forth by the moon, and for the chief things of the ancient mountains, and for the precious things of the lasting hills, and for the precious things of the earth, and the fullness thereof, and for the good will of him who dwelt in the bush. Let the blessing rest upon the head of Joseph, and upon the top of the head of him that was separated from his brethren." After a residence here of twenty years, the above benediction seems to me more applicable to California than to the patrimony of him for whom it was originally intended.

Should this present process of improvement go on, and continue for fifty years to come, it needs no prophet to foretell that California by that time will have become the choicest spot for human residence on earth. I speak of *material* things. Indeed it has become such already. If not, what means this growth and development of the past twenty-five years? What this passionate fondness of all Californians for their adopted State? What this hegira of cultivated and well to do people from the East and "from all lands to make their home here." That California far exceeds the ancient Canaan in its productions and climate and resources no one can doubt who has taken the trouble to compare the two. And the Garden of Eden — barring sin and its effects — whether it excelled this our Garden of Hesperides or not, is a question the debating clubs of the country may find it hard to determine. But alas! no place can be a heaven to a sin-smitten heart! God's immortal child never can find solid rest save in his father's house and in his father's arms. Here as elsewhere man's steps are restless, despite these lavished gifts of God. His eye is often dimmed with tears. His mouth is filled with murmuring and curses. His heart with discontent, and in cases not a few in his hand glitters the knife of the suicide. Milton represents Satan as saying, "Which way I go is hell, *myself am hell!*" Nevertheless there is much in these surroundings. Heaven is heaven to the pure in heart, though a devil could not be happy there.

21

TWENTY YEARS IN SOUTHERN CALIFORNIA

The writer has now reached his seventy-third year! The voyage of life is nearly completed, and the port is almost in sight. At masthead the white signal calls for the pilot. He will soon come on board and take the helm, and ere long we shall glide into the harbor of an eternal rest! And we shall step upon the shores of heaven, the shores of immortality! "Our feet shall stand within thy gates, oh Jerusalem!" There God is gathering the choice of the earth, the saints of all ages, and forming them into a society more joyous and delightful then ever entered the thought of man! Sometimes in his reveries by day and in his dreams by night, the writer looks far off into the azure blue and fancies he sees there the City of God, the holy place of the tabernacles of the Most High. Issuing from its gates of pearl, he sees a train of friends and loved ones gone before, coming down the golden walk to meet and embrace us and conduct us to the heavenly mansions! What a meeting that will be! What congratulations! What introductions to persons we have longed to see! What wondrous sights! What new experiences—and what new endowments to fit us for our new conditions, and for an endless life! An hour that, never to be forgotten, and perhaps never to be equaled!

The hour of our terrestrial birth we have forgotten! Perhaps we were not conscious of it at all. Not so did Enoch and Elijah enter upon the life above, but with eyes wide open, and faculties undimmed. Even so shall we, it is likely, with undimmed vision and every faculty intensely active, cross over the Jordan, and enter into the promised land.

OLD AGE AND LIFE BEYOND SEVENTY

It seems quite in place here, to drop a word upon those who look forward to old age with fear and dread. Not a few imagine that life beyond seventy, is in the main joyless, and usually a burden grievous to be borne. Indeed, there are those who question its desirableness *before* that time, or even at all. There are people well to do, so far as health and property and social position are concerned, who often express the wish they had never been born. They object to the command to "multiply and replenish the earth," on the ground that there is more evil than good in life. More sorrow than joy, more sighs than songs! Indeed, the whole pessimistic school of philosophizing skeptics hold and advocate this doctrine. And if their denial of the desirableness of life, finds support in their experience, it does not highly compliment their faith. Let them talk no more like Hume,[61] of the gloom which enshrouds the Christian religion, despoiling life of all its pleasures. For who ever heard of a Christian wishing he had never been!

Is then life beyond seventy necessarily cloudy? Or may it not, on the other hand, be rich in joys, in sunshine and in song? Were the writer to refer this question to his own experience it would be quickly decided that no part of life equals it in peace and joy, and all substantial good. It is the rich autumn wherein is gathered and enjoyed what was planted in spring and cultivated in summer. The most beautiful colors which gather on the leaves of forest trees, or the cheek of orchard fruits, are those that give grace and glory to ripening days, and accompany the frosts of autumn! No such plethoric stores for man and beast fill the bin, the barn and the cellar, as those which crown the closing year. And are not these things in nature prophetic and suggestive of what will be and ought to be true, of the closing years of a useful and successful life? Let us consider some of the reasons why life beyond seventy may be specially peaceful and happy.

1. On account of its exemption in large measure from care. Active life, immersion in affairs and in business, involves men necessarily in much of forethought and wearisome care. What multitudes are annually killed by it, or prematurely worn out? But in old age these responsibilities are laid upon other shoulders, and the rest is sweet. Sweet like the rest of the laborer when the toil of the day is over.

Thus in my prime, no sooner had I preached one sermon, than the question was upon me, What shall I preach next, and what do the wants of my people require? And there was no rest to the mind, till that message was selected, elaborated and preached.

So when, after much solicitude and labor, a soul was converted, the question at once arose, How shall he be led on the narrow way? How edified and made useful?

2. *Retrospection* is a spring of unfailing pleasure to an old man who has spent an honorable, useful and a truly Christian life.

"Oft in the stilly night
When slumber's chain hath bound me,
Fond memory brings the light
Of other days around me."

This is one of the special objects and offices of memory: To escort the good man back over his past and refresh his spirit with joy, as he pauses at each hallowed spot where was left behind him some token of his love to God, or good will to man. A good act blesses the doer, not only at the time of its performance, but perhaps even more, every time it is reviewed. It hath an eternal fragrance. Memory hath made it immortal!

There is no part of life so given to retrospection as old age, and in extreme age little else employs one's thought. And if indeed we have spent the prime of our days in useful labors, the retrospection thereof will be sweet and blessed.

And "blessed is the man who hath his quiver full of them."

3. The consciousness of *growth and improvement* in our characters and dispositions is in old age a source of pleasure. Conversion lays the foundation of a moral temple whose subsequent growth and symmetry, the angels shall admire, and whose top shall shine even in heaven! But brick after brick, and stone after stone must be laid upon it and story after story must be added. And as it rises it shows its design, and develops the wisdom and glory of its plan. And the man of mature Christian life, who has grown in grace and gotten largely the victory over the world, the flesh and the devil, has happy thoughts to dwell upon, when he thinks of victories won, and improvement made since he was a babe in Christ.

4. The *removal of all doubts of acceptance* with God, is another source of joy to old age. With most persons doubts and clouds hand about the portals of conversion, and often for years, ever and anon, the question, will obtrude itself, "Have I been truly converted?" "Am I His or am I not?" But God has arranged a series of tests along one's path, which brings out to view the principles which really govern us. By the time we reach old age, if not before, these many crucibles through which our spirits are called to pass have removed all doubt as to whose we are and whom we love. Thus having arrived in due time at the full assurance of faith how can we be less than happy at the final settlement of the most momentous question which ever agitated human thought. The writer has heard many a man say, "I would give all that I have to know that heaven is my home, and eternal life secure." Well, reader, it is your privilege to walk with God and

to be allied to him so consciously and so livingly that you *cannot doubt* your acceptance. You can say with Paul, "I *know* in whom I have believed," and with John "*We know* that we have passed from death unto life." It is your privilege to know this before you have journeyed very far on the homeward road. And you are inexcusable, indeed, if when old age has come, you are still a babe, and wearing yet the swaddling clothes of doubt.

5. *Exemption* in large measure *from fierce temptations* is a special relief granted to old age. God has provided that then the passions of the body shall largely have gone to sleep, and they trouble us then little if at all. The world appeals not to us as formerly. We have largely retired from it and its conflicts. Its opinions, once so weighty, are of little weight with us now. Its silver and gold and houses and lands, are fast losing all their value to us. Less too are the assaults of Satan. Perhaps God's guardian angels will not allow him to disturb the old war-worn soldier retired to the hospital, or the sagacious enemy may by this time have become convinced that it will be of no use at this late hour to try to seduce the old veteran from his loyalty to God.

Finally, *proximity to heaven*, the Father's house so near at hand, fills all the valley through which the old man is passing, with peace and joy and unearthly light. After the long and wearisome journey through the wilderness of Sinai, who can describe the joy of Joshua and Caleb when the Lord said to them, "In three days ye shall pass over this Jordan to go in to possess it"? Or that of Elijah, the aged prophet, as, leaning on Elisha's arm, he hastened over Jordan, to meet the chariots sent to escort him to the presence of the King of Glory? Or that of Paul, the aged, now ready to be offered, and the time of his departure at hand, assured beyond a doubt that there was "laid up for him a crown of righteousness!" Let us not think such exultant experiences belong to the past alone. They are, and they have been, the heritage of God's people of every age and every clime.

During a ministry of nearly forty years, it has been my duty and my pleasure to accompany numbers of Christians down to the Jordan, and to watch with them in their latest hours. And judging from their language and their looks, the hours of their supreme joy have been the closing hours of life, those verging upon an eternal day! The Saviour said, "I, if I go away, will come again and receive you to myself." The "coming again" referred to here is, in my belief, this singular revelation of the Master to his people when dying, or about to die. In some cases he comes early, in others, later, but in all he comes.

Dr. Nelson relates the case of an eminent Christian, who, in dying, experienced no such revelation to his departing spirit as he expected. His daughter held his hand in hers, and said, "Father, if the Master comes to you after speech and sight have gone, will you squeeze my hand?" He said, "Yes." At length his hands and feet became cold, a moment more and he would be gone. Just then the Saviour came, faithful to his promise, and the stiffened muscles began to contract, and closing his fingers, strongly pressed his daughter's hand, thus signifying his Lord had come. And if this be the divine arrangement, then may we welcome old age and gray hairs, and go down into the valley, singing as we go, "When I walk through the valley of the shadow of death I will fear no evil, for thou art with me, thy rod and thy staff, they comfort me."

A DREAM OF HEAVEN

I once had a dream of heaven. It was, perhaps, twenty years since. But neither advancing age nor failing memory have availed to efface the vision, or obliterate the picture from my memory, or weaken its influence on my views and life. This was the dream: That I had dropped suddenly dead, and after a few moments of confused thought, like that we experience when awakening out of sleep, I found myself in the city of New Haven, Conn. I was standing on "The Green," as we used, sixty years ago, to call the Central Park. But "the City of Elms"—my beau ideal of civic beauty in college days—was no more there, save only its site. The old stuccoed Statehouse was gone. So, too, were the college dormitories and halls of science, the stately elms also, and even the temples of worship! Gone they were, but in their places were structures, and a scenery more beautiful than tongue can tell! Trees indeed, there were, arching the long streets as of yore, but they were transfigured—spiritualized! glorified! And I stood entranced by their beauty, much as some of us remember to have been, as we have walked out into a forest some bright wintry morning, and beheld everything bejeweled and glittering with icicles; the great trees, bending under a weight of glory, and glittering in the morning sun. And not only the great tree's trunk, and limbs, and tiny twigs, but even the grasses were strung with diamonds, and sparkled in the rays of glory.

Such a scene, so familiar to those who have lived in wintry lands, and the impression it makes, will best convey to the reader the impression made upon me by the trees which embowered the streets of the paradise my dream revealed. Streets, indeed, there were, but they were enlarged to avenues, generous in width, and a thousand miles in length. Residences, also, but not crowded, were on every side, but they seemed as pure and holy, spotless and ethereal, as if made of crystal or glass. No two were alike, and each had some peculiarity, all its own, which was the admiration of all. No walls or fences divided these celestial mansions, and they reminded me of Euclid street in Cleveland.

Persons, too, I saw, not in throngs, nor often walking singly, but gathered in social groups, as if on some joyful visit. While looking through the long avenues, the door of a palace on my right opened, and down the steps walked three persons, and crossed the green before me and entered another, whose door *opened and closed of its own accord.* I had never conceived of such beauty before, nor of such elastic steps, and harmony in motion. Such purity of force and diction. Such sprightly suggestions, and such quick and apt replies! Perfectly happy they seemed in each others' society. And now and then there came melting upon my ear strains of music, rich and rare, beyond all former conception. But what impressed me most of all was, that I saw *no place of worship,* nor any form of God, my Maker, nor of Christ, my Saviour. But presently I felt within, stealing over all my spirit, a sense of divine love, a pulsation from the great heart of God, like a wave of the great ocean, flowing into all the bays and inlets connected with it. And then my heart throbbed back responsive, and then the divine wave returned, revealing God's love to me, so much more intimately and delightfully than sight could do, that I could not bear to have substituted for it the more distant revelation of a form to the eye, however glorious it might be. And I saw that every heart in that delightful land was intensely conscious of these throbbings of divine love, and was also joyfully responsive to them, and that *this constituted the supreme bliss of heaven.*

This, reader, was a real dream, not made up and tampered with for effect, but related as it came and went. I have told it, not as a revelation, but as *a dream.* Yet I cannot rid myself of the conviction, that in it I gained a true conception of what will constitute the great river of the water of life above. Not the outward adornment of the Celestial City, not its exemption from sin and sorrow, and death; not its transcendent heights of knowledge; not its songs of unearthly melody; nor yet its society, delightful as that may be, made up of dear kindred and loved ones, and the saints of all ages too. All these, and more, no doubt, will be there for us to admire and enjoy. But that which shall surpass them all, and leave them far behind, will be those impulsations of divine love which shall fill all hearts, and unite them forever to the Lord.

And I think I understood better than before why John was inspired to write those startling words:

"And I saw no temple therein; for the Lord God Almighty and the Lamb are the temple of it."[62]

APPENDIX

INTRODUCTION [1898 edition]

By Rev. J. H. Fairchild, D.D., President of Oberlin College

There is nothing so interesting to the human heart as human experience; and this volume, setting forth scenes in the life of Rev. Sherlock Bristol, presents a wider range of experience in many lines of thought and action, and a greater variety of adventure, than are often found concentrated in a single human life. The book contains much that is amusing and inspiring. The same earnest purpose pervades the book that has characterized the life of the author from childhood to old age, and few I think can read it without being stimulated to higher endeavor and a more worthy life. It may be quite possible to question the wisdom displayed here and there in an emergency, as in most human lives, but the earnestness of faith and courage, often mightier than wisdom, are seldom found wanting.

It was my privilege to become acquainted with Mr. Bristol at the beginning of his college life at Oberlin, and the life-long friendship which resulted may explain somewhat the interest with which I have read the record of his life; but I cannot imagine that any one who has a particle of sympathy with the struggles and efforts of an earnest soul can read this book without similar interest.

NOTES TO TEXT

1. The second edition of 1898 had an introduction by J. H. Fairchild, the president of Oberlin College, which was placed before the Preface and Table of Contents; it is a slightly guarded encomium of Bristol, in whom Fairchild found "earnestness of faith and courage," if not always "wisdom" in an emergency. For the full text, see the Appendix.

2. This is Bristol's first reference to the notion of holiness or Christian perfection that loomed so large in his experience (see the Introduction for discussion of this doctrine).

3. This was a term used commonly and by religious agencies to refer to those missionaries who labored at home (mainly in the western districts) rather than in foreign missions. The American Home Missionary Society (AHMS) was founded in 1826 to encourage and coordinate such efforts, especially among Congregationalists and Presbyterians and their allies.

4. In the Old Testament, Nimrod was "a mighty hunter before the Lord" (Gen. 10:9), while Esau "was a skilfull hunter" (Gen. 25:27).

5. The Sabbath or Sunday School was at this time still a new institution. Its original British aim of teaching literacy in a pious setting to the children of the poor had been changed to the aims of teaching the Bible to the young and encouraging their conversion to evangelical piety. The American Sunday School Union had been founded in 1824 as an interdenominational voluntary association for the purpose of furthering such goals.

6. Sir William Blackstone (1728-80) was a famed English jurist whose *Commentaries on the Law of England* was the basis for the teaching of law in nineteenth-century America.

7. Nathaniel W. Taylor (1786-1858) was, from his influential professorship of theology at the Yale Divinity School (which Bristol calls the New Haven Seminary), one of the foremost adapters of strict Calvinism to the needs of the evangelical revivals. He gave greater scope to human freedom and responsibility than the older Calvinism had seemed to do. The Divinity School had been founded in 1822 and was long under the impress of his theological system. For more about Taylor, there is the excellent study by Sidney Earl Mead, *Nathaniel William Taylor, 1786-1858: A Connecticut Liberal* (Chicago: University of Chicago Press, 1942).

8. In the temperance movement of the early national period (and

later), persons were encouraged to sign a pledge committing themselves to
stop drinking alcoholic beverages. The American Temperance Union was
founded in 1833 out of several earlier societies and sponsored temperance
lecturers who denounced the evils of liquor and encouraged the signing of
the pledge. Before that time there had been no general opposition among
Calvinists and evangelicals to the use of alcohol.

9. Phillips Academy in Andover, Massachusetts, had opened in 1780
as a school for boys, chartered by and named after Samuel Phillips, who
had held several public offices in the state. Its aim was to combine classical
studies with moral instruction. Its relationship to Andover Theological Seminary, an institution founded in 1808 for the training of Congregational
ministers, was close until the seminary was moved in 1908.

10. The American Education Society had been founded in 1826 as
yet another one of the evangelical voluntary associations which, it was hoped
by their founders, would together "christianize" the land. It supported
promising though impecunious young men who desired to enter the ministry.

11. The American Colonization Society, organized in 1817, had as its
goal the manumission of slaves and their resettlement in Africa. At first
many of the New England clergy supported it for humanitarian and missionary reasons (it was hoped the returning Africans would plant Christianity
in their native continent), but by 1830 reformers had judged it a failure as
well as a device of slaveholders for ridding themselves of troublemakers,
and abolitionists began to denounce it.

12. Levi Woodbury (1789-1851) was first a governor of New Hampshire and then one of its United States senators; in 1834 he became secretary
of the treasury in President Jackson's cabinet.

13. Asa Mahan (1800-1889) was educated at Andover Seminary and
while a pastor in Cincinnati sympathized with abolition. He came to Oberlin
as the choice of the Lane Seminary rebels who left Lane because of its
compromise with slavery and was president of the newly founded Oberlin
College from 1835 to 1850. He was closely associated with the evangelist
Charles G. Finney in the development of holiness or perfectionist doctrine,
a subject upon which he wrote extensively.

14. The colonial pastor and theologian Jonathan Edwards (1703-58)
was an important source as well as a great inspiration to ninteenth-century
American evangelicals. As a young man at Yale he had drawn up a series
of resolutions on moral and spiritual matters that became notorious for their
strictness.

15. This is the first mention of the great evangelist Finney, who was
the most important influence upon Bristol. He came to Oberlin in 1835,
not long before Bristol arrived there, and served as professor of theology
as well as pastor of the First Congregational Church. From 1851 to 1866
he was president of the college. But he still managed to continue his revival
tours, taking long absences from his college duties. For details about Finney's
career and especially his Oberlin years, see Keith J. Hardman, *Charles Gran-*

dison Finney, 1792-1875: Revivalist and Reformer (Syracuse, N.Y.: Syracuse University Press, 1987).

16. From its beginning Oberlin was associated with the perfectionist theology being taught there by Mahan and Finney, who began to develop this teaching at about that time.

17. Jonathan Edwards was often called the "Elder Edwards" to distinguish him from his son, Jonathan Edwards, Jr., (1745-1801), who was a longtime pastor of the Congregational Church in New Haven and an influential theologian in his own right.

18. Yale Divinity School. See note 7.

19. "New School" referred to the modified Calvinism that had arisen especially with N. W. Taylor and such popular preachers as Lyman Beecher. Bristol saw the Oberlin theology as just a further extension of Taylor's giving greater scope to human freedom. For detailed discussion of these theologies, see Frank Hugh Foster, *A Genetic History of the New England Theology* (1907; rpt. New York: Russell and Russell, 1963).

20. This is of course Nathaniel W. Taylor. See note 7.

21. Mark 5:1-20; Luke 8:26-36.

22. These were the "Christians," or Disciples of Christ, a denomination that had developed out of the work of Barton Stone and Alexander Campbell (hence "Campbellite"). They taught that faith was not a supernatural act of grace but a straightforward and rational decision to believe in Christ and be his disciple. They were fond of public debates with proponents of other denominations. Against their views, Bristol argued on behalf of the need for a supernatural regeneration by the Holy Spirit.

23. Mark 15:34. Words spoken by Jesus from the cross. Calvinists had long maintained that these words represented a "cry of dereliction," as Christ, bearing the sins of humankind in a substitutionary atonement, bore (temporarily) the full weight of God's wrath against sin. Bristol follows a long Calvinist tradition in using this passage to magnify the heinousness of sin.

24. The American Home Missionary Society (see note 3) was wary of the abolitionist sentiments of those educated at Oberlin because it hoped to avoid such controversial issues in order not to cut off potential support for the organization.

25. An incident occured to Bristol when he was returning to Ohio for his work as pastor at Franklin which was expanded into an additional chapter for the 1898 edition. Stopping at Albany to catch a canal barge to Buffalo in the autumn of 1842 (according to Bristol), he encountered a young man whose money had been taken by a trio of ruffians. Coming to his rescue, Bristol regained the money and helped the young man on his way. The young man, who was going to Oberlin to begin his studies there, turned out to be Charles Livingstone, younger brother of the famous African missionary and explorer David Livingstone. Charles Livingstone reported the help he received to his family in Scotland, and Bristol was rewarded

with a gift of some books sent by them. He also later received a letter of thanks from David Livingstone, then in Africa, and corresponded with him several times thereafter; *The Pioneer Preacher* (New York: Fleming H. Revell, 1898), pp. 320-25; for the account of Charles Livingstone (which is dated 1840 not 1842, and is in a surviving letter and so must be a more accurate dating than Bristol's), see Robert Samuel Fletcher, *A History of Oberlin College: From Its Foundation through the Civil War*, 2 vols. (Oberlin, Ohio: Oberlin College, 1943), II, 540-41. But Charles Livingstone does not tell of being rescued from robbers, only of getting help to get to Oberlin: did the aging Bristol remember poorly an incident that he had not included in the earlier edition of his work, or did the younger Livingstone avoid alarming his family about the roughness of conditions in America?

26. The brothers Arthur and Lewis Tappan were wealthy New York merchants and ardent evangelicals who supported many of the missionary and reform causes of the "benevolent empire." They were especially committed to abolition and their gifts and support made the founding of Oberlin College possible. But they both went bankrupt in the panic of 1837. Nonetheless they managed to continue their support and labors on behalf especially of the antislavery cause.

27. H. C. Bowen moved to New York City from Connecticut and made his fortune working for the Tappan brothers. He married Lewis Tappan's daughter. He was active in founding the Plymouth Congregational Church in Boston, where Henry Ward Beecher was later the famous pastor. He founded *The Independent,* a religious newspaper to advance the causes of Congregationalism, evangelicalism, and antislavery. It quickly became one of the leading religious papers in the country. There is much about Bowen and his paper in Altina L. Waller, *Reverend Beecher and Mrs. Tilton: Sex and Class in Victorian America* (Amherst: University of Massachusetts Press, 1982).

28. Orthodox and evangelical Congregational churches were sometimes locally dubbed "Trinitarian" to distinguish them from Unitarian churches, many of which had been Congregational parishes that had become Unitarian but still retained their original name.

29. James G. Birney (1792-1857) was an abolitionist from Kentucky, who had freed inherited slaves in 1834. He was an agent of the Colonization Society, later executive secretary of the American Antislavery Society, and twice candidate for president of the United States on the Liberty Party ticket. He worked closely with the evangelical abolitionists. He figures largely in Gilbert H. Barnes, *The Antislavery Impulse, 1830-1844* (1933; rpt. New York: Harcourt, Brace & World, 1964); for a biography, see Betty L. Fladeland, *James Gillespie Birney: Slaveholder to Abolitionist* (Ithaca, N.Y.: Cornell University Press, 1955).

30. I Samuel 10:11-12.

31. Joshua Leavitt was a Yale graduate and Congregational minister who edited the influential *New York Evangelist.* He worked closely with the Tappans and Theodore Dwight Weld in the cause of abolition.

32. Isaiah Rynders was a United States marshall who was prominent in New York City politics as a Tammany Hall leader in the Democratic party. He was said to have great influence on elections because of his control of the more "turbulent elements" in the city, and had helped defeat Henry Clay and the Whigs in New York in the 1836 election (see *The National Cyclopedia of American Biography* [New York: James T. White & Co., 1893], 3:386).

33. The Broadway Tabernacle was the New York City congregation of which Finney had been pastor from 1836 to 1837, even after he had gone to Oberlin. It proved too difficult for him to maintain his posts in both New York and Oberlin and so he resigned the New York pastorate. The tabernacle building had been purposely built for Finney's ministry and for the advocacy of antislavery. See Susan H. Ward, *The History of the Broadway Tabernacle* (New York: Trow, 1901).

34. The American Missionary Association had been organized by abolitionist New School Congregationalists in 1846 at Albany as a protest against the compromises the other evangelical societies of the Benevolent Empire were making with slavery. After 1865 it did educational work among former slaves in the south.

35. George Whipple was one of the Lane Seminary rebels who left that institution in 1835 in order to come to Oberlin. There in 1838 he was made professor of mathematics but resigned in 1847 to become corresponding secretary of the American Missionary Association. See James H. Fairchild, *Oberlin: The Colony and College, 1833-1883* (1883; rpt. New York: Garland Publishing, 1984), pp. 289-90.

36. "Free" as an appellation attached to a congregation usually meant that it supported itself without pew rentals so that all the seating was free and open to the public. In this period such churches among Presbyterians and Congregationalists were typically evangelistic and Finneyite, and often antislavery.

37. From the parable of the "Good Samaritan," Luke 10:31-32.

38. The Señora de la Soledad mission was one of the early missions established on the California coast by the Spanish Franciscans. Southeast of Monterey, it was founded in 1791.

39. In 1846 Maine passed the first prohibition law of any of the states; "Maine Law" became proverbial for such a statute.

40. Free Will Baptists began to found congregations under that name in New England in the latter part of the eighteenth century. They adopted an Arminian or free-will theology rather than the Calvinism more usual among Baptists. They were often opposed to slavery. Later many of their northern congregations united with the main body of Baptists in that region.

41. From 1852 to 1862, though from 1859 to 1861 he was in Elmwood, Illinois, as Congregational pastor, and only came back to Wisconsin for the remainder of 1861 and the first part of 1862.

42. This is a reference to Numbers 21:8-9, where the brazen serpent

set up in the wilderness healed those who looked upon it; in Christian interpretation this had long been taken as a typological prefiguration of the cross of Christ. The remark of Felix to the apostle Paul is found in Acts 24:25.

43. This passage from Deuteronomy (32:35) was the text for Jonathan Edwards's famous sermon "Sinners in the Hands of an Angry God."

44. This river was the longest tributary of the Snake River, winding for 425 miles, often through deep canyons. Gold had been discovered in this region in 1860.

45. Council Bluffs, in southwest Iowa on the Missouri River, was named from a council held there between Lewis and Clark and their Native American contacts in 1804. It was an important supply point for westward routes during the gold rush years.

46. "Miss Bright Eyes," or Susette La Flesche, was a Pawnee woman who told moving stories of the harm done the Native Americans by whites. Daughter of an Omaha chief, she won sympathy for her cause by a speaking tour in the eastern United States during 1879.

47. Raids were widespread in Idaho country and nearby during the 1860s. Fort Laramie is in southeast Wyoming. See Robert M. Utley, *The Indian Frontier of the American West, 1846-1890* (Albuquerque: University of New Mexico Press, 1985), pp. 71, 122.

48. Fort Bridger was in southwest Wyoming, and had been founded as a supply post on the Oregon and other trails west in 1843.

49. Clement Vallandigham was a member of congress from Ohio from 1858 to 1863; a strong proponent of states' rights, he opposed the war against the Confederacy, for which he was court-martialed.

50. Fort Hall was near present Pocatello in southeastern Idaho.

51. One of the plagues that Moses called down upon Pharoah and the Egyptians in order to gain the freedom of the Israelites from bondage, Exodus 9:20-24.

52. Thus Bristol lays claim to having found the site upon which the city of Boise was established in 1863.

53. The original text, which was still not corrected for the 1898 edition, reads 1884; but it makes no sense unless the date 1864 is intended, and so I have emended the text accordingly.

54. This is one of Bristol's few references to the Civil War. Its infrequent mention is surprising since he was such an ardent abolitionist.

55. Lyman Beecher (1775-1863) was one of the leading clergymen of antebellum America. Serving both Presbyterian and Congregational churches, he was a leading exponent of revivals and benevolent societies. He had been president of Lane Theological Seminary in Cincinnati when the majority of its students bolted in order to study in the more congenially antislavery atmosphere of Oberlin.

56. Ripon College in Wisconsin had been founded as a college in 1863 by western evangelicals, mostly Congregationalists. The town, which went

back to an early Fourierist Utopian community, was a center of abolitionist sentiment.

57. That is, to California and back from New York in 1851-52, and from San Francisco to New York in early 1864, after he had left Idaho and gone on to California in order to return to Wisconsin from there.

58. Although wild boars from Europe were imported into California for hunting in 1925, at this early date these boars must have been just feral pigs that had escaped domestication and inhabited the brushlands of coastal California.

59. Charleston, South Carolina, was struck by a severe earthquake in 1886; damage was extensive.

60. This last chapter was considerably rewritten with much new material added for the new edition of 1898. Instead of this chapter title, it was entitled "Fourscore and Beyond," and reported that the author was then in his eighty-fourth year and "as busily employed" as before. Bristol recounted how he had donated or sold at half price hundreds of copies of the first edition of *The Pioneer Preacher* to the American Home Missionary Society, the American Board of Commissioners for Foreign Missions, the American Missionary Association, and the Seamen's Friend Society for placement in libraries provided for ships. This led to the necessity for what Bristol calls a "third edition," the publication of 1898 (the *National Union Catalogue* provides evidence of only two editions—perhaps there had been a second printing of the first edition in 1887). He also comments on the extensive correspondence he engaged in relative to the question of Christian holiness. The rest of this new final chapter simply rewrote the material on the advantages of old age and then reproduced verbatim the section on "A Dream of Heaven," *The Pioneer Preacher* (Chicago: Fleming H. Revell, 1898), pp. 326-28.

61. The eighteenth-century English philosopher David Hume counted for nineteenth-century evangelicals among those infidel authors, such as Thomas Paine, whom they were fond of attacking.

62. From Revelation 21:22.

INDEX